Filicide-Suicide

Also by Kieran O'Hagan

CRISIS INTERVENTION IN SOCIAL SERVICES

WORKING WITH CHILD SEXUAL ABUSE

THE ABUSE OF WOMEN IN CHILDCARE WORK (*with Karola Dillenburger*)

EMOTIONAL AND PSYCHOLOGICAL ABUSE OF CHILDREN

COMPETENCE IN SOCIAL WORK PRACTICE (*editor*)

CULTURAL COMPETENCE IN THE CARING PROFESSIONS

IDENTIFYING EMOTIONAL AND PSYCHOLOGICAL ABUSE

COMPETENCE IN SOCIAL WORK PRACTICE (*editor, 2nd Edition*)

THE VERDI SOLUTION

Filicide-Suicide

The Killing of Children in the Context of Separation, Divorce and Custody Disputes

Kieran O'Hagan

To Paul Grant — with thanks

Kieran O'Hagan

20th March 2014

palgrave
macmillan

© Kieran O'Hagan 2014

All rights reserved. No reproduction, copy or transmission of this publication may be made without written permission.

No portion of this publication may be reproduced, copied or transmitted save with written permission or in accordance with the provisions of the Copyright, Designs and Patents Act 1988, or under the terms of any licence permitting limited copying issued by the Copyright Licensing Agency, Saffron House, 6–10 Kirby Street, London EC1N 8TS.

Any person who does any unauthorized act in relation to this publication may be liable to criminal prosecution and civil claims for damages.

The author has asserted his right to be identified as the author of this work in accordance with the Copyright, Designs and Patents Act 1988.

First published 2014 by
PALGRAVE MACMILLAN

Palgrave Macmillan in the UK is an imprint of Macmillan Publishers Limited, registered in England, company number 785998, of Houndmills, Basingstoke, Hampshire RG21 6XS.

Palgrave Macmillan in the US is a division of St Martin's Press LLC, 175 Fifth Avenue, New York, NY 10010.

Palgrave Macmillan is the global academic imprint of the above companies and has companies and representatives throughout the world.

Palgrave® and Macmillan® are registered trademarks in the United States, the United Kingdom, Europe and other countries.

ISBN 978–1–137–02431–2

This book is printed on paper suitable for recycling and made from fully managed and sustained forest sources. Logging, pulping and manufacturing processes are expected to conform to the environmental regulations of the country of origin.

A catalogue record for this book is available from the British Library.

A catalog record for this book is available from the Library of Congress.

Typeset by MPS Limited, Chennai, India.

Dedicated to the 224 children killed by parents who once loved them.

Contents

List of Figures and Tables viii
Preface ix
Acknowledgements xii

Part I Filicide: Its Principal Features and Catastrophic Effects
1 Oh my God ... I made a mistake ... 3
2 Features of filicide: more common than we think 18
3 Learning from the Greeks 33

Part II A Study of 224 Filicide Killings, 1994–2012
4 Filicide literature and research 51
5 The results of a study of filicide and familicide 72
6 Mental illness and filicide killings 114

Part III Dispelling the Myths, Working Towards Prevention
7 To kill out of love ...? 135
8 The legislative context 151
9 Jackie's story 169
10 A way forward 184
Postscript 204

References 213
Index 225

List of Figures and Tables

Figures

5.1	Days on which killings occurred	105
5.2	Age of parent at the time of killing	106
5.3	Age of victims	107
5.4	Age and gender of victims killed by fathers	108
5.5	Age and gender of victims killed by mothers	108
5.6	Suicides and attempted suicides by mothers and fathers (%)	110
5.7	Method of killing	111

Tables

5.1	Filicide fathers	74
5.2	Filicide mothers	84
5.3	Familicide fathers	92
5.4	Number of filicides and familicides per day of the week, 1994–2012	105
5.5	Age and number of victims	109
5.6	Revenge-retaliation	111

Preface

Former colleagues in academia and social services may raise an eyebrow on reading the word 'custody' in the subtitle, and the phrase 'custody and access' which appears numerous times throughout the book. Are these not words and phrases confined to the lexicon dustbin by implementation of the 1989 Children Act? An explanation is called for.

The replacement words for 'custody' and 'access' are 'residence' and 'contact'. It was relatively easy for professionals to make the transition, basically for two reasons; first, few, if any, professionals were entirely relaxed about the use of terminology which had an unmistakeable whiff of conflict about it. The original (Latin) meaning of the word 'custody' is safekeeping and protection, which is exactly what it should always mean. But after a century of rising divorce rates and the predictable disputes over children accompanying them, the words 'custody' and 'access' acquired a different meaning, not just for parents separating and divorcing, but also for that whole range of professionals likely to have become involved as a consequence. 'Custody' was then often perceived as a concept emerging from the marital and/or relationship battlefield of a courtroom. Those awarded 'custody' (nearly always mothers) were perceived by their partners as the winners. The partners not only perceived themselves as losers (of their children), but were often stricken by a sense of loss of authority, power and control, which could remain a deep and lasting source of resentment. Given such perceptions of 'custody', that other term 'access' was regarded by many of its recipients as little more than a sop, as provocative as it was demeaning. Little wonder social workers, lawyers and magistrates welcomed the 1989 Act's removal of such contentious terminology from all subsequent deliberations on the welfare and safeguarding of children.

The second reason for the ease with which the replacement terms 'residence' and 'contact' were quickly assimilated within childcare law and practice was because they didn't just sound less contentious, they actually meant something different. Residence did not and could not mean: winner takes all, as custody had often been perceived. On the contrary, the place of residence should interfere as little as possible with the child's relationship with both parents. Each parent retains full parental responsibility and with it the power to act independently unless this is incompatible with a court's order, regardless of who has a residence order.

The new 'contact' order was also wider in scope. Rather than mere access, it provided for the child to visit or stay with the parent named in the order, and it grants that person the right to exercise all his or her parental responsibilities subject to not doing anything incompatible with a court order. Where direct contact (for whatever reason) is considered inappropriate, the court may authorize indirect contact, by telephone or letter, for example. The other parent would be expected to facilitate these alternatives.

Who would have forecast in 1989 that a quarter of a century later, these new concepts of 'residence' and 'contact', indisputably preferable to those they replaced, are barely acknowledged outside of the professions for whom they were especially formulated?. The general public do not recognize or use them. The press stubbornly continues referring to 'custody and access' disputes. Popular magazines, soaps and cinema do precisely the same. Jo Spain, a family law solicitor, recently lamented on her company website: 'I keep on hearing about custody ... There is now in English Family Law no such thing as "Custody".'

And she is right. But no matter how many times the same truths have been uttered, the nation as a whole simply isn't listening.

That might be reason in itself, when subtitling a new text, to use either the old or the new. Use the word 'residence' and keep up the good fight in the hope that someday, somehow, the general public will accept and know exactly what you mean; or, use the word 'custody' and be assured that everybody will at least think that they know what you mean.

So why decide on the latter?

The subject matter of this text may be of interest to the public, as much as to professionals in family and childcare law, social work and child protection, to whom it directly speaks. It is not about horrible, sustained, intensifying abuse and neglect of children by parents (or more often, substitute parents) who are clearly incapable of loving them. It is about a phenomenon that in many ways is more inexplicable and frightening: the instant killing of children by those who have never ceased professing their love for them.

In this context, the matter of whether or not to use the old terminology or the new seems not all that important. In the 128 cases identified, all occurring long after 1989, there is no indication whatsoever that the changeover and the subtle differences in meaning had any influence on the tragic outcomes. There is good reason to believe, however, that in the spiralling deterioration of relationships, the majority of protagonists central to the tragedies thought mainly in terms of 'custody' rather than 'residence' and 'access' rather than 'contact'.

There are limits of course to the extent to which an author will strive to reach a wider audience. Chapter 8 is about the legal frameworks which provide opportunities for professionals to prevent filicide tragedies. The old terminology 'custody' and 'access' is unceremoniously ditched for the duration of that chapter.

I hope the reader can at least understand if not forbear the inconsistency.

Acknowledgements

This has been a difficult project, and I am indebted to many in completing the task. A number of Coroners were helpful in discussion and correspondence, and in facilitating attendance in their courts. Many Children's Safeguarding Boards were commendably prompt in response to my requests. Camilla Howley and Geraldine Jentz dug deep into the relevant archives. Elizabeth Jones, solicitor for Liverpool City Council, scrutinized the section in Chapter 8 on child protection law, thankfully making some necessary corrections. Lorraine Blackwood of Vincents Solicitors kindly arranged and accompanied me on a number of visits to someone at the centre of a filicide tragedy, who was willing to talk to me. Sandra Flynn, of the Centre for Mental Health and Risk at University of Manchester, was exceedingly generous with her time, directing me along the most productive routes. Paul Grant, producer of the acclaimed *File on 4* report on Family Annihilators, helped on numerous occasions. The BBC gave permission to quote a mother's searing words on the death of her children. Merseyside Police personnel helped in discussions about new laws and a new culture in tackling domestic violence.

Jackie (obviously not her real name), whose story is the subject of Chapter 9, allowed me to explore in depth her tragedy over a 12-month period. I remain in awe of her resilience, sense of humour, and total lack of sentiment and self-pity.

My wife Maura once again tolerated my two-year hibernation! But she also for the first time had to cope with an author whose subject matter brought him perilously close to the brink!

The project would not have been completed without my daughter, Christine. She edited ceaselessly and rigorously, and guided me through the expanding and increasingly oppressive maze of differing filicide classifications, assuring me at all times that the effort would be worthwhile. It was not without humour, either.

Part I
Filicide: Its Principal Features and Catastrophic Effects

1
Oh my God ... I made a mistake ...

Introduction

Children die in many different ways at the hands of their parents. For the general public, and for future researchers and administrators, they then become statistics. Statistics tell you nothing about what a child endured or experienced preceding the killing; and very little about the perpetrator or the circumstances leading up to the death. Yet it is these factors that may leave indelible memories and provoke powerful emotions in the lives of family members, neighbours and friends. Without such factors, the bare statistics, accumulated over time, are unlikely to move us, or enlighten us about a deepening tragedy in family life. More importantly, such factors may also contain lessons, enabling professionals to minimize the risks of similar killings in the future. In this book, the narrative will often pause on statistics, probing what they do not tell us as much as what they do. The second chapter will give details of the book's contents, but this first chapter is different: it will focus almost entirely on three cases. They belong to that category of filicide in which the method of killing is drowning. This is a relatively short chapter, but it has numerous objectives: (i) to quickly transport the reader into the core painful realities of filicide; (ii) to describe the events leading up to one particular killing; (iii) to highlight the exploitation, abuse and suffering endured by all the children; (iv) to question generally held assumptions about the mental health of perpetrators, particularly revolving around the motivational delusions attributable to them; and, finally, (v) even though the book will make its own contribution to the 'statistical field', and encourage workers to familiarize themselves with all relevant research findings, this chapter will expose the limitations of statistics. Subsequent chapters will contribute in pursuit all of these objectives.

When something more than killing is required

Drowning is commonly chosen by parents as a method of killing their children. Andrea Yates (O'Malley, 2005), perhaps the most infamous name in maternal filicide history, managed to drown all of her five children. The bathroom is frequently the location of the killing, particularly for very young children. They are simply held under water for a long enough period. It doesn't require a great deal of physical strength to hold a young child's head under the water. Resistance is easily overcome. There is little or no noise. There is usually no unsightly bruising or blood.

Within that broader segment of filicide by drowning, however, there is a sub-category in which the drowning is a more explosive culminating point of a sequence of events, than a mere killing. The perpetrator, mother or father, may actually perceive that sequence of events to be more symbolically important than the actual drowning itself. This book is fundamentally about filicide killings in the UK, but these powerful and symbolic drowning incidents take place all over the world. Here are a number of them which have occurred during the past couple of decades:

- In Co. Wexford, Ireland, a 40-year-old father stabbed his wife to death. He then plied his two sons, aged 10 and 6, with alcohol, strapped them into the car and drove at speed off a pier into the sea.
- In South Carolina, USA, a 25-year-old mother released the handbrake of her car on a steep incline which went down into a deep lake. Her two children, aged 3 and 1, were sleeping on the back seat.
- In Victoria, Australia, a 36-year-old father drove the car containing his three children, aged 10, 7 and 2, into a dam. The father escaped.
- In the Midlands, UK, a 42-year-old father drove his car with his two children, aged 6 and 5, into a river. The father and the oldest child escaped.
- In Humberside, a 28-year-old mother clutched her 2-year-old daughter and leapt from the Humber Bridge, one of the most notorious suicide locations in the UK.

- In New York State, a 25-year-old mother drove the car containing her four children, aged 10, 5, 2 and 11 months, into the Hudson River. The oldest child escaped.
- In Denmark, a father threw himself and his 1-year-old daughter over a bridge, after a furious row with his wife. Both died.
- In Lancashire, a 33-year-old mother sedated her husband with sleeping tablets, rendering him unconscious, then strapped her two children, aged 7 and 3, into her car, and drove it into the murky sea at a nearby dockland.

The common factor in these eight cases is conflict in the relationship between father and mother at the time of the killings. The conflict may have been generated or was exacerbated by other factors, such as separation, custody and access disputes, domestic violence, mental illness, or extra-marital affairs. The killings appear to have been a final symbolic act that was intended to, and was certain to, end the conflict and ensure a lasting sense of devastation in the bereaved parent.

Psychological profiling is more bearable than unspeakable suffering

Whenever these types of 'sensational' filicide killings take place, drowning or otherwise, they are the subject of much media attention. Numerous 'experts' are called upon to comment. These experts are invariably asked: how could a parent be driven to the point of doing something like this? The experts have never met the parent, and know nothing about him or her, but that does not prevent them offering theories, explanations and psychological profiles of 'typical' filicide perpetrators. What is conspicuously lacking in these post-mortem analyses is any reference to or any attempt to discover precisely what the children were experiencing in the moments, hours or days leading up to their deaths; it is their killers who are the sole object of interest, for the media and public alike. For family and friends, the children are an unimaginable loss, the source of much trauma and anguish. But for the public at large and the media serving it, they are mere appendages in the tragedy. They will soon graduate though (or be relegated depending on one's point of view) to the role of statistics. Unlike the children seared into our collective consciousness, such as

Victoria Climbié, Baby P and Jasmine Beckford, the filicide victims of marital break-ups are then quickly forgotten about.

There are reasons why these filicide victims are forgotten about, which will be explored in later chapters, but suffice to say at this point that their experiences are often as brutal, nightmarish and destructive as anything endured by those iconic victims in the literature of child abuse. In one sense at least, they endure far more: they are the ultimate pawns, the victims of blatant parental exploitation that has no parallel in any other area of family and childcare work. Worst of all, they are sometimes old enough to realize what is being done to them; they actually see, hear and understand how and why they are being exploited, and they are left in no doubt whatsoever about the intentions of the killer before he or she perpetrates the final act.

Here is the real-life story of one of those children, her sibling and her parents. It is based upon (i) the three-week-long trial of the father, which was given extensive coverage in press, radio, television and the internet; (ii) eye-witness accounts of the killing and the events immediately preceding it; (iii) the judge's summing up; and (iv) a serious case review by the local safeguarding children's board. Fictitious names have been given to all individuals involved, and some material facts have been altered.

Case study 1

The parents of 5-year-old Gillian Rogers and her 6-year-old brother Michael had long separated but the issue of the father's access to the children remained unresolved. Mr Rogers wanted more access. Mrs Rogers, who had custody, did not want him to have any more access.

Contrasting fortunes

The dispute had been ongoing for two to three years. During that time, there was a marked contrast in the fortunes of both parents. Mrs Rogers' situation had stabilised quickly after the separation. She remained in the marital home, had a job, and was well integrated within the community and the school which the children attended. Mr Roger's situation deteriorated rapidly. He was a self-employed mechanic, who lost his workshop (and therefore his job) through debt. He also had to leave his rented accommodation, which compelled him to return to the home of his former wife and three older children. His health deteriorated too, and he was prescribed anti-depressants. He was increasingly reliant on alcohol.

Premeditation

On the day before the incident, Gillian and Michael stayed overnight with their father in the home of his former wife, Sandra. The three older children by that first marriage were there too. The oldest, Karen, was aged 20. Mr Rogers spoke to Karen about his predicament. He said to her at one point that he might go to prison, and he asked Karen would she look after her stepbrother Michael and her stepsister Gillian if that indeed happened. Karen would later testify in court that she interpreted these strange words as meaning he intended to do harm to the children's mother.

On the following morning, Mr and Mrs Rogers had a ferocious argument over the telephone. Mrs Rogers was angrily complaining about the children not being at school. Mr Rogers retorted that the children were never going to school again, and that they were going with him. He told Mrs Rogers to step outside of her home, that he was on his way to her house, and that she would have ten seconds to say goodbye to her children. He told her that she would never see them again.

Even though both children were made aware on numerous occasions of the unhappy state of affairs in the parental relationship, this telephone conversation must have increased their fears and anxieties considerably. We know the children heard it, because Michael said so, in a hand-written letter he wrote of his own volition, 12 months later, to the judge presiding over his father's trial. He was aged 7 then.

The children needed reassurance. They needed comforting. What they got was an enraged and determined father incapable of responding to their needs. He quickly bundled the children into the car and sped towards the home of their mother. He was consumed and driven by the goal which he had publicly pronounced only minutes before: their mother was to have a final sighting of her children, and then she would never see them again.

Nothing to lose, or maybe just bluster

Mrs Rogers had done what he demanded: she was waiting on the pavement outside her door. She felt powerless, helpless and afraid, just like thousands of other parents caught up in bitter acrimonious custody disputes often feel, when the 'other' parent has the children. But Mrs Rogers knew better than anyone else that her predicament was much worse; that the stakes had got much higher. The acrimony between her and Mr Rogers had intensified alarmingly. She was acutely aware of her husband's burdens and misfortunes; his bankruptcy, homelessness and debt; his sense of humiliation in having to depend upon the generosity of his former wife, and of his increasing dependency on prescription pills and alcohol. Perhaps she thought as she waited anxiously on the pavement, that in his misery and in his rage and threats, he felt that he had nothing to lose. These were all sound reasons for her to be very scared indeed.

Conversely, however, she might have thought (and hoped) that it was all bluster and drama; that he was meaning to frighten and hurt her, but that he would not so deliberately and so callously hurt their children. He had after all threatened the children before, 15 months ago to be precise. She told the court about this. It was during another of their rows about contact with the children. She said Mr Rogers told her that if he couldn't have the kids, then she certainly wasn't going to have them. That had frightened her enough to call the police (the police had been called to the home on many occasions). The threat never materialised. Surely then, she may also have thought, he would not carry out this latest more explicit threat, particularly when he had advertised it so dramatically during the telephone call. Surely he wouldn't do anything rash, so publicly, on the street.

The children's nightmare begins

Mr Rogers' car pulled up sharply outside his former family home. The children could now see their mother standing on the pavement, a welcome sight. They had been frightened by the telephone row between their parents, and by their father's consequential rage and the manner by which he had unceremoniously bundled them into the car, and then his near-reckless speed. This 'welcome' sight of their mother, however, did not alleviate them of their distress. Like any 5- and 6-year-old, they instantly recognised in her face something akin to the fear and anxiety they had both just experienced themselves. This was indeed their mother, but without the big smile and the open arms. They had never seen her so tense before, so visibly scared, preoccupied not with welcoming them home, but staring at the face of the father who had yelled at her that this was the nearest they would ever get to returning home. They were not permitted to get out of the car. Their mother wasn't given the opportunity to get into it. They remained locked in, in the back. Their distress increased markedly, and Mrs Rogers' fears for her children intensified.

A witness at the scene testified, as did Mrs Rogers herself that Mr Rogers pulled up only for seconds, to afford her, as he had threatened, nothing more than a final fleeting glimpse of her two children. She begged to have her kids back, but Mr Rogers kept saying 'No!' The other witness then heard him say: 'They're going to die.'

A blinding hatred

Instead of sitting in their classrooms chatting and joking with their friends, as they normally would have been doing around this time, Gillian and Michael were being systematically terrorized. The emotional and psychological abuse being inflicted upon them was of a nature and intensity that, even had they been rescued at that particular moment, they would have been severely traumatized. They had just heard their father say that they were going to die, and the horribleness of those words was wholly compatible with his behaviour, with the expressions on his face, the tone of his voice, and above all the hatred in his eyes. Amazingly, he had said they were going to die, but he never once looked at them. He was utterly oblivious to them and the suffering he was causing them. He only had eyes for the woman he was tormenting.

Mrs Rogers recalled for the court what she described as vile contortions in Mr Rogers' face as he sat in the 'driving' seat, watching her, in effect mocking her helplessness. She vaguely recalled his use of the word 'river' somewhere in among his tirades and his threats.

A futile attempt to save them

It was that word 'river' that made Mrs Rogers dive at the door handle of the car. She knew now that he was deadly serious. She knew how he was going to kill her children. She could see the children as he had intended, the terror in their eyes, their faces separated by a cold car window. And she could hear them screaming. She could not for another second bear the crushing, insufferable sense of her own powerlessness.

Her fingers never reached the door handle. He sped off, towards a nearby field and the river; he drove so fast that another witness who was in the field at the time believed he must have floored the accelerator. He clearly wanted to ensure maximum lift-off from the banks of the river. He wanted the car to be submerged completely, with his children trapped in it.

Losing power and control

Mr Rogers left a number of 'suicide' notes in the car. One of these blamed his wife, and boasted that the children were with him now. If it was his intention to die with his children, as this typical suicide note suggested, his efforts failed abysmally. He could well have chosen a more effective means of suicide and murder, one that did not pose the risk of pain or any great inconvenience to him personally. He could also have chosen a means whereby he controlled events, at least until the dastardly deed was over. Mr Rogers, however, chose a method that was fraught with uncertainty from the outset, that was guaranteed to wrest all power and control from his hands, that would cause him extreme pain and terror as he nearly drowned, and perhaps most significantly, that triggered a crisis in which he not only lost control, but also, his original conviction and intent. Even the most knowledgeable experts in submerged cars cannot predict with confidence what happens to a car and its occupants after lift-off. Mr Rogers was most unqualified to make such a prediction himself.

Unexpected and unintended outcome

Somehow Mr Rogers and Michael escaped from the vehicle, but Gillian remained trapped in the passenger seat below. Emergency services had been called instantly. When a police inspector and a sergeant arrived, they threw a line in the direction of Mr Rogers, and noticed that he made no attempt to grab it. Near to him was what the police first regarded as a floating bundle, but then realised it was a small child. The inspector jumped into the water and brought Michael to the bank where he was treated by paramedics. Mr Rogers was able to make it to the bank on his own. He testified that he had made repeated unsuccessful attempts to rescue Gillian from the front passenger seat where she was presumably strapped in. This was not verified by witnesses.

Gillian spent two hours in the totally submerged car in the freezing cold water before being rescued by specialist divers through the car's sun roof. A paediatric consultant said that she was pulse-less and without signs of life. She was given oxygen before being airlifted to the nearest Children's Hospital. There she received cardio pulmonary resuscitation but she remained asystolic. Subsequent tests revealed extensive brain damage and a severe heart injury. The breathing tube that was inserted was removed and she was pronounced dead, three days after the incident.

The reality of drowning

Some time in the future Michael may be able to say precisely what he experienced during those moments from the time his father sped away from his mother's desperate attempts to reach the car door, to the time that he found himself struggling to breathe and to survive in the freezing waters of the river. As for Gillian, her suffering defies description.

Ron Shaw is an aquatics director and operations manager for public swimming pools who exposes the 'myth about drowning that survives to this day ... that it is a painless, almost pleasant way to die' (1992, p. 1). He details the process of drowning: the blockage of the trachea and the consequential respiratory arrest; the limiting of the body's ability to exchange gases and provide oxygen to the blood; the water being drawn into the bloodstream through the lung's alveoli, the dilution causing an electrolyte imbalance in the body which can bring on fibrillation in the heart, the pressure in the chest and throat; the eyes clouded and the ears bursting. For any normal fit human being, it is nothing short of agony. For a 5-year-old, terrorized by her father's behaviour in the minutes before, the physical and mental suffering can barely be imagined.

The judge in Mr Rogers' trial seemed to have a reasonable grasp of the enormity of the crimes he had committed and the suffering he had caused. Unusually for Crown Court judges in these highly complex cases that originate in fractious separations and disputes over contact with children, his comments on Mr Rogers' actions were scathing and condemnatory: 'These crimes were born of anger and self-pity,' he said. 'You betrayed the trust of these defenceless children who were screaming and crying in terror ... they looked to you for support and protection.' He sentenced Mr Rogers to 16 years for the murder of Gillian, and eight years, to run concurrently, for the attempted murder of Michael.

The nature of the abuse

What is it that makes the case of Gillian so different and so much worse than the many cases in which a parent kills a child and commits, or attempts to commit suicide? The degree of suffering she endured was certainly exceptional, but so too is that of many filicide victims. The answer to the question may not be so obvious, and could never be elicited from statistics. Mr Rogers chose not just to murder his children, but to immerse them in the final phase of a relationship in which his sole motive and driving force were hatred and revenge. He consciously gave them a very specific role during that final phase. First, he had to create the conditions which would terrorize them and, then, their terror was to be exhibited to the mother at a chosen moment when it was impossible for her to do anything about it.

When the judge remarked that the children 'looked to you for support and protection', he was giving some indication of the extent to which Mr Rogers had effectively anaesthetised his moral and emotional antennae. The judge was in effect reminding Mr Rogers that what he did to his children before attempting to kill them was subject them to experiences that were certain to provoke in them the emotions of *panic, fear, terror, bewilderment, acute distress, anguish* and *shock*.

When small children feel and express emotions like those, any normal parent would take them in his arms and hold them lovingly and tenderly until those awful emotions had subsided. This comforting would usually be accompanied by reassuring words. But, bizarrely, and yet inescapably, those were precisely the emotions that Mr Rogers needed to provoke in his children. He needed emotionally distraught children to present to his wife in a situation and context in which she was helpless to do anything about it. Two children sitting in the car happily playing with their iPods would have had little impact other than been a source of reassurance to their waiting mother. Mr Rogers was hell-bent on doing the opposite to reassuring their mother. The more extreme the emotional pain and the visible anguish of Michael and Gillian, the greater would be their mother's fear and terror. And the more he controlled and intensified her sense of helplessness as she watched her children suffer, the greater his sense of gratification and achievement. But he was not to know that these perverse thoughts and feelings would evaporate the moment he hit the water.

Case study 2

Fourteen months later, just as Mr Rogers was about to go on trial, another filicide drowning tragedy which attracted worldwide publicity occurred in New York State (Parker, 2011). A 25-year-old mother drove herself and her four children, aged 10, 5, 2 and 11 months, into the Hudson River. The similarities with the Rogers case are striking: (i) the killings occurred immediately after a ferocious row between the mother and her partner; (ii) the children without any notice or preparation were unceremoniously bundled into a minivan; (iii) there was a history of domestic incidents and violence to which the police had often been summoned; (iv) the mother was fearful about leaving her children with her partner (as she had to do often, because she worked and attended college; her partner was actually facing the prospect of prosecution for neglect of one of the children); (v) just as Mr Rogers had felt the need to give some hint of his intentions to his eldest daughter, this young American mother had the same need. Before she left the house after the ferocious row, she phoned a relative and told her that she was going to do something terrible. A few days previously, she had chosen a much wider audience. On her Facebook page she had posted a stark message: *'I'm sorry... everyone forgive me please for what I'm gonna do...This is it!!!'*. In the minivan she told the children that they were going to die with her; (vi) the mother's mental health had become a matter of concern to her family and friends; in the weeks before the incident, she had been ringing many of them and apologising if she had ever done anything untoward to them; and, finally, (vii) just as Michael had miraculously done, this mother's eldest child, aged, 10, managed to escape from the submerged vehicle and alert the authorities (Watkins, 2011).

Case study 3

In the UK, a few years earlier, a 28-year-old woman carefully prepared to murder her 2-year-old daughter and kill herself by leaping from the Humber Bridge, clutching the child. More than one hundred people have committed suicide at this location since the bridge was opened in 1975. The mother, highly educated and professionally qualified, would leave a will, including 28 envelopes, each containing a different photograph of her, and all ironically addressed to the daughter she was about to kill. She wrote on her stomach, as well as in suicide notes, that her husband was to blame for her actions. They had had a protracted and bitter dispute which ended with a court deciding her husband should have custody of the child. She thereafter found life intolerable.

Life was not extinguished, however. Astonishingly (in the views of the experts and contrary to the grim statistics), both mother and child survived. They were in the water for 45 minutes before being rescued. The mother suffered a fractured spine. The child was treated for hypothermia. When she had recovered from the ordeal, the mother was charged with attempting to murder the child. She pleaded guilty to this charge. She was sentenced to 18 months imprisonment, and was released halfway through her sentence, by the Court of Appeal, on the rarely invoked grounds of 'mercy'.

More similarities

At first glance, this case seems to have nothing in common with the previous two, but it is in fact remarkably similar in key respects. First, there were survivors in all three cases: a father and child in the first; the oldest child in the second, and a mother and child in the third. One of the difficulties in filicide research is that more often than not, there are no survivors to interview, because the perpetrators have succeeded in killing both the children and themselves. In our three case studies, the survivors were potentially invaluable witnesses. Second, all three were premeditated, determined and carefully planned filicide acts (though not so well executed). The core purpose and the all-consuming desires were to kill the children, and they had clearly hinted at something catastrophic in the conversations with others, in Facebook postings, and in suicide writings. Third, all three perpetrators were to varying degrees motivated by revenge or retaliation. They perceived their partners as the principal source of their misery, and they undoubtedly wanted them to share some if not all responsibility for the killing(s), and to endure a pervasive guilt as a consequence. Fourth, the perpetrators underwent some kind of metamorphosis at the precise moment of killing, or attempting to kill their children. This is the most intriguing and the most revealing of all the similarities.

Delusions

As well as revenge, all three perpetrators suffered varying degrees of depression and were driven by *delusion*. This is defined as 'false opinion or belief which cannot be shaken by reason' (Drever, 1953, p. 63). They believed that killing their children and killing themselves was the right thing and the only thing they could do. They expended considerable time and energy, and displayed a near-fanatical determination in achieving this perverse goal. But then something extraordinary happened in each incident. It was witnessed by the two surviving children in the first and second case studies, and by the surviving mother in the third.

When 6-year-old Michael in case study 1 decided of his own volition to write to the judge in his father's trial a year after he nearly drowned, he recalled the moment the car hit the water and his father saying: 'What have I done?' It is both a question and a statement that in its tone, content and doubt, is utterly incongruent with the father's delusions and his determination and intentions so visibly and audibly displayed in the hour preceding the crash. Despite the child's fear and terror at the time, he managed to reply to his father's 'daft' question by telling him he had done 'something really bad ...'

In case study 2, when the 10-year-old child who escaped into the icy waters of the Hudson River and was picked up by a passing woman driver, he blurted out everything that happened in the last few seconds of his family's lives. As the car hit the water and immediately sank, his mother had said: 'Oh my God! I made a mistake ... I made a mistake ...' The mother then frantically tried to put the car into reverse, but it was too late. The 10-year-old consistently repeated these fixed unwavering memories to investigators many times over.

In case study 3, the barrister defending the mother during her trial for attempted murder, made much of the depression she was suffering (as a consequence of losing her child in the custody dispute) and the delusions under which she was living. He said his client believed that her actions 'would lead to an afterlife where she could be with her daughter in a place where they could be happy together' (StokeS, 2006). The Lord Chief Justice and his colleagues hearing the mother's appeal for 'mercy', however, chose to focus on something entirely different; the noble Lord declared that: '... the moment she hit the water she came to her senses and shouted for help'. She not only shouted for help, but she somehow kept the child's head above the waterline for 45 minutes. The Lord Chief Justice remarked that she had 'saved the life' that she had 'tried to end' (BBC News, 2007).

The fragility of delusion

What is the significance of these cases? It seems that the impact of crashing into the rivers and being engulfed in icy cold water instantly shattered the delusions and the murderous convictions that were driving all three perpetrators. One parent then tried and succeeded in escaping, leaving his youngest child to die alone. That is not meant to cast any aspersions in respect of a lack of courage or an abundance of cowardice; it is merely to emphasise that his long-festering intent of killing himself and his children was instantly replaced by an almighty physical and mental effort to save his own life. The second perpetrator experienced precisely the same. She too was hell-bent on killing herself and her children, and obviously had been so since she posted her apologies for what she was going to do on Facebook. But that conviction, that delusion that she had to do it because it was the right and the only thing to do, was instantly turned on its head; she admitted to 'making a mistake', and she then instinctively, but futilely did the opposite; she tried to reverse the minivan out of the river. The third perpetrator had exactly the same conversion. She acknowledged that in a moving testimony during her trial:

> When I was in the water and (-------) was screaming, scared and cold, it was me who felt the most pain. My child was now suffering more than before. I'm forever grateful for those who saved my little princess. In seeing my child so poorly and so scared I knew that I had made everything worse.
>
> (Stokes, 2006)

Thus, three people wanted to kill their children by drowning and to drown with them; they were absolutely determined to bring that about. Those three same people strove to do the opposite as soon as they were enduring an apparently unanticipated, but very real physical discomfort brought about by the coldness, wetness and darkness, and of course, the reality of the threat of death. They didn't want to die after all. Their festering murderous delusions about the worthlessness of their lives, and their revenge and retaliation motives in taking the children with them, all dissolved instantaneously.

In inquests relating to filicide killings, delusions are often cited as a cause. In court trials of parents charged with the murder of their children, delusions have been the pivot around which psychiatrists for the defence and prosecution provide conflicting evidence in ascertaining degrees of responsibility. The delusions of the perpetrator often underpin the belief of many professionals that filicide killings are unpredictable and unpreventable. The principal goal in this book is to demonstrate that most of them are predictable and preventable.

Conclusion

Hopefully this chapter has achieved some of its objectives. The first objective was to quickly transport the reader into the core realities of filicide killings; the second and third were to concentrate on one particular case (Michael and Gillian) and demonstrate the perverse nature and magnitude of suffering and exploitation that can be inflicted on children; the fourth was to question generally held perceptions and assumptions about 'delusion' which is one of the most frequently occurring concepts in filicide literature and research; this has implications for many other widely held views about filicide; and the final objective was to highlight the limitations of statistics in understanding a phenomenon that child protection agencies know little about. This book is not about the killing of children through mounting repetitive abuse, cruelty and neglect; nor is it about the increasing number of child fatalities perpetrated by parents living in squalor and helplessly addicted to drugs; nor is it about child victims of lightning catastrophic mental health breakdowns in otherwise stable, functioning happy families. It is primarily about the phenomenon of children being killed by 'loving' parents, often ruthlessly and brutally. Many of them are consciously or unconsciously exploited as pawns, before, during and after increasingly fractious relationship breakdowns. Consequential and deteriorating mental health problems may impinge to varying degrees on the final outcome, but ultimately, the children are used as tools of revenge and/or retaliation. Such factors will be explored often, and in depth. The underlying objective in this text is to sustain focus on the children; to ensure that the conventions of textbook writing (imparting knowledge and understanding, principles and professionalism) do not convert those children into mere statistics, unwittingly denying the reality of their existence, their individuality, their uniqueness, and their fate.

2
Features of filicide
More common than we think

Introduction

The tragic events of the three cases recorded in Chapter 1 may appear extreme in every respect. In the first case in particular, for example, the cruelty and exploitation of the children reached new depths of hideousness. Yet there are many features of the three cases which are common in day-to-day family and childcare work. This chapter will identify and explore those features.

Cases in which there is the potential for filicide will always be exceptionally challenging for professionals. Unlike in the many categories of child abuse, such as sexual abuse, emotional and psychological abuse, neglect, social deprivation and so on, there is not a body of literature and research on filicide specifically aimed towards preparing and equipping professionals. But there is an expanding library of studies on individual filicide cases. These are called serious case reviews.

Just over a decade ago, child killings resulting from sustained cruelty and neglect were usually the subject of highly publicized and publicly attended inquiries. Today, for all non-accidental child killings, the authorities are obliged to set up a *serious case review*. Initially, these reviews were cloaked in secrecy and confidentiality, which made little or no contribution towards understanding filicide killings. The public could only see the flimsiest version (called an executive summary) of the overall report. In June 2010, however, the government instructed local authorities to make serious case reviews available in their entirety. This chapter will critically examine the emergence of serious case reviews and their relevance to filicide killings. It will conclude with a detailed preview of the contents and objectives of remaining chapters.

Not so unique?

There are many features of the three case studies in the previous chapter which we might regard as extreme: the sustained and deliberate cruelty inflicted on the children (particularly in case study 1); the revenge motive, the advance notice of the intention to kill, the symbolic sensationalism in the method of killing, and the mass killings themselves, of four children under six years of age. Not many professionals, fortunately, encounter such tragedies, or are given responsibility for preventing them. But family and childcare professionals in particular, are nevertheless familiar with many of the features of filicide cases. These include relationships disintegrating, separation, divorce; dispute over custody and access; domestic violence, police involvement, mental health problems; and the exploitation of children. All of these filicide features will be explored and discussed throughout this text, but at this point each of them warrants a brief comment to demonstrate that they are all common challenges which childcare professionals confront on a daily basis.

Relationship breakdown

The UK has for many years had one of the highest divorce rates in the world. It had been steadily decreasing during the past decade, but the Office of National Statistics (2011) shows that the number of divorces in England and Wales in 2010 was 119,589, an increase of 4.9 per cent over the previous year. The total for 2009 was 113,949. Significant as these figures are, they tell only half the story in regards to the actual number of parents who separate.

Unlike the downward trend during the past decade in the number of married people divorcing, the number of unmarried, cohabiting couples has increased dramatically. In the decade 1996 to 2006, it increased by 65 per cent, from 1.4 million to 2.3 million (Office of National Statistics, 2011). Consequently, the number of births outside marriage has rocketed to almost 50 per cent of the total, and is forecast to go well beyond that by 2016 (Office of National Statistics, 2013). Although the ONS does not provide accurate figures for the number of cohabiting couples who separate, the Millennium Cohort Study (Benson, 2009) initially focussing on 10,000 mothers who gave birth in 2000–01, is the most reliable indicator to date on this issue. It calculates that unmarried cohabiting parents are at least twice as likely to split up as married parents, regardless of income or education; more significantly, 35 per cent of the former are likely to have split by the time their offspring reach the age of 5, compared to 9 per cent of the latter. This suggests that the ONS divorce rate is much less than the *total* number of parents who are separating, and that the children of married and unmarried separating parents combined are much younger than the ages which ONS provides in respect of divorced parents alone. Whether their parents are married or cohabiting, however, the impact of separation on children can be severe, which is one of the reasons why so many childcare professionals become involved.

Relationship breakdown is the most conspicuous and significant characteristic of the filicide cases in this study. It is also one of the most common features encountered in childcare and child protection work. Its immediate and lasting consequences are the essence of the major challenges that workers face in ensuring the welfare and protection of children.

Disputes over custody and access

Separation and divorce after a relationship breakdown can be a carefully orchestrated, mutually consensual arrangement, involving children old enough to understand what is happening, and why. But most often it is not, which is precisely why social workers, lawyers, court welfare officers, probation officers, guardian ad litems, judges and mediation counsellors, get involved. The purpose of involvement, whether through public or private law, is predominantly to ensure the welfare of the child. Most parents experiencing the trauma of separation and all the bitterness and sense of betrayal that might ensue are the least likely people to cordially agree to a custody and access plan; on the contrary, custody and access for many separating parents represent the first and most contentious battleground. Achieving suitable access arrangements can be a formidable challenge for the professionals and for the courts. In the vast majority of filicide cases in this study, one quickly sees that within the disagreements about custody and access, is the potential for unleashing destructive and suicidal forces. Professionals in family and childcare work may never encounter filicide, but they are more than familiar with these potentially violent situations.

Tensions, rows, and recriminations

Social workers often sense the deep underlying tension in relationships which have broken down. The tension may manifest itself in total separation; a determination by both parents to avoid each other, not to be in the same room, not to share meals, children or friends. It may manifest itself in an entirely different way: explosive rows triggered by the slightest provocation, accusations and counter-accusations, walkouts with doors mightily slammed. Other parties may be drawn into the dispute, ostensibly to support and help, but invariably, unintentionally, exacerbating every aspect of the dispute. Tension and mutual ill-feelings will rise. Each parent may think that decisive action is necessary: separation, divorce ... some kind of final solution.

These are also the behaviours and processes evident in the preceding weeks and months leading up to the cataclysmic end in many filicide cases. Witnesses later testify that the relationship rapidly deteriorated, that rows became more frequent, that threats and violence ensued. Many groups of professionals are thoroughly familiar with these scenarios. In the vast majority of cases which they deal with, parental relationships do not degenerate into murderous thoughts and impulses, but seldom can they be sure of how near or how far off such thoughts were.

Violence and the threat of more violence

Over 40 per cent of male perpetrator cases in this study had incidents of domestic violence. Many of them were serious enough to necessitate police intervention; some of them led to prosecutions. Saunders (2004), on behalf of Women's Aid Federation of England, studied 13 cases of filicide in which 29 children were killed. Domestic violence was a recurring theme in 11 of these cases.

Few if any of the professionals already mentioned in this chapter have not encountered cases of domestic violence and witnessed its effects. Walby and Allen (2004) estimated that there were 12.9 million incidents of domestic violence against women and 2.5 million against men in a single year. Even allowing for the fact that the vast majority of these incidents went unreported, the police dealt with nearly one million *recorded* cases of domestic violence in the year 2009–10 (Home Office, 2010). In addition to police and social workers, many other professionals deal with domestic violence and its effects on a daily basis. These include after hours crisis intervention teams, staff in refuge centres, and perhaps most important of all, nurses and doctors working in hospital accident and emergency centres.

Mental health problems

Social workers responsible for investigating child abuse referrals and implementing child protection strategies are well aware of the prevalence of mental illness among parents who have neglected their children, or who have abused them physically, emotionally or psychologically (Farmer and Owen, 1995; Pritchard, 2004). Practitioners and researchers in child maltreatment since as long ago as the 1950s have identified mental illness as a causal or contributory factor in child abuse (Baldwin, *et al.* 1982; Orraschel *et al.*, 1980; Pollitt, 1965). Researchers have consistently estimated the number of diagnosed mentally ill parents being investigated and monitored by child protection agencies to be in the range of 25–35 per cent (for example, Falcov, 1996; Hetherington *et al.*, 2002; Oliver, 1985). This figure approximates with the number of diagnosed mentally ill perpetrators of filicide (Flynn *et al.*, 2009; Gilbert, 2008; Somander and Rammer, 1991). Depression is the most common mental illness of parents in both filicide and child abuse research (Belsky and Vondra, 1989; Corby, 2000).

Exploiting the child

In the first chapter, a father who is involved in a bitter and protracted custody dispute, uses his children as pawns, exploiting them to the extent of emotionally and psychologically abusing them, terrorizing them, and then attempting to kill them. His ultimate objective, motivated by revenge, was to inflict incalculable suffering on the children's mother.

Childcare professionals and divorce and family law solicitors are all well aware of the extent of exploitation of children. Twice within a four-month period in 2011, Sir Nicholas Wall, President of the Family Division (i.e., the country's principal Family Court judge) felt the need to go public on the issue (BBC News Online, 2011).

He talked about the dramatic increase in the number of children who 'have to somehow survive between the warring parents'. Here are some quotes from both of those addresses:

> Children are often very damaged by the way family disputes are settled in adversarial court cases.
>
> Parents use children as weapons in divorce.
>
> Children are both the battlefield and the ammunition.
>
> There is nothing worse for most children than for their parents to denigrate each other.

The danger in this disturbing trend lies in the fact that using children, in the judge's words, as a *battlefield*, and as the *weapon* and the *ammunition* of choice, in other words as the ultimate pawns, their parents are in essence not just vengefully exploiting them, but exposing them to substantial risk of a violent death. The dividing line between such a cataclysmic outcome and the general misery inflicted upon children unwittingly used in parental conflicts may be a very thin one indeed.

Filicide: a neglected field

Despite the similarities discernible between the comparatively unknown world of filicide and the well-worn field of family and childcare work, there remains a huge discrepancy in the level of expertise, practice training, literature and research available for each. Unlike in many of the different categories of child abuse (that is, physical, emotional, psychological abuse, and so on) there is not a body of literature and research specifically aimed at preparing and equipping professionals who may find themselves in potential filicide situations. There is, however, an expanding library of studies on individual filicide cases. These studies are called serious case reviews. Unfortunately, they have, since their inception, been cloaked in secrecy and have contributed little to the overall learning. Their major contribution has been to stifle public and professional debate about filicide killings, and to further entrench the view that such killings cannot be predicted or prevented. That is a view strongly challenged by Women's Aid (Saunders, 2004), by feminist researchers (Johnson, 2005; Kirkwood, 2012) and by subsequent chapters in this text. It is necessary to look at the origin and evolution of serious case reviews, herein after referred to as SCRs.

The antecedents of serious case reviews

The Maria Colwell Report was published in 1974 and the Victoria Climbié Report, in 2003 (Department of Health and Social Security, 1974; Laming 2003). The Colwell Report was instrumental in the formulation of the 1975 Children's Act. The Climbié Report directly led to the radical paper *Every Child Matters* (DfES, 2003) and to the subsequent 2004 Children's Act. Between those dates an additional 70 child abuse inquiry reports were published. Many of them, particularly the 32 reports published between 1974 and 1985 (the year of the Jasmine Beckford Report) influenced in varying degrees the milestone 1989 Children Act. Nearly all the reports (and none more so than that on Victoria Climbié) were based upon public inquiries in which individual professionals and their managers were called upon to give evidence and to be questioned and cross-questioned by counsel for the various parties. The inquiries were also helped by written submissions from interested lay persons and family and childcare experts.

A cheaper, more secretive and much less explosive alternative

In 1991, the government produced its paper *Working Together Under the Children Act* (Department of Health, 1991b). Whether it was intended or not, this was a first step in establishing SCRs as a viable and much cheaper alternative to child abuse public inquiries. The *Working Together* paper has been revised many times, with whole chapters devoted to the purposes of and the processes involved in conducting SCRs. The primary purposes are spelt out in the opening pages of every SCR:

> To establish what lessons are to be learnt from the case about the way in which local professionals and organisations work

individually and together to safeguard and promote the welfare of children; identify clearly what those lessons are both within and between agencies.

(HM Govt., 2010, p. 234)

It is interesting to contrast this strictly formal, non-informative bureaucratic speak with the opening pages of some well-known child abuse inquiry reports, such as that on Jasmine Beckford, for example. It tells us that:

> Jasmine died at the age of 4½ ... as a direct result of several manual blows ... Jasmine was a very thin little girl ... emaciated as a result of chronic under-nourishment ... Apart from stunted development, she had been subjected to parental battering over a protracted period ... to say nothing of the psychological battering she must have undergone ...
>
> (Blom-Cooper, 1985, p. 2)

The opening paragraph of the report on Victoria Climbié (Laming, 2003) is more succinct, but even more searing. It says that Victoria was 'transformed from a happy little girl into a wretched and broken wreck of a human being' (1.10). This may not be the language one expects from the higher echelons of the judiciary, but, in both cases, one cannot help sensing that the inquiries have been rigorous, and that they are going to be exceedingly disturbing to read.

Exclusion of the public and public scrutiny

In contrast to the transparency of public inquiries, SCRs were cloaked in secrecy. The public and the press were excluded from the whole process. The completed SCRs were made available only to a small group of people, chiefly those who had contributed to and/or participated in its production. A tokenistic, curiously named *executive summary* of the main report was provided for the public. This summary was usually no more than six or seven pages long, more than half of which consisted of (i) direct quotes from the *Working Together* stipulations; (ii) a list of contributors; and (iii) a lengthy list of recommendations for improvements. The summary had little substantive information on the circumstances of or contributory factors to the children's deaths.

A welcome change?

The number of SCRs has increased dramatically since 1991. Sidebotham (2012) calculates there are now over 100 produced each year. Consequently, the number of child abuse public inquiry reports have dwindled to zero, the last and most notable being that of Victoria Climbié (Laming, 2003). The advantages for agencies of SCRs over child abuse inquiry reports cannot be over-estimated: no more daily public exposure and rigorous cross-questioning of managerial and frontline child protection staff; no more ridicule and pillorying of individual professionals by the tabloid press; no more need for public apologies by CEOs (since the public had been deprived of seeing the SCRs), and perhaps most appreciated of all, the public would no longer have to hear excruciatingly painful details of the suffering endured by the child, with the consequent clamour for heads to roll.

Resistance to change

The government periodically reviewed SCRs when revising the *Working Together* paper (Brandon *et al.*, 2009; Brandon, *et al.*, 2011, Department for Education, 2008a, 2008b, 2009; Ofsted, 2010; Sidebotham, 2012). The relevant authorities and agencies approved of the now wholly entrenched culture of secrecy and anonymity. Eleven out of 14 respondents in the 2009 consultation exercise 'indicated explicitly that they were not in favour of publication of full SCRs' (Department for Children, Schools and Families, 2009, p. 5). Only one respondent favoured publication.

The most persistent objection by the authorities to publication of whole SCRs revolved around the issue of confidentiality and data protection. Even with redaction, and anonymity, it was believed that the overview reports had too much information, allowing the press and public to identify the family. This was sensible in respect of SCRs dealing with non-accidental injury to children, which perhaps had never been publicized, and it was both sensible and necessary in respect of professionals involved in such cases. But that same objection was not as strong in respect of SCRs of filicide killings. At the time of the killings, photographs of family members, plus their names, ages, addresses, schools, and employment, were repeated ad nauseam in every newspaper and in every news bulletin. This intense media interest lasted a week or so, and then it died away. In three, six or twelve months time, however, the interest was rekindled during the trial of the perpetrator (if the perpetrator was still alive) and/or during an inquest on the victims. And of course, there was the internet.

A change of direction

No one could have predicted that the 2009 consultation on publication would be the last, or why. In March 2006, Peter Connelly, known as Baby P, was born. He died in August 2007. His short life was one of neglect and sustained physical, emotional and psychological abuse. Medical staff discovered more than 50 injuries on his body in a blood-stained cot. In an eight-month period before his death, he had received 61 visits from social workers, health workers, and police. His mother was jailed in 2009 after admitting causing or allowing his death. Her partner and lodger were both convicted of causing his death and sentenced to 12 years and a minimum of three years respectively. These three individuals were publicly named after a court order granting them anonymity was lifted in March 2009.

The politicization of Baby P

Why did this case attract so much attention? Equally shocking murders of toddlers occurred *before* and *after* Baby P became public. The case of Baby P, however, was different in crucial respects: (i) he lived and he was tortured and beaten to death in Haringey, the same authority castigated in the child abuse inquiry report on the death of Victoria Climbié (Laming, 2003); (ii) in February, 2007, a social worker whistle-blower sent a letter to the Department of Health expressing her concerns about Haringey's child protection failings shortly after Lord Laming's devastating report; and (iii) after the convictions of the three people involved, Ed Balls, Minister for Children, felt compelled to order an inquiry into events surrounding the death of Baby P, more specifically, into the role of the local authority, the health authority and the police, a much wider brief than that of merely 'learning the lessons' of SCRs. This was the beginning of the politicization of the case, leading to (i) sustained media scrutiny and comment; (ii) public revulsion and sweeping condemnations; (iii) unprecedented argument and debate in Parliament about the ramifications of the Baby P case; (iii) resignations, including that of Haringey's Council Leader and his deputy; (v) the sacking of managerial and frontline staff; and (vi) not one, but *two* serious case reviews (the first was rejected by Ofsted) and each of them in their entirety available online, a decision made by the incoming coalition government in the teeth of opposition from their predecessors and most agencies.

Policy reversal

The death of Baby P was the catalyst for change, but change itself was inevitable when the coalition took power. The Shadow Children's Minister Tim Loughton had written an article three months before taking office, which could have left no one in any doubt as to the fate of the secret SCRs:

> In addition we must be able to show that the lessons of previous failures have been learnt and acted upon. When those lessons are secreted in unpublished Serious Case Reviews (SCRs) accessible by only a small number of people, the public have no way of judging what the lessons were and if there have been genuine attempts to resolve outstanding problems. When the thin executive summaries of those reports are revealed as bearing little relation to the underlying report, and when a subsequent Serious Case Review later trots out the same old shortcomings in the same authority, it is little wonder that the public suspect cover-up and obfuscation.
> (Loughton, 2010a, p. 5)

Consequently, on the 10th June 2010, Loughton instructed all Directors of Children's Services and Local Safeguarding Children Boards that the overview report of SCRs should be published and made available, 'appropriately redacted and anonymized to protect the privacy and welfare of vulnerable children and their families' (Loughton, 2010b).

Criticism of SCRs

Despite Loughton's directive, of the 147 SCRs initiated since, only 28 have been published, according to the journal *Professional Social Work* (Navqi, 2013). Yet 28 voluminous reports represent a significant advance in transparency. Studying them, we can now understand not just why resistance to publication was (and remains) so strong, but also the level and nature of criticism of SCRs from the government's own commissioned research. Brandon *et al.*'s (2011) specific focus on SCR recommendations revealed the astonishing figure of 932 recommendations in a mere 20 SCRs which occurred in 2009–11. The vast majority of the recommendations were for new procedures and training. Very rarely were the recommendations evidence-based. There was little or no awareness in any of the recommendations of the links between deprivation and child maltreatment. The authors commented that: '[Safeguarding Children Boards] need to take responsibility for curbing this self-perpetuating cycle of a proliferation of recommendations and tasks and allow themselves to consider other ways of learning from serious case reviews' (ibid., p. 2).

Sidebotham (2012) warned about the proliferation of new procedures. He indirectly criticizes the mechanism by which material is accumulated for the review, which can be a purely administrative exercise overseen by the panel chair person. Something more is required: 'The current approach, based primarily on a review of records with or without interviews of practitioners, does not encourage learning' (ibid., p. 4), which of course is supposed to be the *raison d'être* of SCRs.

Are filicide killings neither predictable nor preventable?

SCRs on filicide cases have invariably concluded that the killings are neither predictable nor preventable. Since virtually nobody outside of those who produced them were permitted to read them, it was a view unlikely to be contested. Now it has to be contested, because, even though still subject to redaction and anonymization, SCRs reveal a great many shortcomings in how agencies and individual professionals responded. We will look at some of the SCRs on filicide killings in more detail in subsequent chapters, but suffice to acknowledge at this point that professionals may have, through their words, actions and more commonly their omissions, unwittingly contributed to the deteriorating relationship dynamic and to the individual social, emotional and psychological disintegration that so often precedes a filicide act. Conversely, comprehensive, rigorous assessment of risk (the most glaringly common omission revealed in SCRs), and the readiness to intervene on the basis of the conclusion reached about risk, may have saved lives. It may be some time before the authors of SCRs can admit to either of these possibilities. Only then will frontline professionals truly 'learn the lessons' and discard the debilitating pessimism of believing that every filicide killing was neither predictable nor preventable.

Chapter content

Chapter 3 will complete Part I of the book. It will provide definitions of the terms which frequently appear in filicide literature; these include homicide, infanticide, neonaticide, uxoricide, femicide and familicide. The book's primary focus is on filicide in the context of marital conflict, relationship breakdown and custody and access disputes. Mental illness is a common feature in many of these situations. The cases looked at have an additional set of criteria which differentiates them from all other categories of filicide. The chapter will also look at filicide within a historical and cultural perspective.

Chapter 4 will review the substantial body of filicide research and literature that has accumulated over six decades. Although there are countless areas of diverse study within filicide, the chapter will focus on five discernible strands that predominate: (i) the concentration on female perpetrators; (ii) reviews of original and contemporary literature and research; (iii) the accumulation of basic data on all aspects of filicide killings; (iv) a feminist-sociological perspective on filicide; and (v) publicized personal testimony from bereaved mothers.

Chapter 5 will present the findings of this study on 128 cases of filicide and familicide which occurred in the UK between 1994 and 2012. They are divided into three categories: (i) filicide perpetrated by fathers; (ii) filicide perpetrated by mothers; and (iii) familicide (that is: the annihilation of whole families) perpetrated by fathers. These findings are presented in the usual empirical manner, but additionally, each case is listed, giving the children fictitious names and their actual ages, and the means by which they were killed.

Chapter 6 will look at the mental illness context of many filicide killings. One of the inevitable casualties of marital conflict, of fractious separation and/or custody and access disputes, is the mental well-being of one or both of the protagonists. Recent inquiries into filicide-suicides by mothers suffering from depression will be explored.

Chapter 7, the opening chapter of Part III will critically explore the origins and development of the concept of 'altruism' or 'love' as a motivating factor in filicide. This concept is rooted in filicide research of the 1960s, and is frequently advanced as an explanation for the killings. There are risks in this 'explanation' which need to be acknowledged.

Chapter 8 will explore the legislative context. There are three main pillars of legislation relevant to the vast majority of filicide and familicide cases. These are: legislation pertaining to (i) domestic violence; (ii) mental illness; and (iii) child protection. In each of these areas there has been an unprecedented amount of new legislation, much of it driven by the failures of specific agencies in preventing filicide tragedies in the past. Frontline professionals, particularly police, mental health and child protection workers have now much greater opportunities and powers to intervene in potential filicide cases in the future.

Chapter 9 will present a case in which a father killed his children and committed suicide on learning about his wife's affair with another man. This particular case is chosen for two reasons: first, it has a substantial number of features identical to those in many other cases presented throughout the text. Second, the author has been granted an extraordinary degree of contact with the surviving parent, in which so many aspects of the case, normally ignored in filicide literature, have been addressed in depth.

Chapter 10 suggests a way forward in terms of attitude and approach. It is addressed primarily to all frontline professionals encountering potential filicide challenges, and to their trainers, supervisors and managers. It summarizes the knowledge base underpinning good practice; it identifies three common types of filicide situations, focussing upon the most significant risk factors in each of them, and it provides case histories to illustrate how lack of knowledge and failure to assess risk, particularly when domestic violence or clandestine affairs are prominent features, may allow the relationship dynamic spiralling towards filicide, to accelerate.

Summary

The context in which filicide killings take place, and the events leading up to them are not unfamiliar to most frontline professionals in family, childcare, and child protection work. They often work with couples whose relationships are fast disintegrating in mutual bitterness and recriminations, which increase the potential for a filicide conclusion. Professionals need to recognize and acknowledge that potential.

Child abuse inquiry reports, many of them held in public, have been replaced by SCRs, in accordance with the government's (1991) paper, *Working Together Under the Children Act 1989,* and in its subsequent revisions of that paper. SCRs have had little or no impact on child protection law, nor have any of them been considered worthy enough (as have many inquiry reports) to have been included in the mandatory reading lists of professional training courses. They have been much less rigorous and challenging than most child abuse inquiry reports. They were compiled and completed in secrecy, and none of their stages of development were subject to challenge by either family members or public representation.

It is only since 2010 that SCRs have been made available to the public. Public and professional scrutiny can only enhance their quality and learning potential. We may in the future learn details such as: what professionals said or did on a particular visit, what was the specific purpose of their action and words, and what their ultimate goal was. Public and professional scrutiny may also inhibit the authors of SCRs from habitually telling readers that the filicide killings, which the reviews are discussing, were unpredictable and unpreventable. Some filicide killings are undoubtedly neither predictable nor preventable; but when *every* filicide is judged likewise, the *raison d'être* of SCRs, which is to 'learn lessons', may be impossible to attain.

3
Learning from the Greeks

Introduction

The sudden killing of children by parents occurs in differing contexts and for different reasons. The victims may be any age between newly born and late teens. The unborn too may be victims. The perpetrators may be fathers or mothers aged between teens and old age. A parent or both parents may be killed besides the children. The motivation and the objectives of the perpetrators may be similar or they may vary enormously. Such a multiplicity of factors has given rise to different sets of explanatory terminology. This chapter will begin with the most basic classification in filicide study: naming and defining specific filicide acts.

'Filicide' is the main focus of interest in this text, particularly when it occurs in the context of marital, separation and divorce conflict, and/or in custody and access disputes. Mental illness is also an important contextual backdrop which can exacerbate any of those conflicts and disputes. There are additional criteria which will be identified and explored in this and subsequent chapters: (i) suddenness; (ii) unexpectedness; (iii) inexplicability; (iv) children not a subject of concern for childcare agencies; and (v) the perpetrators' professions of love for their victims.

A brief look at filicide in history will follow. The antecedents of filicide, in respect of both the act and the context, stretch back to the dawn of time. Not only was it perpetrated in every known culture and society, but it was also the subject of classical literature and drama. *Medea*, which is fundamentally about revenge filicide, remains one of the most frequently performed plays since it was first produced by Euripides in 431 BC. It is worth more than the cursory glance given to it by many present-day filicide researchers. Its characters, relationships and motivations will be considered in the light of prominent contemporary filicide cases.

Definitions of the filicide act

The terminology of child killing does not easily evoke the horror and the terror at the core of the experience. Take 'filicide', for example, a rather soft, innocuous, pleasant-sounding term, which, when it appears in the title of a learned journal, gives not the slightest hint of the suffering and cataclysmic consequences endured by victim and family. But for Latinists, the reality may be more immediately apparent. The 'cide' in filicide, derived from the Latin *cida,* means to cut or to kill, and 'fili', derived from the Latin *filius* and *filia,* means son or daughter. With the verb *to kill* established in the Latin 'cide', then, it has been quite convenient to attach a whole string of words referring to other categories of victims: familicide, infanticide, neonaticide, fratricide, parricide, matricide, feticide, uxoricide, gendercide and femicide. The *suï* in the Latin *suïcïda* means *of oneself,* which makes the meaning of suicide perfectly clear. Many acts of filicide and familicide are followed by the suicide of the perpetrator. With the exceptions of feticide (terminating the life of the foetus) and suicide, homicide embraces all of these terms, meaning as it does, the killing of one human being by another. Femicide is the 'misogynous killing of women' (Radford and Russell, 1992) and uxoricide is more specifically the killing of a woman by her husband. The following definitions are of terms which will appear most frequently in this text.

Neonaticide is the killing of a new-born child within the first 24 hours of life. The perpetrator is typically a mother, in her teens, often alienated from her parents, with no social support, an unwanted pregnancy, and no prenatal care (Resnick, 1970). This is in marked contrast to *abandonment* by teenage parents, who, despite suffering similar deprivation and circumstances, somehow cannot conceive of killing their new-born; they may leave him or her on the steps of a doorway, where they know he or she is certain to be found.

Infanticide is the killing of a child in his or her first year of life. UK law (The Infanticide Act, 1922) specifies that infanticide is perpetrated by the infant's mother, though, strictly speaking, the perpetrator could be anyone. Fathers cannot be charged with infanticide under the UK Act.

Infanticide and neonaticide are by far the most prevalent forms of child-killing worldwide. In western countries, infanticide is often a result of mothers suffering postnatal depression or postpartum psychosis (either of which may be used in defence mitigation). In India and China, in particular, neonaticide and infanticide of girls occur on an industrial scale (Warren, 1985; Wu *et al.*, 2006), so much so, that the ratio of boys over girls in great swathes of both countries has reached a staggering 125:100 (Zhu *et al.*, 2009). The Chinese Academy of Social Sciences (2010) recently forecast that within ten years, one in five young Chinese males (equivalent to the whole male population of the US) will be unable to find a bride because of this ratio. China's one-child policy is obviously a major factor in the unprecedented incidence of infanticide and neonaticide, but in Asia as a whole, there are additional and potent historical, cultural, and economic reasons underpinning what the demographer Eberstadt refers to as 'overweening son preference' (2010, p. 72).

Familicide has not been so clearly defined in the literature. The term itself would suggest, on the basis of its Latin origins, that the whole family is killed. This is the view of Ireland's Health Service Executive (2011) in its inquiry into an increasing cluster of murder-suicide incidents in that country. But some maintain that if either parent and one or more children is killed by the remaining perpetrator parent, a familicide has been committed (Johnson, 2005; Kirkwood, 2012; Wilson *et al.*, 1995). There are many variations in these types of killings. Most indeed do conclude with the suicide of the perpetrator, but not all the children may be killed; or, stepchildren may be specifically targeted or spared. Sometimes, the intention clearly seems to be the killing of the whole family followed by the suicide of the perpetrator, but the planning has not been as meticulous as it needed to be, or, the execution of the plan has lacked competence. There may also be numerous children, some in their teens, who manage to escape, mentally scarred but physically unscathed. Other children may have been attacked, but survived the injuries. Familicide in this text will mean the actual or attempted sudden annihilation of a whole family including the suicide of the perpetrator, invariably the father. The context of familicide is often similar to that of filicide: marital relationship problems, but there can be additional factors, such as businesses failing, bankruptcy, or mental illness. Mental illness is generally perceived as a major contributory factor in cases of filicide, though the annihilation of a whole family including the perpetrator greatly limits the scope of post-deaths analysis.

Additional criteria

This text will focus primarily upon filicide killing of children by a parent in the specific context of conflict revolving around domestic and marital relationships, mental illness, separation, divorce, and custody and access disputes. The word *separation* has numerous meanings in filicide other than the commonly accepted, literal meaning of two parents parting. Parents may perceive themselves to be separated when their partners are away for long periods. They may feel separated by way of social isolation, mental illness or drug addiction. Clearly the marriages or partnerships of such parents face huge challenges.

Additional criteria, which will narrow the focus considerably, and eliminate many categories of cases which have been included in homicide and filicide studies, are as follows:

1. The killings are inflicted suddenly and/or without warning, though much planning may have preceded them.
2. They are totally unexpected, by family members, relatives, friends, and work colleagues.
3. They are inexplicable, not just to the remaining members of the family, neighbours and friends, but also to professionals who may have been attempting to provide a service.
4. Even though there may be involvement in the family by child protection agencies, generally, the children's safety and welfare have not been a matter of concern.
5. The killings are perpetrated in the main by parents who have in the past, repeatedly professed and amply demonstrated their love for their victims, a love witnessed by family and friends.

This set of criteria is the complete opposite to that found in many categories of child killing, particularly that category containing fatalities which are the consequence of deliberate, sustained physical abuse, neglect and cruelty (Emery, 1985). To take the first and second criterion above, for example; one could hardly say that the death of Victoria Climbié or Jasmine Beckford was either *sudden* or *unexpected*; on the contrary, considering the bestiality to which they were both subjected over such a long period, and the number of internal and external injuries they both endured, it is much more surprising that they did not die sooner. And in the fifth criterion above, the contrast with child abuse and child neglect fatalities could not be starker. There can be no *love* in the action of a parent or partner who systematically deprives a child of the basic necessities of life, i.e., food, shelter, clothing, protection, nurturing and care. The frequent beatings and torture inflicted on many of the subjects of child abuse inquiry reports would strongly suggest that some form of psychopathic hatred or sadism, rather than love, was the driving force behind the killings.

Child killing in history

Child abuse literature in general and filicide studies in particular predictably include an opening chapter or section on the prevalence of abuse and child-killing in history. A usual starting point is Greek myth and the Medea story, though Warren and Kovnick, (1999) give us 'archaeological evidence' of child sacrifice 7000 years ago. A few thousand years later, Aristotle and Plato were strongly advocating neonaticide for all defective births. The Old Testament is littered with references to filicide sacrificial killings. In II Kings the Sepharvites sacrificed their children in fire to the Sepharvaim gods, Adrammelech and Anammelech (17.31). In Jeremiah (7.31) we learn of God's wrath on the 'sons of Judah' who 'burn their sons and daughters' in the valley of Hinnom, in sacrifice to the god Molach, 'something which I did not command', says God; 'nor did it come into my mind' (Jeremiah, 7.31). It certainly came to his mind when he struck down Egypt's first born (Exodus 12: 29) and when he sided with Joshua who took an oath in his name proclaiming that anyone attempting to rebuild the walls of Jericho would only do so by laying their first-born in the walls' foundations, and their youngest son to be laid beneath the gates (Joshua 6.26). These biblical references may have been the inspiration for the subsequently increasing practice of interring newborns in the foundations of buildings, bridges and dykes (Radbill, 1974; Stern, 1948).

Elsewhere, life was similarly precarious for children. In Assyria, sons and daughters could be burnt on the altar as a penalty for a breach of contract. In 310 BC, the Carthaginians offered hundreds of children up to the gods when besieged by the Greeks. They were burnt to death. Infanticide was routine throughout Africa, the Middle East and Asia. In Rome, the Laws of the Twelve Tables actually declared it illegal to rear a child with a defect or deformity, and the Roman law *Patria Potestas* gave fathers an absolute legal power over their sons that included the right to kill them, in infancy (Zigler and Hall, 1989). In the Americas, the Mayas, Incas and Aztecs regularly indulged in the sacrificial killing of their children (Davies, 1973, 1995; Hammond, 1982). In Japan, babies who were surplus to the normal requirements of one or two children, were disposed of by infanticide or desertion (Kuono and Johnson, 1995) and in the Scandinavian countries, until the 1850s, fathers also had a similar law to that of ancient Rome giving them the power of life or death over their newborns (Werner, 1917).

Interesting, though not particularly relevant

Of what relevance is all this? One of the tendencies in current filicide literature, when providing these brief historical reviews, is to use terms like 'child killing', 'infanticide', 'child sacrifice', and 'filicide' synonymously. It unhelpfully blurs important distinctions of context and culture. There seems to be an underlying, conscious or unconscious need among writers to identify common threads of ideas and practices between the old and the new, no matter how barbaric or culturally alien one may be perceived by the other. The reality is that the historical examples of child-killing we've just looked at, tell us very little about current-day filicide, and nothing at all about the filicide tragedies which are, intermittently, and increasingly, coming to our attention.

Interestingly, historical drama and fiction, which comparatively, rarely touches upon filicide killings, can be more relevant. Goethe's *Faust* contains an infanticide perpetrated by Margaret, but her seducer suggests she acted under delusion, a common enough reason advanced by many defence lawyers today. Sartre's *No Exit* tells of Estelle, who drowned her child, the result of an illicit affair with a man much younger than her aging husband. In the Hispanic legend,

La Llorana (the weeping woman), Maria drowns her two children in revenge for her lover's rejection of her. In Mauriac's (1959) *Thérèse*, the central character, having failed to murder her husband, is trapped in a hopeless and meaningless existence, and sets about killing herself. Thérèse has one last look at her sleeping child Marie, and recalls the many accounts she has read of 'desperate women who had taken their children with them to the grave' (ibid., p. 89). Acknowledging that she is 'a monster', she nevertheless lightly kisses Marie, and experiences something 'from deep down in herself' that prevents her from killing the child.

Medea

Nearly all filicide literature mentions *Medea*, written by the Greek dramatist Euripides, three and a half thousand years ago. The Medea Complex is a phrase coined to denote the revenge motivation of the central character. It is worth spending a little more time on this particular work, as it is highly relevant in attempting to understand the specific category of filicide on which this text is primarily focussing. Here is a synopsis, and if you can temporarily suspend belief that it is merely a drama from ancient Greece, based upon Greek myth (Grave, 1955), you will immediately detect its resonances with many present-day filicide killings.

> Medea's marriage to Jason was an elaborate affair, steeped in religious ceremony and blessed by the gods to whom they swore their mutual love and loyalty. But then Jason deserted her for a much younger bride, the daughter of royalty. Medea is nearly driven mad by this treachery. Observers frequently detect her thirst for revenge. The social and economic consequences of the marriage breakdown are dire. She is friendless in an alien city and culture, and the bitter passionate way she has reacted to her husband's behaviour compel the authorities to banish both her and her children. The chorus of the play sense that Medea is hell-bent on some terrible deed of revenge. They futilely try to caution her, warning her of dangers of excessive grieving. She tells the chorus she wants to die. Her husband tries to reason with her, but succeeds only in incensing her. She plots her revenge. She kills his new bride, and the bride's father, Creon, who had intended

banishing Medea into exile. Medea then perpetrates the ultimate revenge on Jason by killing their two children. She does not kill Jason himself, leaving him, she thinks and hopes, to rot in his own misery and guilt.

An impulsive need to kick out

A storyline like this of course, does not necessarily make great drama, but it is the character of Medea and the innermost turmoil of her mind as she embarks upon her fatal journey of revenge that make it a great play, and which brilliantly recreate, as no other work of fiction or drama has ever done, the awful reality for both perpetrators and victims of modern-day filicide tragedies.

In the opening lines of the play, Medea is in despair, lamenting the fact that she and her husband are now enemies, their mutual bonds of love severed for ever. Her distraught nurse tells us of Medea's continuous weeping, suffering and fasting, after learning of Jason's desertion for a younger, more beautiful woman. The nurse later observes how Medea's relationship with, and her responses to the children, change; even the way she looks at her children is different. She really isn't seeing them; they are merely a projection of their father: She openly curses them, hoping they may perish with the father and that the house in which they dwell may collapse all round them.

Quite an extreme reaction, one may think, but few frontline childcare workers will be too shocked. Many single parents, male and female, suddenly engulfed by the catastrophe of a partner deserting them for a younger, and/or richer, and/or more secure alternative, and the dire economic and social consequences that may ensue, will, very naturally, have an impulse to kick out at the world around them. Because the person who has inflicted this fate upon them is no longer available, and, worse still (in the eyes of the aggrieved one, is lying in the arms of a new lover), the kicking out may be specifically aimed at their ever-present, living embodiment, namely, their children. Medea's vitriol towards her children is simply a statement of mind, of hatred and fury, but not yet a statement of intent. The nurse replies to Medea's despair with one of the most resonant and incisive lines in the play, asking her how can she, in all conscience, hold her children responsible for the treachery of their father?

Creon, the bride's father, decides to take precautions before any likely revenge. He banishes Medea, telling her that it is better that he incurs her hatred now, than to be kind and regret it later. Medea pleads not to be banished, for the sake of her children! She reminds Creon that he too is a parent and whatever he thinks and fears about her, he should at least be kind to them. This is another developing and resonant theme, and cruelly ironic: the killer appears to be increasingly and conspicuously concerned about the children in the hours preceding her killing them. She is permitted to remain for another 24 hours, time enough, she tells the chorus, to do what Creon feared.

Guilt money

In the trials and inquests of todays' filicides, we frequently hear of the furious rows between the warring couples. None of them have ever been recorded, but we learn something of their essence, in the testimony of a remaining parent, or a close neighbour, or a long-standing friend. The deserting parent is aware of the impact of their action, and seeks somehow to mitigate its effects. When that parent is a male, who is socially and financially upgraded by the move, what better way to mitigate than to offer financial assistance to the bereft woman?

That's what Jason does, and it makes Medea incandescent. In the climactic row that dominates the middle of the play, she accuses him of the worst of all human vices: shamelessness. She casts up to him every sacrifice she has borne for him, including her freedom. She reminds him of his marriage vow, and she ridicules his so-called fatherhood, abandoning his children to wander as beggars.

Pushing the prospective killer over the edge

Jason makes a terrible mistake. He tries to reason with this passionate fury. He tries to justify his actions. He even tries to argue that it is in their children's interests that he should abandon them. His reply turns into a lecture. Medea can sense his gratification in controlling and cleverly marshalling his arguments. He becomes smug and condescending. There is a supercilious tone in his voice. He isn't capable of realizing the yawning gap he has created and which he is emphasizing at this very moment: a social and material gap; a huge imbalance of power, influence and wealth; above all, worlds apart in their emotional and psychological well-being. He is basically telling Medea to get a grip ... accept her lot, and be thankful.

The audience realize that for Medea, this is the tipping point: they hear her cry out that she will kill her children, and that no one will be able to rescue them.

As we will see in later chapters, this most paradoxical of intentions is quite common in the thinking of many filicide perpetrators today. The children have to be rescued from 'something awful'. That might mean being rescued from poverty, or from being deprived of the 'love' of the perpetrator who intends to commit suicide; or from the abomination of another 'stranger' parent caring for them, and so on. Words to the same effect are frequently included in suicide notes.

Medea explains why she seriously intends to kill her children. Her original intention of killing the threesome, the new bride, her father and her deserting husband has been overtaken by a desire for a much greater revenge. Something more cataclysmic is required, something that Medea tells the audience, they may not want to hear: Jason, she has decided, will not see his children alive again (it is a decision and declaration almost identical in words and marital context as in two of the three cases in Chapter 1).

Reality stranger than fiction

Life can be stranger than fiction. Here are the details of another of the drowning filicide cases listed in the first chapter.

In October, 1994, in South Carolina, Susan Smith, 25, fed her two toddlers, Michael, 3, and Alex, 14 months, their favourite pizzas, then wrapped them in winter clothing, strapped them in her burgundy Mazda, drove them to the edge of a lake, and parked it on a steep decline. She later told the authorities that she intended ending her own life, as well as the lives of her children. But she didn't. She released the brake as they slept, and watched the car accelerate towards the waters.

The day before, her boyfriend, Tom Findlay, handsome and rich, the 'most eligible bachelor' in the college they both attended, had formally ended their relationship with a letter that would, during and after Susan's trial, become infamous (Montaldo, 2011). Her defence team would make much of the devastation the break-up had wrought on this vulnerable young mother.

Much of the content of this letter is eerily familiar to that in Jason's speech to Medea, particularly its total lack of empathy. It is overbearingly self-righteous, vain and condescending. The beginning is typical: he is giving her the bad news that their relationship is finished, but prefaces it by telling her he knows how highly she thinks of him. He combines the shock-horror news of his leaving her with a conviction that she will make a great wife to some lucky man. He even cautions her to take her time in finding that man, commenting that she can be a bit 'man-crazy', and that if she is prepared to wait, the right man will come along. He is critical of her morals, having seen her kiss another man when she and he were supposed to be in a meaningful relationship. He warns her about where this can lead, saying how he would regret her becoming a disreputable person. If she wants to 'catch' someone as nice and wonderful as him, he tells her, she is going to have to behave equally nice. Just as Jason does to Medea, he holds out the prospect of employment and security: if she is ever stuck for a job, he tells her that his father, apart from the business he owns, is mighty influential in the town, and knows everyone there is to know. Just get in touch!

Tom eventually gets tired making such a good case for himself (just as Jason got fed up justifying himself to Medea) and signs off the letter, telling Susan of the late hour (11.45 p.m.) and how sleepy he is. His letter is slightly more incredulous and insulting than Jason's speech if only because he didn't have to face the recipient when he was writing it. No doubt, had she been facing him, Susan Smith would have been every bit as incandescent as Medea, and would have fierily interrupted his long, self-congratulatory, self-righteous epistle at every opportunity.

There is no way to prove the unanimous view of everyone who knew her and the lawyers who defended her that Tom's letter was in effect a death sentence for her two children, but it seems perfectly plausible that it was at least a contributory factor in her rationale that she had to do something cataclysmic in response (Rekers, 1998). Just like Jason's speech to Medea, the letter is a crude, blatant proclamation of the imbalance of power in the relationship between Tom and Susan.

Resolve and cunning

Medea is a more sophisticated character than Susan Smith, and more aware. When she announces her intention, she tells the audience that just because she has been treated with such contempt by Jason, she should not be thought of as a weakling. When the chorus urge her not to kill her children, she reveals the ultimate motivator compelling many filicide killers today: she is killing the children to inflict the greatest pain upon her estranged husband. The chorus helplessly turn to the audience, asking them how can a parent look her children in the eye as she drenches her hands in their blood? We often ask that question too, when we read of the latest filicide-revenge case.

There is no answer. Medea is deaf to their protestations. She is now in the phase of deceit and planning. She must make her peace with Jason, convince him that she has come round to his way of thinking. She apologizes profusely, asking him to forgive her for kicking up a great big fuss about nothing. She reproaches herself for behaving so badly against those who are only really trying to help her, and so on. Jason is naïve enough to explain her changed behaviour as her having had time to reflect on his superior wisdom!

In the following chapter, there will be many examples of filicide perpetrators similarly deceiving, allaying whatever anxieties or fears their partners may have had just before the children were killed.

A weakening of resolve

Medea as it turns out, is not as ruthless and as determined as she thought. As the hour approaches, she frequently bursts out crying. At one point, when she looks into the eyes of her children, she wonders whether or not she has the 'courage' to do as she intends. All kinds of doubts and insights assail her, the most important of which is her realization that killing her children purely for revenge will undoubtedly cause her much mental anguish, perhaps even more torment than that which she intends to inflicts upon her husband.

This phase of the play raises important questions: how many contemporary filicide parents experience the ebb and flow of doubt and resolution (just as Mauriac's Thérèse did) as they continue to come into contact with the child, as the child repeatedly looks them in the eye and the only thing the perpetrator can see, apart from their child's love and their innocence, is the reflection of themselves as their child's killer?

Medea cannot now bear to look at her children. Even their fragrant breath, their happy and innocent voices, their heavenly tender touches ... these all burden her with insufferable guilt. She orders them to get out of her sight.

No turning back

But the doubts and the guilt remain. She counters that by willing herself to arm and not weaken. She tries to banish the recurring memories of having brought the children into this world; she steels herself to forget about her love for them as she kills them; she resigns herself to mourning for them thereafter.

She charges into the house and slays the children as they scream in terror. The murderous deed was never actually displayed in ancient productions (unlike today when the scene usually takes central stage to gratify the modern craving for explicit blood and gore). Such explicitness is unnecessary, as the lines which the children speak, and the sounds they make (both of which are clearly heard), more than adequately convey the extent of the evil and the carnage.

Fiction turned into reality

This depiction of a heinous crime, which shocked even the audiences of ancient Greece, has since converted to reality in virtually every western country, no more so than in the US and in the UK. There are no large amphitheatres, packed tight. More likely, the scenario is a semi-detached in quiet suburbia. The only observers are other family members; who may experience the same fate; the only witnesses, helpless neighbours hearing the children's screams and trying in vain to break down the locked doors.

A reality that officialdom avoids

One of the most conspicuous features in modern-day responses to filicide cases is to say as little as possible about what the children actually endure. It is too painful, too shocking, too abhorrent. No one could disagree with that. Thus a child may have been stabbed 47 times by a deranged parent and the Coroner calmly abbreviates that nightmarish scenario to: '*the child died due to a single incised wound to the neck*'. Perfectly correct, too, from a purely factual and legalistic basis. Another child gasps for breath and hopelessly tries (over minutes that seemingly turn into hours) to fend off the hands determinedly intent on keeping the child's terrified face submerged in the full bath, and the Serious Case Review abbreviates that experience to '*a drowning*' of a child called '*AW*'. That is the way we expect officialdom to respond, totally without emotion and sentiment, cold and objective. But it does nevertheless mirror a universal reluctance to even think of the reality, the nightmarish reality which befalls so many filicide victims. There is no running away from, or avoiding, or concealing that reality, in Medea. She charges at the children with knives raised. They try to escape and endure moments of the utmost panic and terror, before she finally catches up on them. The 'lucky' one was the first to die; the remaining child had to watch it, knowing what was coming next. As many cases in the following chapter will reveal, that is another feature of modern-day multiple filicide killings: a child has to watch their siblings die, knowing they will suffer the same fate.

Process, the missing factor in research

The play *Medea* is relevant to contemporary filicide studies because of its analysis of the processes leading to the filicide act. It also shows how familial, political, spiritual and sociological factors (not the least of which is the role and status of women in ancient Greek life) may impact upon those processes. This is a weakness in current literature and research on filicide: we have endless statistics on every detail, like age, gender, class, education, employment, mental health, antecedents of violence, and so on, and we have countless psychological profiles of perpetrators. But there are no real attempts to identify *processes*, the social, emotional, psychological, material, spiritual, interactive and crisis processes leading simultaneously and interconnectedly, to the killings. Nor is there anything in the literature and research about the process of doubt, the inevitable doubt that many would-be killers experience before the act.

Whatever limitations *Medea* may have, by virtue of the fact that it is merely a drama three and half thousand years old, about characters whose status and lifestyles are as distant from us as those of Shakespeare's kings, it nevertheless provides character and motivation that are utterly convincing. This chapter has referred to a number of recent cases that demonstrate that fact. There are many more.

Summary

The terminology of child killing has considerably expanded, and definitions are needed to differentiate between distinct categories. *Filicide*, derived from the Latin *cida*, means to cut or to kill, and 'fili', derived from the Latin *filius* and *filia*, means son or daughter. *Familicide* is the killing of a whole family and is invariably carried out by the father, who then commits suicide. Familicide by definition, always includes acts of filicide. *Neonaticide* is the killing of a new-born child within the first 24 hours of life. *Infanticide* is the killing of a child in his or her first year of life. *Infanticide* and *neonaticide* are by far the most prevalent forms of child-killing worldwide, and are carried out on an industrial scale in much of China and India.

Child killing was prevalent throughout history, and archaeological evidence for the sacrificial killing of children 7000 years ago, has been discovered. In the ancient world, fathers had absolute power over their children, and those born with any kind of defects were quickly disposed of, not just because parents wanted to avoid the stigma it caused, but also, because some states actually compelled parents to get rid of them. The Old Testament is littered with stories of child killing and child sacrifices.

The play *Medea* is often referred to in filicide literature. Euripides was the first writer to imaginatively explore in depth the contexts and the processes of one particular filicide killing. Although written and produced in ancient times, its characters and actions are often similar to those found in modern-day filicide cases: the desertion of a partner for another, the consequential sense of devastation and loss, the depression and despair developing into a hatred and thirst for revenge ... these are all common themes in many filicide cases. Those who study and/or work with modern-day filicides, repeatedly hear, in courtroom trials, in Coroner's inquests, and from victims, families and friends, that the perpetrator killed the children and spared the partner to ensure the greatest suffering for the latter. That is precisely what Medea said of her intention to kill her children three and a half thousand years ago; it was a means of inflicting the greatest pain and torment on her husband, Jason.

The profundity and relevance of *Medea* will ensure that filicide researchers will continually refer to it, and that students from the level of GCSE to PhD, will continue to study it, for at least another three and half thousand years.

Part II
A Study of 224 Filicide Killings, 1994–2012

Part II

4
Filicide literature and research

Introduction

This chapter will critically review research and literature on filicide. It will begin by identifying five distinct strands that are discernible in the evolution of filicide study: (i) the concentration on female perpetrators; (ii) reviews of original and contemporary literature and research; (iii) the accumulation of basic data on all aspects of filicide killings, (iv) a feminist-sociological perspective on filicide, and (v) personal testimonies from bereaved parents. The chapter will focus on contributions in each of these strands, charting their influence and exploring their limitations.

One of the most striking features of the first 40 years of research into filicide is its focus upon maternal perpetrators. It is also a feature of research and literature on mental health and family and childcare. The reasons why researchers focus far more on women, and, some of the implications, will be explored.

There is now such an abundance of filicide literature and research that critical reviews are increasingly appearing. They are helpful in pointing out inconsistencies and variations in the methodologies, target groups and criteria in the research. They also provide, compare and contrast much of the basic data (the third strand) that has accumulated from individual research on all aspects of filicide killings. These include data on the prevalence of filicide, the age and gender of both perpetrators and of victims, motivation, the method of killing and the marital and/or relationship status between the perpetrators and their partners.

An emerging fourth strand in filicide literature is of particular relevance to frontline practitioners. It focuses upon male perpetrators and domestic violence. The filicide killings are perceived by the authors as part of a continuum of violence against women. Women are not only the bereaved victims of many filicide killings, but they have also been the victims of prolonged physical, emotional and psychological abuse by the same perpetrators. The most prominent of these feminist and/or sociological perspectives on filicide will be reviewed.

The final strand consists of personal testimonies from the main victims of filicide, the bereaved parent, left to cope with the killings of her children, and often, the suicide of the perpetrator. Long after their tragedies, they provide harrowing accounts of the immediate aftermath and of the long-term consequences.

Research strands

Researchers and writers in filicide literature are candid in their criticism and self-criticism. The review by Flynn *et al.* concluded: 'The quality of the literature on filicide is limited with many inconsistent findings' (2009, p. 38). Kirkwood went further, writing of 'the often contradictory research findings' (2012, p. 8). Friedman, Hrouda *et al.* (2005) admit to a lack of standardization in filicide research, and Kauppi *et al.* (2010) speak about limited data and the lack of comparisons groups. Many of these shortcomings will become more evident in this chapter, and they compel this writer to approach the topic from a different perspective. Looking at the literature and research in its accumulated entirety over the past 60 years, there are, despite all their disparity and lack of consistency, discernible patterns or strands which can tell us something about the evolution of filicide research, about its narrow foundations, its limitations and achievements, and its relevance. There are actually five discernible strands in the literature and research. They are loosely connected, though interdependent. They have, by and large, different origins, methods and outcomes. They are all worthy of examination:

- The study of female perpetrators, which dominated all filicide literature over many decades.
- Comprehensive reviews of original and contemporary literature and research.

- Research primarily seeking basic data (for example, frequency, age and gender of victims and of perpetrators, method of killing and weapon use, the state of relationships between parents).
- Feminist-sociological research based upon the perception that filicide killings are merely an extension of violence against women.
- Personal and publicized testimony of mothers whose children were killed by their fathers.

We will look at all five strands.

The focus on women in filicide literature and research

A well-established tradition

If one looks at the reference section of filicide research papers written between 1960 and 2000, one is struck by the enormous imbalance between the number of contributions which focus on women perpetrators and those that focus on men. Writers and researchers repeatedly draw the reader's attention to this fact (Alder and Polk, 2001; Harder, 1967; West, 1965). Why does this imbalance exist? Before answering that question it is only fair to point out that filicide research is no different in that respect from other categories of social welfare and medicine-based research studies. Mental health literature and research for example, particularly in the second half of the last century, reveals a predominant focus on women (O'Hagan and Dillenburger, 1995). Perhaps the die was cast much earlier though, with Freud and Jung both concentrating to a large (and not particularly objective or healthy) degree on their female patients. Similarly with child abuse and child protection literature and research, these fields of study have also predominantly focussed on women (and still do) often to the total exclusion of men. It is hardly surprising. Women are the principal carers. They are available and receptive, often confined to their homes and their maternal responsibilities, often dependent on welfare, their children the subject of concern by visiting social workers. They are a limitless potential source for the substantial band of researchers wanting to question them. Although their male partners are very often the principal source of risk to the children (O'Hagan, 1997), they are the most difficult to locate and engage, and (more often than not) the least cooperative.

Convenience of location and the compliance of the subject

The reasons for the preponderance of women-focussed research in filicide studies include some of the above, but a more telling reason is that many of the earlier studies relied on women perpetrators who had been incarcerated in jails or psychiatric institutions, or half-way houses between the two (Cheung, 1986; McGrath, 1992; Harder, 1967; Korbin, 1989). Under the 'care and supervision' of powerful medical and psychiatric personnel, and, at best, misunderstood but more commonly despised, feared and loathed by the public for killing their children, there could not have been a more compliant and conveniently located body of subjects who had been responsible for all types of maternal filicides, particularly neonaticide and infanticide. One gains some sense of this power and helplessness duality in one of the earliest and most often quoted paper in filicide literature, Resnick's (1969) 'Child murder by parents: a psychiatric review of filicide'. Resnick looked at 131 cases of filicide going back as far as 1750. That figure comprised 88 mothers and 43 fathers, probably the greatest majority of maternal over paternal perpetrators in filicide literature. The case histories provided are almost exclusively those of women, including two very lengthy histories obtained through interviews preceded by the administering of sodium amobarbital.

The missing contexts

There is nothing unusual about such practices given the period in which they were carried out (Pilgrim and Rogers, 1993); they were symptomatic of a reality which existed then: the vulnerability of women diagnosed as mentally ill, and the virtually limitless power of psychiatry in the institutions in which they were incarcerated (Chesler, 1972; Showalter, 1987). What is of much more significance, however, are the case studies themselves, which betray the fixation of psychiatrists on the mind of the patient and their childhood experiences to the virtual exclusion of other significant aspects of the patient's life preceding the filicide act. For example, in the first case, we learn of a 31-year-old mother, married to a military pilot, who drove herself and her 5-year-old daughter off a cliff, then smashed the skull of the child who had survived the cliff fall. We learn a good deal about this woman: about her parents and her repressed and fear-laden upbringing, her sense of inadequacy on the birth of her last child; her two extra-marital affairs, her attempted suicide; her feeling that she wasn't satisfying her husband sexually. We also learn that the apparent trigger for this event was her husband, the day before, telling her she wasn't wanted by either him or the four children and that she should go. All of this information reaffirms the impression of female helplessness and vulnerability (and probably guilt and blame), but in truth, it tells us nothing about key milestones in the developing, deteriorating relationship between her husband and herself; nor anything about the social, emotional, psychological, cultural and material processes generated by and between a husband and a wife, which must have been leading inexorably towards the filicide act. Resnick adheres to the psychoanalytical stance: this mother killed her child to 'vent the anger that her own mother would never have tolerated' (1969, p. 331). He suggests that she and another of his female patients, in their suicide attempts after committing filicide, were attempting to reunite with their own mothers.

This typical 1960s psychoanalysis, whatever its efficacy or merit, certainly had the effect of absolving the husbands of any responsibility for the filicide acts; more importantly, it would have stifled any professional inclination to spend some time looking at the marital, family and social dynamics which no doubt fuelled the crises that preceded the killings.

Literature and research reviews

One of the most recent and comprehensive review of filicide literature and research is that carried out by the University of Manchester's Centre for Suicide Prevention (Flynn *et al.* 2009). This was commissioned by the Department of Health, Social Services and Public Safety Northern Ireland (DHSSPSNI) after the publication of an inquiry into the death of a young mother and her 9-year-old daughter (Boyd, 2008). The mother killed her daughter and then committed suicide.

The review by Bourget *et al.* (2007) also provides a comprehensive look at existing literature, and concentrates on what the research tells us about the differences and similarities between filicide offences committed by men and women. It seeks to recognize causes and to contribute to both prediction and effective intervention strategies. Stanton and Simpson's earlier review sought to 'make sense of filicide and identify future research directions' (2002, p. 1). As with Bourget *et al.*, it included literature and research on the deaths of children through abuse and neglect.

Friedman, Hrouda *et al.* (2005) critically reviewed literature and research on maternal filicide only, listing 42 separate studies, with the age of victims and the number of subjects, and the filicide category to which they belong (that is, neonaticide, infanticide, and so on). Marleau *et al.* (1999) produced a ground-breaking piece of research on ten paternal perpetrators underpinned by a review of the limited amount of relevant literature at the time. A decade later, West *et al.* (2009) had much more substance in terms of quality and quantity for a review on all existing research on paternal filicide. McKee and Shea's study (1998) is less of a critical review and more of a context for their analysis of 20 cases of maternal filicide. Kauppi *et al.* (2010) extensively used available research and literature as a backdrop to their review of 200 filicide cases in Finland over a 25-year period.

Basic data

The prevalence of filicide

Studies of available data bases demonstrate the difficulty of determining and comparing filicide rates among countries with vastly differing reporting and classification systems. For example, Flynn *et al.* (2009) quote an American government report revealing that in 1998, 31,000 newborns and babies were abandoned in public places, particularly hospitals; 32 per cent of those abandoned in places other than hospitals, died. The US government may actually have encouraged this abandonment trend with its 'safe haven' laws, ensuring that mothers who do this at designated sights, preferably hospitals, will not be prosecuted (Porter and Gavin, 2010). The US has not yet tried to calculate how many abandoned babies and newborns are not so lucky as to make it to a hospital or refuge. If that is a difficult task for the US, then how much more difficult for the authorities in rural India, China, Bangladesh or Nigeria? We simply don't know (of any country) how many children in their first days and weeks of life are being abandoned or killed. The veracity of statistics on the totality of filicide, therefore, must always be in doubt as long as neonaticide and infanticide remain categories of filicide killings.

Homicide-filicide: the need to differentiate

Johnson remarks on the 'dearth' of facts and figures relating specifically to filicide, and speaks for many when she says: 'the only way to approach this offence is to study the related areas of homicide and suicide as it relates to family killings' (2005, p. 105). Be that as it may, it becomes quite noticeable in research literature how the two terms homicide and filicide appear to blend as one, with little or no differentiation made (Bourget, 2007). Somander and Rammer (1991) include extra-familial killings perpetrated by strangers, or, by relatives other than parents, in their 'filicide' study. Additional derivative terms are also used: 'intimate homicides'; 'intimate partner homicides' (Kirkwood, 2012); 'spousal homicide' and 'consortial homicide' (Liem *et al.*, 2009). This tendency can be confusing when it pervades whole papers.

The problem stems from the 'umbrella' nature of homicide. It covers all types of killings. Marzuk *et al.* (1992) and Liem *et al.* (2009) identify filicide as a significant and prevalent category of killing within homicide. Filicide is always homicide, but homicide is not always filicide. Some publications purporting to be about filicide provide comprehensive figures on child homicides, but do not specify the number or the nature of filicide killings which is the principal subject being written about. Flynn *et al.* (2013) provide a clear differentiation between homicide and filicide, as do Putkonen *et al.* (2009) whose article is aptly entitled 'Differences between homicide and filicide offenders'.

Contrasting sources of data

A further complication in the UK is that the homicide statistics are provided by two separate bodies, the Office of National Statistics (ONS) and the Home Office, and there is considerable discrepancy in the figures which they provide. The reason may well be that the ONS figures are based upon the cause of death as determined by a coroner, whereas the Home Office criminal statistics are based on the number of cases which lead to prosecution or conviction for homicide. In the Home Office's figures for 2010–11, there were 56 child homicides, of which 36 of the children were killed by a parent or step-parent (Smith *et al.*, 2012). There is, as one might expect from these kinds of statistics, no information on the context and circumstances of the killing, nor any information on the family structure and the precise relationship between perpetrator and victim. The Home Office cautions that these figures are subject to change as cases progress through the court.

Bearing all these factors in mind, let's consider the principal areas of inquiry in filicide research:

- the gender of the perpetrators
- the age of the perpetrators
- the age of the victims
- the gender of the victim
- the perpetrator's relationships with spouse/partner
- the victim's relationship with perpetrator
- the method of killing
- filicide-suicide
- motivation.

The gender of the perpetrators

There are many filicide studies which find that the majority of perpetrators are men (Christiansen *et al.*, 2007; Kaplun and Reich, 1976; Mouzos and Rushford, 2003); and there are probably just as many which find that the majority of perpetrators are women (Karakus *et al.*, 2003; Kauppi *et al.*, 2010; Myers, 1970; Putkonen *et al.*, 2011; Resnick, 1969). There is another strand of research which finds that the numbers of mothers and fathers who kill their children is roughly equal (Alder and Polk, 2001; Bourget *et al.*, 2007; Lucas *et al.*, 2002; U.S. Dept of Justice, 2011).

Even allowing for the differing sources and classification systems used in filicide literature and research generally, some of these results are surprising. Filicide, the killing of a child by his or her parent, is a constituent part of familicide, which is the annihilation of the whole family, including the suicide of the perpetrator. The literature and research are unanimous in finding that perpetrators of familicide are invariably male (Friedman, Hrouda *et al.*, 2005; Léveillée *et al.*, 2007; Stanton and Simpson, 2002). Because familicide nearly always involves multiple killing of siblings, one might reasonably think that research dealing with the whole spectrum of filicide-familicide killings, even including neonaticide and infanticide, would show that more fathers kill their children than mothers.

The age of perpetrators

Friedman and Resnick (2007) concluded from their review of infanticide research that the perpetrators were predominantly female and in their early twenties. d'Orbán et al. (1979) revealed a mean age of 24.6 years for maternal mothers generally. Marleau et al. (1999) gave a mean age of 32 of the ten male perpetrators they studied. Léveillée et al.'s (2007) 75 perpetrators, male and female were aged 36 and above (not specified). Liem and Koenraadt (2008) researched 161 perpetrators, 82 women and 79 men. The mean age of the women was 30.5, and of the men, 34.2. Karakus et al. (2003) found a mean age of 26.1 for women and 36.1 for men (41 fathers and 44 mothers). Flynn et al. (2013) studied 195 cases of male perpetrators and 102 cases of female perpetrators. Each group had the same median age of 27.

There are wide discrepancies in the age ranges chosen for various studies. The youngest male perpetrator in Bourget and Gagne (2005) was 20; the oldest, 76 (mean age, 39). In Liem and Koenraadt's (2008) study, the age range of female perpetrators was 18–58 (mean age 30.5) and for male perpetrators, 19–72 (mean age 34.2); in Flynn et al.'s (2013) study, the age range of males was 15–70 (median 27) and of females, 14–50 (median 27).

The age of the victims

Researchers are unanimous in the view that children aged 0–12 months are the most vulnerable (Marks and Kumar, 1993; Mouzos and Rushforth, 2003; Paulozzi and Sells, 2002). But fatalities among this group (referred to as infanticide and neonaticide) are often the consequence of protracted child abuse and neglect (Crittenden and Craig, 1990; O'Hagan, 2006). Apart from infanticide and neonaticide, the 4–7 age group does seem to be a particularly vulnerable one in filicide killings generally (Alder and Polk, 2001; Kauppi et al., 2010; Rodenburg, 1971; Somander and Rammer, 1991).

Kauppi et al. (2010) noted a significant difference in victim age between maternal and paternal perpetrators, a mean of 1.6 years and 5.6 years respectively. Marleau et al. (1999) gave a mean age of 5 for the 13 victims of 10 paternal perpetrators.

There is apparently no consensus in filicide research about the upper age limit of victims, which can range from 13 (Bourget and Gagne, 2002) to an incredulous 35 (Bourget and Gagne, 2005).

The latter not only distorts the mean age of Bourget and Gagne's 77 victims (7) but implies a study so wide-ranging that it would contain filicide cases of little relevance to the subject of this and many other texts. Furthermore, such ranges limit the usefulness of comparison study, and accentuate the vastly different contexts in which filicide can occur.

d'Orbán (1979) divided ages into seven bands, beginning with under six months; then six months–one year; one year–under two; two years–under three, and so on, until the last band, five years and over. She then disclosed how many children in each band were killed by each of the six categories of maternal perpetrators she was studying, that is, mentally ill, mothers who battered to death, neonaticides, and so on. Thus we learn that 11 children under 6 months old were battered to death by their mothers; nine 2-year-olds were killed by mentally ill mothers; two 4-year-olds were killed by retaliatory mothers, and so on. This kind of research would be useful if replicated on a much larger scale.

The age of child victims may be influenced by certain variables. For example, Bourget et al. (2007) suggest that parents who commit suicide after the filicide are likely to have killed older children, and the parents who do not commit suicide after the filicide are likely to have killed younger children. This view is supported by the research of Lucas et al. (2002) and the review of Stanton and Simpson (2002). Daly and Wilson (1988) made the same findings, but specifically about filicide mothers rather than parents. d'Orbán (1979) and Cheung (1986) found that mothers who were mentally ill were more likely to kill older children, and young mothers, among whom there was very little mental illness, were likely to kill younger children.

The gender of the victim

Research has consistently demonstrated no significant difference in the number of male and female victims of filicide (Kirkwood, 2012; Mouzos and Rushforth, 2003). Some research suggests that older male children are more likely to be victims of fathers (Kunz and Bahr, 1996; Maguire et al., 1993). Liem and Koenraadt (2008) found that male victims predominated in all categories of their 309-victim total, but predominated by how much, is not specified. Flynn et al. (2009) contend that the research in general shows roughly equal rates for each gender. West *et al.*'s (2009) review of the literature on paternal filicide demonstrates precisely the same.

The perpetrator's relationships with spouse/partner

The key question here is not about the relationship in general, but its state at the time of the filicide killing. Researchers consistently report that couples are separated, estranged, in dispute over custody and access, and that many of the perpetrators had mental health problems which were worsening. Liem and Koenraadt (2008) reported that 20 out of 79 (25 per cent) fathers had killed as a reaction to the threat of divorce or separation. Eight men (10 per cent) killed the spouse as well as the children. Bourget and Gagne (2005) reported that a 'rupture of the marital relationship' (not specified) had occurred for 24 (40 per cent) of fathers in their study of male perpetrators. Of the 49 men diagnosed mentally ill, 27 (55 per cent) had experienced separation preceding their action. The three retaliatory killings which they identified had also followed upon separation. Marleau *et al.* (1999) and Bourget *et al.* (2007) both note that rows about infidelities preceded filicide killings. d'Orbán (1979) reported that 'severe marital stress' with their husbands or cohabitees was endured by 58 (71 per cent) of 82 convicted female perpetrators. Sixteen of the women were living alone with their child(ren) at the time of the killings. West *et al.* (2009) reviewed seven studies of male perpetrators and found that 32 per cent of the accumulated total were estranged from their spouses and living alone when they killed.

The victim's relationship with perpetrator

Increasingly, children are having to adapt to substitute father and mother figures in their lives, that is, step-parents and/or cohabitants. There is wide variation in filicide research about the inclusion of non-biological parents. Friedman *et al.* (2005), for example, only included biological mothers and fathers, and would not have considered any of the cases which have been the subject of official inquiry reports, in which step-parents and cohabitants figure so prominently in the deaths of children (Reder *et al.*, 1993). In contrast, Liem and Koenraadt (2008) and Somander and Ramner (1991) included step-parents, and/or foster and adoptive parents. Karakas *et al.* (2003) even included cases in which the precise relationship between substitute father perpetrators and victims was unknown.

The method of killing

Somander and Rammer (1991) looked at 96 children under 15 years old, killed in Sweden over a ten-year period. Strangulation, shooting and stabbing were more frequently used in the killing of very young children, which is partly at variance with Lewis *et al.*'s (1998) study, who found that weapon use was more likely to be relied upon in killing older children. Flynn *et al.*'s (2009) review of the literature concluded that 27 per cent of neonaticide killings were caused by asphyxiation; 22 per cent by drowning and 14 per cent by exposure. In contrast, Mendlowicz *et al.* (1999), who looked at 53 neonaticides in Rio de Janeiro between 1900 and 1995, discovered that most of the victims (77.4 per cent) were killed by various forms of wounding.

d'Orbán's (1979) study of female filicide offenders in Holloway found that 37 of their victims out of a total of 98 died from being repeatedly hit or thrown; 13 were suffocated; 13 were drowned; 13 were overdosed on drugs; 9 died from neglect and abandonment; 4 were gassed, 4 stabbed, 3 set alight, 1 scalded; and 1 electrocuted. Resnick's (1969) study showed that 9 per cent of victims were killed by firearms (a relatively low figure in a US context perhaps explained by the fact that two-thirds of the perpetrators were female). In Bourget and Gagne's (2005) study of male perpetrators in Canada, 26 (34 per cent) of a total of 77 victims were killed by firearms. Lewis *et al.* (1998) concluded that the women who used weapons (knives or guns) were more likely to be unemployed, to suffer delusions and hallucinations, and to be psychotic, than the women who did not use weapons.

Filicide-suicide

Flynn *et al.* (2009) and Friedman, Hrouda *et al.* (2005) both concluded that findings relating to perpetrator suicide varied considerably. In maternal filicide studies, Friedman, Hourda *et al.* (2005) established that the number of mothers who committed suicide ranged from 16 to 29 per cent. In paternal suicide, the number of fathers who committed suicide was between 40 and 60 per cent. The authors suggest that the higher rate for fathers was consistent with the higher rate for men who commit suicide generally.

Kirkwood (2012) described research by Australia's Homicide Monitoring Program (NHMP) in which 291 children were killed by their parents in 239 incidents between 1997 and 2008. There were multiple killings (not specified) in 39 of these incidents. Seventeen per cent (41) of the total number of parents committed suicide. Sixty per cent (24) of this total were mothers and 40 per cent (16) were fathers. In contrast, Flynn *et al.* (2013) looked at 342 filicide perpetrators (male and female) in the UK over a ten-year period (1997–2006) and found that out of 45 suicides in total (median age, 37), 28 (56 per cent) were men. In 14 of the cases, a spouse/partner or ex-spouse/partner was also killed.

Motivation

Resnick (1969) identified five types of cases and named them in accordance with the motivation he attributed to them. Strictly speaking, some of these types tell us nothing about motivation, but they enlighten us about the context and circumstances in which the killings take place.

- *'Altruistic' filicide:* These killings are perpetrated according to Resnick, 'out of love'. There are two subgroups within this type: (i) when a parent kills the child and commits suicide (or seriously attempts to), claiming (in a suicide note) that they could not part with their child and had to 'take the child with them'. (ii) Parents kill to relieve their child of pain, an interminable or incurable illness. Resnick reveals that altruistic killings were the most prevalent (38%) in his research of 131 filicides.
- *Acutely psychotic filicide:* These killings are perpetrated by parents undergoing or stricken by an acute psychosis, or epilepsy, or delirium. It often involves hallucinations and commanding voices, and may occur when an 'affecting impulse is translated directly into a violent reaction' (1969, p. 77).
- *Unwanted child filicide:* This type of killing may include neonaticide and infanticide. It also applies to those rare cases when older children are killed because they are regarded by the parent as a hindrance to their career or relationship with a new partner.
- *Accidental filicide:* Resnick used this term because he believed homicidal intent was lacking. It could apply to some fatal child abuse cases discussed in earlier chapters.
- *Spouse revenge filicide:* This occurs whenever a spouse kills the child as a means of inflicting the greatest hurt on his or her partner. Resnick found only 2 per cent of his group of male perpetrators and 3 per cent of his female perpetrators were motivated by

revenge, whereas, in a much later study, Liem *et al.* (2009) found that 25 per cent male and 5 per cent of female perpetrators were so motivated.

Later classifications on motivation

d'Orbán (1979) and Cheung (1986) modified and extended Resnick's classification to include *battering mothers*. This is the beginning of a move away from classifying strictly according to motive (much too problematic) and reverting back to the task of merely identifying types of filicide, some of which may merely imply what the motive for the killing is. They introduced the much broader-based *mentally ill mothers*, covering all forms of mental illness, and they incorporated Resnik's altruistic motive into *mercy killing*. They replaced his revenge category with *retaliatory killing*, indicating the influence of Scott (1973a), who was preoccupied with what he believed were primitive, violent impulses underpinning many filicide killings.

Diversity and disparity

One of the most prominent features to emerge from the second and third strands of filicide research and literature is the diversity of: (i) the subject; (ii) the method; and (iii) the conclusions. We have already seen that diversity in factors such as the gender of perpetrators and the age of victims. Liem *et al.* (2008) uniquely included *attempted* filicides in their research. We learn at the outset that a total of 161 perpetrators killed 309 children, and that of that 161 total, there were an unspecified number of would-be perpetrators who attempted to kill their children but failed. This seems potentially fraught with difficulty from a research point of view, but the authors argue that 'from a forensic mental health perspective those accused of a fatal crime may resemble those accused of an attempted fatal crime' (ibid., p. 169). They are researching the characteristics of offenders, and since those who failed to kill were nevertheless tried and convicted for attempted murder, it would suggest they are likely to share many of the same characteristics as those who succeeded in killing. In the findings of this current study, presented in the next chapter, two perpetrators, one male and one female, are included for precisely the same reason.

Filicide: an extension of male violence

The fourth strand of filicide literature and research focuses upon male perpetrators and domestic violence. The filicide killings are perceived as part of a continuum of violence against women. Women are not only the bereaved and devastated victims of filicide killings, but they have also been the victims of prolonged physical, emotional and psychological abuse by the same perpetrators.

The proponents of this strand have contributed to and agree with much of the findings in mainstream filicide research. But their own findings have also convinced them that many filicide killings *are* predictable and preventable. They usually stress this very point in the opening pages of their work (Ewing, 1997). The evidence they provide, albeit from small sample groups, is convincing. We will consider the recent work of three of them.

When agencies and professionals fail the victims of domestic violence

Saunders (2004) looked at 29 cases of filicide killings in 13 families in England and Wales, which had occurred between 1994 and 2004. Domestic violence and obsessive control that was dependent upon the threat of violence were pervasive features in 11 of the 13 families. Violence against the mother was not recognized as 'significant harm' to the children who witnessed it. In many of the cases, well known to family and childcare agencies, the children were neither seen nor spoken to by professionals. In three of the cases, court orders were granted which gave the fathers, who were known to be excessively violent, unsupervised access to their children. Some of these court decisions were made despite advice to the contrary from family and childcare professionals. Mental health was an issue in nine of the 13 cases. Professionals were ignorant of the risks mothers faced in deciding to separate and/or leave abusive relationships. Five of the fathers killed their children for revenge.

Saunders analyses many of these cases, exposing major shortcomings in professional practice, non-adherence to basic principles in *Working Together to Safeguard Children*, and an appalling ignorance of the dynamics at play and of the risks inherent in domestic violence situations and immediate post-separation periods.

The voice of survivors

Johnson (2005) reached similar conclusions in her study of 15 filicides perpetrated by seven fathers in Western Australia. These cases revolved primarily around separation. The partners (all married except one) had striven sometimes for years to separate, due to prolonged abuse and/or violence against them and their children. They had finally succeeded in separating, overcoming all kinds of obstacles, that is, apologies, pleas, bribes, and even their own families advising them against separation. But the violence did not cease. The men simply didn't accept separation. Countless incidents of threats and violence were recorded by the women after the separations. This tendency was also noticed by Saunders (2004) and Ewing (1997). Johnson says the agencies seemed incapable of an adequate response, and the risks to the children were 'either ignored or minimised' (2005, p. 20). She believes that in some of the cases, the risks were apparent 'for years prior to the offence' (ibid., p. 32).

Johnson is particularly critical of the legal system and family courts. She encounters exactly the same bizarre experiences as those documented by Saunders in England and Wales (see above); for example, women in fractious custody disputes being advised (warned) by their legal representatives that their disclosure of domestic violence perpetrated against them, without irrefutable evidence, could be disadvantageous in the final analysis and judgment by the court. She writes of the inconsistencies of response when abused women apply for Violence Restraining Orders, and more importantly whenever such orders lapse or are breached. Johnson regards the police as a crucial agency in the matter of domestic violence, but laments their lack of training and preparation for the assessment and risk of further violence. She notes that when disputing parents separate and enter that post-separation phase in which many filicide killings occur, the police still regard further attacks by men on their partners merely as a continuation of domestic violence; the reality is that these post-separation attacks are much more dangerous than the original domestic violence; they indicate that the men may be seeking and are determined to inflict a more terrible and final violence, exacting the ultimate revenge on their former partners. The risk to the children cannot be overestimated at this point.

Johnson acknowledges the limitations of a research study focussing on such few cases. But its strength lies in the authentic voice of the main victims of domestic violence culminating in filicide: women suddenly bereft of everything meaningful to them in life; the catastrophic effects on their mental health and their emotional lives, on their social status and relationships. Some simply didn't survive.

Gender differences in filicide motivation

Kirkwood (2012) investigates filicide killings in the context of separation and the 'prior family violence' of each of them. She notes the predominance of psychological and psychiatric perspectives in filicide literature and research. Her perspective is distinctively sociological and feminist. She reviews much filicide literature, but she focuses more on research findings on the homicide killings of women generally, by their male partners. Kirkwood cites numerous research studies which demonstrate that the majority of the killings are perpetrated following 'a considerable period' of violence against the women. She recognizes that most filicide killings are of very young children and they occur as a consequence of long-term abuse and neglect, but she rightly points out that violence against the mother is a significant factor in many fatal child abuse and neglect cases.

Kirkwood focuses upon eight cases, each of which she regards as an extension of, or extreme expression, of violence against women. All of the cases occurred within the context of separation. Kirkwood is well aware of the difficulty of determining precisely what the motivation is for filicide killings. She compiles a list of problem areas that researchers have encountered in this task, for example, limited number of studies, different methodologies, substantial overlap in the literature of established categories of motivation, and so on, but she nevertheless categorizes her eight cases as retaliatory (revenge) filicides. In at least three of the cases, that categorization is more than justified. In the first one, a filicide killer phoned the mother of their child numerous times before the killing, telling her exactly what he was going to do and why: 'to get back at you' (ibid., p. 39); in the second, the killer is obviously gratified in telling the mother that she will now suffer for the rest of her life; in the third case, the killer boasts to a friend that he will avenge his wife by killing the children, after the breakdown of their relationship, the separation, and her partnering with another man. These three cases are indisputably revenge killings, but the remaining cases are not so clear-cut. There are suicides and suicidal attempts; there are diagnoses and clear indications of depression; and there are lengthy court cases, in which opposing sides argue about the mental state of the defendants.

Unlike Saunders (2004) and Johnson (2005), Kirkwood examines six cases of maternal filicide. These cases also occur in the context of separation, but the contrast with male perpetrators is stark. There are none of the hate-laden, blatant revenge-driven suicide notes or conversations made by the men. There are many expressions of love and regret at having to kill the children, but certainty also that it is the right thing to do, and, from the delusional and/or severely depressive perspective of some of the women themselves, the *only thing to do*. These mothers all set out to commit suicide, five of them succeeding, But the prospect of leaving their children without a mother, or leaving them with their father, or, risking them being taken into care ... consequences like these convince some of the women of the need to 'take their children with them'. Kirkwood finds significance in the fact that four of the women were victims of domestic violence, the implication being that such violence may not only increase the risk of a father killing his children (and his partner) but also may contribute to the spiralling emotional and psychological disintegration preceding many killings by mothers.

An overview of filicide literature does not entirely support this dichotomy of cause and effect between men and women. Many filicides are committed by men afflicted with the same type of mental illness, predominantly depression, borne by so many single mothers who kill. And, as the results of the current study will show in Chapter 5, there have been numerous killings by mothers driven and motivated by similar negative emotions of aggression, rage, jealousy and revenge, as those motivating men.

Personal testimonies of the victims of filicide

This final strand that contributes to our understanding of filicide is very different to the previous four, and it is expanding. Mothers who have experienced unimaginable horrors, and who have endured years of trauma and seclusion as a consequence, have decided to speak out. At least 25 bereaved mothers in the current study have told their stories in documentaries, newspapers and journals.

These may range from a film clip lasting two or three minutes, to a recorded conversation of 15,000–20,000 words. Journalists have been instrumental in encouraging these women. At least three mothers have, with the help of journalists, written books (Schaap and Korsgaard, 2008; Thomson and Ross, 2011; Williams, 2013). Tallant (2011) is a distinguished and award-winning Irish journalist who wrote an excellent text on filicides and familicides in Ireland. Like all journalists, she does not reveal her sources, but it would appear from the detail and penetration of her writing that she has had access to bereaved parents or those very close to them.

There are 'no holds barred' in many of these contributions. Words like 'evil' and 'monster', 'hate', and 'never forgive' are commonplace. There is detailed biography, tracing the parental relationships from their very beginnings, through crisis after crisis, revealing worrying personality traits like possession and control, and frightening levels of repetitive domestic violence. There can also be empathy for the 'monster'. Addley (2004) records a mother, subjected to physical and psychological abuse that drove her out of the home with her children, yet who acknowledges that at the time of the killings her husband's position was dire. He had lost everything, and his mental health was deteriorating. She is able to imagine herself in that position, and understand why her filing for divorce may have been the last straw. She wishes that things could have been dealt with more sensitively.

One of the most terrifying revelations for many of these bereaved parents, long after the killings, is the premeditation and planning their husbands resorted to. This the survivors can only interpret as the most extreme form of revenge. To be plotting and planning for weeks at the same time as maintaining an air of normality, or to be sitting beside or opposite to the woman upon whom he will inflict untold suffering ... these are images that take root and torment, and are nearly impossible to eradicate. Schaap and Korsgaard (2008) describe how a husband waylaid his estranged wife by arranging a birthday party in his home for their son. When mother and son arrived, he detonated a bomb intended to kill all three. The mother survived.

These kinds of personal testimonies must conform to the core demands of journalism, publishing and other media outlets: they must help sell copy. But that does not detract from their contribution to understanding. The majority of them reveal relationships and processes common in filicide cases generally (such as domestic violence, obsessive control, imbalances of power), thereby casting more doubt on the contention that the killings are neither predictable nor preventable. Probably, however, their more important function is therapeutic. The mothers are given a purpose in life. They no longer allow themselves to be defined as 'perpetual tragedy' because of the barbarism of their former partners. Many of them succeed in forging new lives, in charitable and therapeutic enterprises, and in starting afresh in new relationships and, again, in giving birth.

Summary

Five distinct strands of focus are detectable in filicide literature and research. The first is the exclusive concentration on women in the earliest years of filicide study. The authors were mainly psychiatrists and/or medical directors in prisons and hospitals in which maternal filicide offenders were incarcerated. The perspective of study was predominantly psychoanalytical, with little or no reference to the familial, social, environmental or cultural contexts in which filicide killings took place. The critical reviews of filicide literature and research, which are now quite numerous, and which constitute the second strand, amply display this gender bias; it was not until the 1990s, that researchers seriously attempted to focus on male perpetrators. The third strand of the literature is the accumulated basic data arising out of the research studies on various groups of perpetrators. This includes data on the prevalence of filicide, the age and gender of perpetrators and of victims, relationships between victims and perpetrators, and the method of killing and motivation for killing. The lack of standardization in approach and methodology in each of these areas is apparent from the outset, and the consequential variations in results entirely predictable. The fourth detectable strand in filicide literature is a feminist-sociological perspective, in which filicide killings are perceived as an extension of male violence. These studies expose the nature and extent of violence suffered by the mothers of filicide victims long before the killings take place. They graphically portray the entrapment that many mothers endure, and they expose the inadequacies of agency response. The fifth and final strand emerges in the personal testimony of bereaved mothers, who choose to publicize their experiences through interviews for newspapers and journals, or write about the experiences themselves. Most of them recall relationships and patterns common in filicide cases generally. The main beneficiaries of publication, however, are the women themselves; it can be immensely therapeutic, opening up various opportunities, and rescuing them from a devastation and suffering that once threatened to be permanent.

5
The results of a study of filicide and familicide

Introduction

Each case in which there is the sudden killing of a child by a supposedly 'loving' parent is unique, yet every single case has the same consequences: devastation, chaos, suffering on an unparalleled scale, and suffering and loss etched in the memories of friends and loved ones for a lifetime to come. Such consequences are often lost in the statistics of Chapter 4, and in anonymized, massively redacted serious case reviews. They are also largely invisible in psychological profiling of the perpetrator, and in ideological perspectives that aim to locate the cause of filicide in the structure of the family, the oppression of women, or aggression in men.

There is a well-established convention that researchers do not concern themselves about suffering. But there are no good reasons why frontline professionals and the public at large should not be aware of the nature and extent of filicide killings. This chapter presents filicide cases in a framework in which the central focus is on the children themselves: they have an identity, as well as an age and gender; we also learn of the means by which they were killed, and of the level of premeditation and deception that preceded many of the killings. The findings also include the days of the week on which the killings took place, age and gender of perpetrators, incidence of suicide after the killings, and the exceptionally high number of killings motivated by revenge-retaliation.

An ethical dilemma

In Chapter 2, issues of confidentiality and privacy were raised in the light of widespread publicity given to filicide cases. The question was asked: what is the sense of anonymizing and/or redacting whenever countless personal details of family member have been revealed ad nauseam in every local and national newspaper? But there is a moral imperative for maintaining confidentiality in relation to survivors and bereaved family members. The core elements of that moral imperative are choice and respect. Would bereaved parents and surviving family members *choose* to have their names and personal family details published all over again? Can we claim to *respect* them in accordance with our ethical codes if we name and publish without them having the opportunity to *choose*? The answer to both questions is clearly 'no'.

In Tables 5.1–5.3, neither mothers nor fathers are named, whether they are perpetrators or non-perpetrators, whether they are the bereaved parent or the partner who committed suicide. I have also omitted information about extended family members, friends and neighbours who were sometimes killed because they happened to be visiting the home at the wrong time. There are no details about the ages of parents or about their employment, nor is there identification of other children who escaped, or who were attacked, but survived. There is no hint of addresses or location in which the killings occurred, nor of the dates, nor of the agencies that were called upon to deal with them, or were already dealing with them.

There are some obligations, however, which must be fulfilled: the children's existence must be acknowledged. They must appear as children and not as numbers, and for that reason, each child is given a name (as is the convention in childcare literature), albeit a fictitious one. We must know of their age (crucially necessary in ascertaining and understanding their perceptions and experiences preceding the killings) and, we must know how they died.

Also provided in the following tables are (i) the actions of the perpetrators (including suicide or attempted suicide) immediately before, during and after the killings; and (ii) known contexts in which the deaths occurred (marital break-ups, mental illness, custody and access dispute, and so on).

All of the cases in Tables 5.1–5.3 and Figures 5.1–5.7 occurred between 1994 and 2012. Table 5.1 provides details of 62 filicides

Table 5.1 Category I: Filicide fathers

Case No.	Victims, ages, method of killing	Father's action before, during and/or after killing	Context and circumstances at time of killing	Case No.	Victims, ages, method of killing	Father's action before, during and/or after killing	Context and circumstances at time of killing
1	Hilda, 9 Kim, 6 Rose, 2 Poisoned: carbon monoxide.	**Suicide**, same time and method.	DV; mother seeking divorce; father uses access visit to kill children.	2	Nora, 4 John, 3 Strangled.	**Suicide**, by falling/jumping from tower block.	DV: Mother leaves. Custody dispute. Father becomes threatening and unstable. Killed during access.
3	Joseph, 2 Poisoned: carbon monoxide	Attempted to kill older child; failed. **Attempted suicide**, same time and method: failed.	Marriage break-up; separation; father kills during access visit. Under pressure from Child Support Agency.	4	Satbir, 9 Saroop, 7 Burnt to death in locked car outside mother's home so that mother can witness it.	**Suicide**, same time and method.	Parents separated 2-3 weeks before, after much **DV**. Father believed mother was in a new relationship. Children killed during access.
5	Anwar, 5 Junayd, 3 Thrown from 3rd floor balcony.	**Suicide**. Jumped after throwing the children, head first.	Marital break-up; Father kills on hearing of wife's affair.	6	Jason, 7 Malachy, 6 (both stepchildren) Strangled.	Strangles his wife and children. Flees and **attempts suicide**. Fails, but succeeds 14 years later in prison.	Sacked for theft from employer. Is on anti-depressants; money problems; moves back to location of wife's origins.

7	Jackie 9 Coleen, 7 Janice, 6 Clarence, 6 Poisoned: carbon monoxide.	**Suicide**: same method, same time		Rachel, 5 Raped and strangled.	Took child from home; raped and strangled her; dumped her body nearby.	**DV**: Mother left but still in contact. She did not turn up to a meeting as arranged.
8			Separated 2 months. Heavily in debt to Child Support Agency. Businesses failing. Kills during access, when mother is socialising.			
9	Safiya 14, and Sahna 11, had their throats cut; Ushta 9, had multiple stab wounds; Hasit 2, was strangled.	Killed wife by multiple stabbing. Convicted of all 5 killings.	**DV**: Mother fled to refuge. Father kills two children at home, then tracks her down and attacks her and other two children.			
10				Kieran, 2 Christian 11 mths. Multiple injuries.	Father attacked mother; very serious injuries, then **suicide** by jumping over cliff, holding 2 children.	**DV**: Marital break-up. Police called. Father walked out but returned later to attack his wife and kill the children.
11	David, 7 Daniel, 3, Burnt to death in locked car.	**Suicide**: same time and method.	Partnership break-up. Father sets car alight during access: supposed to be a trip out.			
12				Lorna, 7 Timothy, 4 Eloise, 3 Drugged. Then car set alight.	**Suicide** by hanging.	**DV**: Marriage deteriorates after third birth. Mother has affairs. Couple separate; attempt reconciliation. Father kills children when mother is with another man.

(*continued*)

Table 5.1 Continued

Case No.	Victims, ages, method of killing	Father's action before, during and/or after killing	Context and circumstances at time of killing	Case No.	Victims, ages, method of killing	Father's action before, during and/or after killing	Context and circumstances at time of killing
13	Douglas, 2 Poisoned: carbon monoxide.	**Suicide:** same time and method.	Couple separate two weeks previously. Father can't accept; kills during access trip to seaside.	14	Derek, 7 Jacob, 3 Poisoned: carbon monoxide.	**Suicide:** same time and method. Row with mother just before access. Set house on fire; then killed.	Marital break-up. Long custody battle between parents.
15	Mary, 8 Felicity, 6 poisoned: carbon monoxide.	**Suicide:** same time and method.	Marital break-up	16	Edward, 3 Poisoned: carbon monoxide.	**Suicide:** same time and method.	Marriage break-up and separation; child killed during access visit.
17	Samira, 7 Zhazia, 6 Multiple stabbings.	Stabbed mother to death in presence of children.	Marital break-up: couple in process of divorce; mother re-married in secret; father finds out; kills during access visit.	18	Cedric, 9 Owen, 6 Hanged from beam in garage.	**Suicide:** same time and method	DV: Marriage break-up. Custody dispute. Mother has relationship with another man; they book into hotel night before the killings.

19	Cedric, 9 Owen, 6 Strangled.	Battered and stabbed his wife to death. Convicted: 3 life sentences.	Marital strains: Father claimed his wife was hassling him just before killings.	20	Barry, 4 Battered with lampstand and stabbed. (18-month-old sister attacked but survived)	**Attempted suicide** by stabbing. Succeeded one year later in prison.	Marriage break-up; mother leaves and lives with father's best friend. Father can't cope; admitted to hospital. Kills Barry on discharge.
21	Diana, 2 Poisoned: carbon monoxide.	Collected child for weekend access.	Marriage break-up and separation; DV (verbal). Killing took place 12 weeks later.	22	Jack, 6 Strangled.	**Attempted suicide** on electricity pylons. Convicted of manslaughter.	DV over many years Mother and daughter flee to refuge; Jack remains with father (diagnosed paranoid schizophrenic).
23	Brian, 8 Bertie, 7 Brian had throat slit. Bertie stabbed in neck with a screwdriver.	Self-injury; claimed he and children were attacked by gangs. Convicted: 2 life sentences. **Suicide** in prison only days after conviction.	DV Mother trying to end relationship. Is attacked before children are killed.	24	Aloysius, 12 Cecilia, 9 Christine, 7 Anthony, 3	**Suicide:** Set car alight with him and children inside. All died from severe burns and/or inhalation of toxic fumes.	Marriage break-up. He threatened to kill one month before doing so. In suicide note, father accused mother of complicity. Killed children during access.

(*continued*)

Table 5.1 Continued

Case No.	Victims, ages, method of killing	Father's action before, during and/or after killing	Context and circumstances at time of killing	Case No.	Victims, ages, method of killing	Father's action before, during and/or after killing	Context and circumstances at time of killing
25	Jade, 7 Terry, 6 Colin, 5 Dez, 3 Poisoned: carbon monoxide from a lawnmower in car.	**Suicide**: same time and method. Rang mother to let her hear children die and cry for help.	Marriage break-up: mother tells father she is pregnant to another man.	26	Prasad, 2 Multiple injuries (Older child left unharmed)	Stabbed mother to death; jumped off bridge with child in his arms. **Suicide** multiple injuries.	Believed mother was having an affair with work colleague.
27	Elizabeth, 3 Strangled and beaten.	Stabbed mother to death.	DV Planned murder of wife and child. Father is having affair. Debt problems. History of violent attacks on women.	28	Polly, 4 Elvira, 2 Multiple stab wounds. (youngest child unharmed)	Stabbed mother to death in presence of children; then **suicide** by jumping off a bridge.	DV; separation; court orders against father; custody dispute. Mother in new relationship.
29	Mervyn, 6 Joey, 4 Throats slit, but both survive due to paramedics.	**Suicide** by slicing his own throat.	DV: long history of. Mother leaves; father still visits; has row during access; and attacks children.	30	Maisie, 4 Chloroformed; strangled.	**Attempted suicide** Depression; on antidepressants.	Relationship break-up: Mother having affair; father discovers intimate texts.

31	Lorinda, 9 mths. Shot in stomach.	Shot mother in head. Fled to his family home. Arrested. Tried. Convicted; life sentence.	Couple settle abroad. Father in debt; can't get job; engages in fraud; scouring Internet porn and escort sights.	Marital break-up. Mother had affair over three years but ended it. Predicted husband would kill her.
32	Aaron, 11 Abraham, 8 Hilda, 6 Bludgeoned by a cricket bat.	Killed mother first by same method, then fled abroad. Apprehended; re-turned; convicted.		
33	Laurence, 6 Pushed over balcony; died of multiple injuries; younger child survived.	**Attempted suicide** Father jumped after children; survived. Tried; found unfit to plead. Hospitalised. Coroner says children unlawfully killed.	Ferocious row before incident. Marriage failing; mother in a relationship with another man; father threatens to 'take children'.	Partnership break-up and separation. Child regularly brought by mother to home of father. Ferocious row when mother arrives late. Mother attacked.
34	Noel, 15 months. Multiple stab wounds after frenzied attack.	**Suicide** with knife.		
35	Catherine, 5 Alex, 3 Asphyxiated.	Tried; convicted. Suffered depression, but of 'sound mind' when killing.	Relationship failing. Father discovers text between mother and another man; kills children when she is at a concert.	Relationship break-up separation. Mother tells father it's over.
36	Angela, 12 Stan, 5 Multiple stabbings.	Father also kills mother and two relatives. Tried and convicted.		

(continued)

Table 5.1 Continued

Case No.	Victims, ages, method of killing	Father's action before, during and/or after killing	Context and circumstances at time of killing	Case No.	Victims, ages, method of killing	Father's action before, during and/or after killing	Context and circumstances at time of killing
37	Jerry, 6 Stabbed to death.	**Suicide** by electrocution, in prison, awaiting trial.	Marriage break-up; mother and son walk out 2/3 weeks before killing; son has weekend visit to father.	38	Kevin, 6 Lois, 4 Kevin had stab wounds; died of smoke inhalation.	Father physically removes mother from home. Kills both children; sets home alight. **Suicide** with knife.	Marriage failing. Mother is having affair while husband is away from home. She tells husband about affair.
39	Rory, 4 Multiple stabbing. Sister stabbed 14 times but survives.	Father attacks Rory during access visit; then attacks sister. Admits killing to police.	DV: Marital break-up; separation; mother is in relationship with another man. Father awaiting prosecution for rape and use of weapon.	40	Carl, 6 Asphyxiation.	**Suicide** Sets house alight after killing son, then hung himself.	Marriage break-up. Dispute over custody. He believes mother in relationship with another man.
41	Ricky 7 Millie (severely disabled) 25 Multiple stab wounds.	**Attempted suicide** with knife and pill overdose. Tried; convicted.	DV: Marital break-up; separation; mother seeking divorce and settlement. Custody and access dispute.	42	Peter, 6 James, 2 Multiple stab wounds, while locked in car.	Set alight to car after killing them. **Attempted suicide** in car; survived. Tried and convicted.	Marriage break-up; Father resorts to alcohol and gambling. Wants more access to children. Leaves a revenge letter for mother.

43	Alison 7 Oliver, 3 Poisoned: carbon monoxide.	**Suicide:** same time and method. Leaves hoax bomb and revenge note for mother.	DV: Marital break-up Mother leaves.
44	Eliza, 3 Eleanor, 14 mths. Asphyxiated.	**Suicide** by hanging.	Partnership break-up; separation; custody and access dispute; father kills children during access.
45	Terry, 2 Yvonne, 4 Strangled with internet cable.	Father made video of children saying 'bye' to mother. **Attempts suicide** Tried, convicted.	DV. Mother leaves a week before killings. Father discovers her attempts at Internet dating.
46	Warren, 3 Throat slit and abdomen slashed. Younger sister untouched.	Father attacks wife with same weapon, wounding her. Tried, convicted.	Marital break-up; couple decide to separate day before killing.
47	Louise, 11 mths. Stabbed through the head.	Stabbed mother to death; left 2-year-old son amongst carnage; He fled. Tried; convicted; judged sane at time of killings.	Relationship failing; father loses job; has bipolar disorder; heavily in debt; has fled family home on numerous occasions.
48	Gillian, 5 Drowned; her brother escaped.	During access, he phones and taunts mother about killing children; attempts suicide but changes mind.	**DV:** Marital break-up Conflict over custody and access. Police involved. Father loses home and job; resorts to alcohol.
49	Conrad, 6 Poisoned with over-dose of morphine and sleeping pills.	**Suicide:** same time and method, just before mother was due to collect child. Father had custody.	Marriage break-up; separation; dispute over custody and access; mother in new relationship.
50	Ray, 10 Rhoda, 8 Multiple stab wounds	Called police; admitted killings; Tried, convicted.	DV: Marriage break-up; father about to be evicted; children murdered during access visit.

(*continued*)

Table 5.1 Continued

Case No.	Victims, ages, method of killing	Father's action before, during and/or after killing	Context and circumstances at time of killing	Case No.	Victims, ages, method of killing	Father's action before, during and/or after killing	Context and circumstances at time of killing
51	Sonya, 2 Shot dead. Older child escapes.	Father tortures mother before killing her and child; **Attempts suicide**, but failed.	DV over long period; police called many times; mother tries to end relationship.	52	Aniela, 5 Kajetan, 1½ Multiple stab wounds.	Kills mother and three others with knives. **Attempts suicide**. Tried; convicted of manslaughter.	**DV:** Marital break-up. Mother has affair; husband can't cope; attempts to kill himself; hospitalized but discharged early.
53	Noah, 15 months Burnt to death.	Father (and an accomplice) also killed mother and her father. Fled; Tried, convicted of multiple murders.	**DV:** Relationship break-up; mother returns to parents; father begs her to return to him; then threatens her.	54	Ewan, 6 months. Asphyxiated.	Dressed child and placed in bed encircled by toys and flowers. **Suicide:** hanging.	**DV:** Partnership failing; constant rows and violence. Police called. Separation. Killed Ewan during 1st access.

55	Ada, 8 Multiple injuries caused by axe and a knife. A 4-year-old sibling suffered minor injuries.	Kills mother. Flees, attempts suicide. Tried.	Partnership failing; father's work prospects bleak; mother has high-powered job in education.		
56	Shane, 12 Rowena, 8 Christine, 7 Multiple stabbing; throats slit.	**Suicide:** Jumps over cliff.		**DV:** Marital problems. Rows day before. Father sees texts between her and another man. Mother wants to leave.	
57	James, 11 David, 3 Method of death not known yet.	**Suicide:** by hanging.	**DV:** parents separate. Father fears losing custody; mother posts details of new partner on Facebook.		
58	Kirsty, 6 months Burnt to death by father setting house on fire.	Mother and grandmother also burnt to death. Father denies charge. But convicted.		Relationship break-up Separation; father believes mother is in new relationship.	
59	Brenden, 7 Fran, 6 Multiple stabbings.	**Suicide:** knife wounds. Father attacked children in car during access.	Marital break-up; separation. Father 'distraught'. Posts bitter comments on Facebook weeks before killings. Said he was 'sorry'.		
60	Maria, 3 Fatal abdominal injuries; died in hospital.	Father tries to conceal injury; child untreated; pleaded guilty to manslaughter.		**DV:** Stormy relationship; father discovers mother is having an affair. Attacks child.	
61	John, 10 Asphyxiated. Severely handicapped.	Told mother to take younger child away, enabling him to kill John. Defense claimed it was a mercy killing.	Marriage crumbling. Father resorting to alcohol; unable to cope with son's disability; Judge accused mother of complicity.		
62	Unborn child: mother six months pregnant, suffered nine stab wounds and was strangled.	**Attempted suicide** Barricaded himself in home; surrendered; tried; convicted; life sentence.		**DV** History of violent attacks on women; had stabbed mother in previous year, was arrested and charged.	

Table 5.2 Category II: Filicide mothers

Case No.	Victims, ages, method of killing	Mother's action before, during and/or after killing	Context and circumstances at time of killing	Case No.	Victims, ages, method of killing	Mother's action before, during and/or after killing	Context and circumstances at time of killing
1	Alban, 7 Aloysius, 18 mths. Asphyxiated.	**Suicide** by hanging.	Marital break-up. Children killed 48 hours after father said he was leaving.	2.	Keith, 7 Charlene, 5 Clifford, 3 Multiple stab wounds.	**Suicide** by drowning; said to neighbour: she would take children with her.	Marital break-up; separation; mother suffered depression and paranoia.
3	Ben, 3 Vivienne, 2 Drowned.	**Suicide**: same time and method.	Relationship break up and separation; mother develops depression.	4	Garry, 11 (severely autistic) Strangled with his own belt	**Suicide attempt** by cutting her wrists.	DV over many years. Resort to alcohol; left father a month before killing; homeless.
5	Ronald, 8 Carl, 5 Poisoned; carbon monoxide.	**Suicide**: same time and method.	Marriage break-up; father having affair with work colleague; mother cannot cope.	6	Marvin, 5 Ruby, 4 Poisoned: carbon monoxide.	**Suicide**: same time and method.	Marital break-up; separation, divorce; dispute over custody; mother fears she might lose custody.

7	Paul, 5 Stabbed to death; another child attacked with knife and hammer but survived.	Had row with neighbours before attacks. Committed suicide much later by incineration.	Marital break-up; rapid mental health decline. Unsupported, poverty, stigma.	Marriage breakdown and separation. Mental health deteriorates rapidly. Has fears for children's health.
8	Heather, 7 Mark, 5 Poisoned; carbon monoxide.	**Suicide:** same time and method. Mother depressed and delusional. Killed on day children due back at school.		
9	Simon, 6 Poisoned with prescription pills.	**Suicide. Sliced** throat with electric saw. Eight months pregnant. Under psychiatric care for depression.	Marital break-up; Husband about to leave. Mother's depression worsening.	
10	Nahum, 6 Burnt to death; mother set bed alight when he was asleep.	Diagnosed as depressed psychotic and schizophrenic. Many **suicide attempts.**		Mother reluctantly in UK after arranged marriage. No social contacts; can't speak English. Mental health deteriorates rapidly.
11	Owen, 6 Liam, 2 Asphyxiated.	**Suicide** by hanging.	Father leaves for another woman. Row with partner before killings. Had suffered depression in the past. Left suicide notes.	
12	Stella, 9 Stanley, 8 Lethal injection; potassium chloride.	**Suicide** by intravenous drip of potassium chloride.		Marital break-up. Father left 10 days before killings; mother had threatened 'something' if husband left.

(*continued*)

Table 5.2 Continued

Case No.	Victims, ages, method of killing	Mother's action before, during and/or after killing	Context and circumstances at time of killing	Case No.	Victims, ages, method of killing	Mother's action before, during and/or after killing	Context and circumstances at time of killing
13	Bernard, 5 Bludgeoned with heavy instrument while he slept.	**Attempted suicide** by throwing herself from 2nd floor flat. Seriously injured. Tried: convicted of culpable homicide.	Marriage break-up and separation; 5–6 months previously; relocation. History of depression.	14	Lorna, 9 Asphyxiated.	**Suicide** by hanging; mother discharged herself from hospital; suffering depression.	Marriage break-up and separation. Mental health deterioration; mother says she has thoughts of killing Lorna.
15	Adrian, 4 mths. Smoke inhalation and burns	Mother staged arson attack, setting house alight; disconnected fire alarms; confessed; guilty of infanticide.	Postnatal depression Relationship break-up; separation; mother desperate for partner to return. She texts him, hinting at what she might do.	16	Simar, 6 Arjan, 2 Multiple injuries.	**Suicide:** Mother threw herself before fast moving train, holding children.	Postnatal depression; prolonged mental illness following arranged marriage; Father temporarily leaves.
17	Caroline, 6 Strangled with a skipping rope.	Went outside and sat on pavement; admitted killing. Tried; found guilty of manslaughter; jailed indefinitely.	**DV** by both parents. Father left; mother couldn't cope; asked social services to take child.	18	Ralph, 12 (autistic) Drowned.	**Suicide:** Mother persuaded child to jump off bridge, and jumped after him.	Long history of depression and suicide attempts; GP testified that mental state

19	Rashed, 2 Parvez, 1 Asphyxiated.	**Suicide** by hanging.			deteriorated rapidly when she and child's father split.
			20	Arranged marriage; mother brought to large city; has no job or friends; doesn't speak English; does not venture out; rows with husband are frequent and intense.	**Suicide**: Mother set house alight after killings. Mother in new relationship. Had stillbirth two months before killings; suffered depression.
21	Tansila, 6 Battered by blunt instrument. Amina, 5 Strangled.	**Suicide**: method in dispute; all three found in bed.			
			22	DV: Marriage break-up; separation; husband remarrying in country of origin.	Anthony, 10 Beaten to death Kevin 3 Asphyxiated. Mother diagnosed paranoid schizophrenia; detained indefinitely. Marital break-up and dispute over custody and access. Mother's health deteriorates after birth of youngest child.
23	Daphne, 16 Janet, 13 Multiple stab wounds (39 and 37 respectively).	During access; brought them shopping. Bought kitchen knives. Tried, convicted; 33 year sentence. Judge said killings were 'retaliation'.			
			24	Break-up of marriage; husband starts new relationship. Custody battle. During trial mother diagnosed with 'reactive stress'.	Nicola, 4 (mild cerebral palsy) Drowned. Dressed body; took it to hospital. Convicted of murder; received life sentence (15 years). Father told mother to leave days before killing. Alcohol-dependent; suffered post natal depression.

(*continued*)

Table 5.2 Continued

Case No.	Victims, ages, method of killing	Mother's action before, during and/or after killing	Context and circumstances at time of killing	Case No.	Victims, ages, method of killing	Mother's action before, during and/or after killing	Context and circumstances at time of killing
25	Robert, 2 mths. Daniel, 4 mths. Multiple stab wounds	**Attempted suicide** by stabbing. Pleaded guilty to manslaughter. Detained indefinitely.	Relationship break-up; partner leaves. Long term user of cannabis had PND after birth of Daniel. Diagnosed psychotic, paranoia.	26	Jason, 11 Drowned in bath.	Suicide attempt with knife; Pleaded guilty to manslaughter; detained indefinitely.	Separation; husband ceases financial support; mother has huge debts. Depression in months leading up to killing.
27	Kate, 5 mths. Multiple injuries.	**Suicide:** multiple injuries. Mother leapt from balcony with baby in arms.	Immigrant mother. No support/contact with father. Cannabis user. Depression with rapid onset.	28	Bell, 3 Asphyxiated.	**Suicide attempt** with knife; Denied killing; convicted; life sentence.	Mother's 2nd marriage deteriorating; having affair with father of Bell. Paternity dispute. Domestic incidents; police called; custody and access dispute.

29	Havelock, 3 Eliza, 2 Asphyxiated. (2 older children untouched).	Bodies placed in holdall bag; taken to home of father. Convicted of murder; life sentence. (32 years)	Relationship break-up. Mother leaves with children; father re-establishes contact with former girlfriend. Mother sees texts and E-mails between them.	30	Aadi 12, severe learning difficulty Poisoned; made to drink bleach. Younger child untouched.	**Suicide** attempt same time and method. Survives. Psychiatrists unsure about diagnosis.	Marital breakdown. Separation; mental health deteriorates; believes social workers will take child. In conflict with neighbours.
31	David, 14 Steven, 11 Multiple stabbing.	**Suicide:** same time and method.	Father on business trip when killings occurred. Mother has depression/delusions.	32	Rose, 5 David, 11 mths. Asphyxiated.	Fled abroad and killed children. Confessed; tried, convicted; life sentence.	Feared their removal; father arrested; sexual abuse charges; he committed **suicide** in prison.
33	Unborn child, one week before birth due. Poisoned	Confessed to administering poison with intent to procure a miscarriage. Judge said offence was more serious than manslaughter.	Had affair with father of child over 7 years, while married. Tries and succeeds in aborting baby with poison bought on Internet.	34	Kelly, 4 Drowned.	**Suicide:** leaping over bridge.	Marriage break-up; mother suffering depression; custody and access dispute. Mother fearing she would lose custody to father.

(*continued*)

89

Table 5.2 Continued

Case No.	Victims, ages, method of killing	Mother's action before, during and/or after killing	Context and circumstances at time of killing	Case No.	Victims, ages, method of killing	Mother's action before, during and/or after killing	Context and circumstances at time of killing
35	Abraham, 8 Leslie, 8 Cathleen, 5 Multiple stab wounds.	**Suicide attempt** by leaping off balcony. Survived, with multiple injuries.	Marriage break-up. Custody and access dispute; husband in new relationship. In telephone row, she hints at killings as a punishment to him.	36	Calum, 2 Strangled and stabbed.	Admitted to hospital the day before with psychotic symptoms; discharged herself on the same day.	Marriage break-up. Rapid onset of mental illness. After killing, she brought the body to the police station.
37	Paul, 5 Ian, 2 Asphyxiated. Mother had three older children.	**Suicide** by hanging on the day Ian's father is due to collect him.	Single parent: 3 fathers of 5 children. Major issues around custody and access; mother in dispute with fathers of her 2nd, 3rd and 5th children.	38	Sheila, 4 Multiple stab wounds.	**Suicide attempt** by knife wounds; and antifreeze. Massive internal damage. Guilty of manslaughter. (12 year sentence)	Relationship breakdown. Sacked from job. Hints at drastic action in texts to estranged partner.

39	Karen, 4 Asphyxiated.	**Suicide attempt:** Knife injuries; pill and alcohol overdose. Reported the death. Detained indefinitely.	Relationship break up. Father returns abroad. Mother isolated, disowned by family. Mental health deteriorates.
40	Sheena, 7 mths. Asphyxiated.	Kills child after social gathering **Suicide attempt** by slashing wrists. Convicted of infanticide. Detained indefinitely.	DV: Crisis erupts when father tells mother her best friend is expecting his child. Police called often. Mother's mental health deteriorates; cannabis use increases.
41	Alice, 5 Asphyxiated	**Suicide** by hanging Dressed child and placed her in bed surrounded with toys.	Relationship break up; mother life long user of cannabis; treated for depression; unable to hold down a job.
42	Terry, 13 Elizabeth, 9 Multiple stab wounds.	**Suicide:** stab wounds. Bought knives; bought children pizza; attacked during the night.	Father abroad working; mother worried about her job; no history of mental illness. Mother left suicide notes.
43	Lucille, 2 Nearly drowned.	**Attempted filicide-suicide** by jumping off bridge; rescued; child still alive. Jailed; released by Court of Appeal on humanitarian grounds.	Marriage break-up. Custody and access dispute; mother had message written on her stomach blaming father for 'deaths'. He had custody; she was having access.
44	Jason, 5 Poisoned by anti depressant tablets. Three half-siblings unharmed.	**Attempted suicide** Hospitalized. Tried, convicted of manslaughter; diminished responsibility.	Marriage break-up; resisted father having access; prescribed anti-depressants. Had suicidal thoughts; explored suicide sites.

Table 5.3 Category III: Familicide fathers

Case No.	Victims, ages, method of killing	Father's action before, during and/or after killing	Context and circumstances at time of killing	Case No.	Victims, ages, method of killing	Father's action before, during and/or after killing	Context and circumstances at time of killing
1	Bill, 9 Adrian, 1 Children and mother stabbed.	Covered windows. Suicide with knife; tried to set house alight.	Suffered depression in past. Coroner's suggestion: affected by death of son 4 years previously.	2	Grace, 6 Multiple stab wounds Two children escaped, injured.	Stabbed mother to death; suicide with knife. Tried killing two other children.	Fierce row preceding the murder. Father had just lost secure, highly paid job.
3.	Aban, 3 Farrah, 2 Asphyxiated.	Father attempted to kill himself with knife, then hung himself in local park	Repetitive life-threatening DV. Father has suicidal thoughts; issues around culture, identity and asylum seeking	4	Phyllis, 2 Nora, 1 Asphyxiated	Before smothering his 2 children, father killed mother by multiple stabbing, then hung himself.	Family in increasing debt.
5	Albert, 2 Multiple stab wounds. (+ unborn child)	Stabbed mother to death, and child, and then himself. She had struck up new relationship and was pregnant to another man. She had custody of Albert.	Couple separated but father won't accept. Arrested days before for threatening harm. He was undergoing mental health assessment and cautioned to stay away.	6	Freda, 18 Bludgeoned to death by rubber mallet.	Father killed his wife first, then his daughter, and then hanged himself.	Business failing but not catastrophically. Father accused days before of fraudulently receiving £200,000 from supplier.

7	Bernard, 10 Hit with sledgehammer and then died in fire.	After killing Bernard, he sets mother's bedroom ablaze; she is burnt to death; he dies later in hospital, from burns. Earlier had said: "If I can't have my little family, no one can."	Father under care of CMHT: depression, delusion paranoia. Ceased taking medication; discharged himself from hospital. Text and verbal threats to his wife. Told to leave home; he visited at weekends; refused to leave on day of killings, his birthday.
8	Mary, 4 Shot through the head by a Beretta pistol.	Mother left killer months before and has new partner, but keeps in contact, bringing Mary to her father for access. He locks them in, shoots both of them, and then kills himself.	**DV** Custody and access dispute.
9	Kitty, 15 Shot through the head.	Father first shoots dead his wife, then his daughter. He also kills all family's animals; then sets fire to their mansion home.	Business failing, £2 million of debt; house about to be seized on morning of killings. Had told GP of suicidal tendencies.
10	Kathy, 13 Seamus, 7 Barbara, 4, Clídna, 1½ James, 3 mths. Burnt to death	Father spread petrol throughout house and set it alight, late at night	**DV** Father is a convicted sex offender. Authorities about to move in. Mother prepares to leave him.

(continued)

Table 5.3 Continued

Case No.	Victims, ages, method of killing	Father's action before, during and/or after killing	Context and circumstances at time of killing	Case No.	Victims, ages, method of killing	Father's action before, during and/or after killing	Context and circumstances at time of killing
11	Sarah, 16 Stella, 15 Amelia, 10 Henrietta, 3 Burnt to death.	Father locked doors, poured petrol over wife and children as they slept, and set them alight before alighting himself. He died in hospital later.	Cultural conflict; father resents 'Westernization' of daughters. He's less fluent in English; has menial jobs; his wife is a popular community worker, educated, articulate.	12	Ceira 3 Debbie, 6 Stabbed to death.	Father attacked partner and children with knife, then ran car into tree and stabbed himself; succeeded in hanging himself in prison, before trial.	DV over many years. Mother had committed herself to leaving with children after Xmas.
13	Walter, 17 Shot dead.	Father breaks into home from which he's barred; kills son and mother, and himself with shotgun.	Marriage break-up. Mother tells father she wants divorce. Father repeatedly threatens revenge. DV. Served with injunction. He leaves, but returns.	14	Harry, 3 Charles, 1½ Bludgeoned to death. One other child seriously injured; another escaped	Father had been for drink with colleagues after work; attacked family after row.	DV: Father twice arrested for violence. Attempted suicide during 2nd arrest. Both parents in extra marital affairs. Mother was a senior manager in better paid job.

15	Genevieve, 6
Aaron, 3
Shot dead.	Shot mother before shooting children. He failed to kill himself with first shot, and had to use a second.	Family recently moved home and father changed jobs. Enormous debt with creditors about to move in.
16	John, 18
Selina, 16
Laurence 14
Elizabeth 10
Bludgeoned to death by hammer.	Mother is killed same way. A meticulously planned familicide not discovered until 2/3 weeks after. Father hangs himself.	Father: stress-related depression, almost bankrupt; wife having affair with his business partner; He has regular contact with prostitute.
17	Kevin, 7
David, 6
Jack, 2
Bludgeoned with hammer, and then repeatedly stabbed.	Mother killed same way. Father hung himself from banister.	Inquest: depressed about (i) mother's cancer; (ii) threat of bankruptcy; has been bankrupt before; believes he's manic depressive.
18	Geraldine, 10
Francis, 9
Asphyxiated.	Father strangled mother before or after smothering children, then kills himself, carbon monoxide poisoning.	Separated; mother in relationship with another man; father can't cope; leaves suicide note.
19	Elaine, 6
Matthew, 5
Stabbed to death.	Stabbed his wife to death and then himself.	Criminal theft of vital office material may have contributed.
20	Ercan, 15
Tony, 13
Ismail, 6
Stabbed to death.	Children tried to prevent father strangling mother. He stabbed them repeatedly then hung himself.	Father's café business failing; debts mounting.

(continued)

Table 5.3 Continued

Case No.	Victims, ages, method of killing	Father's action before, during and/or after killing	Context and circumstances at time of killing	Case No.	Victims, ages, method of killing	Father's action before, during and/or after killing	Context and circumstances at time of killing
21	Chaitali, 4 Sajani, 2 Bansari, 5 mths. All injected with potassium cyanide.	Watched video of executions before killings. Father probably last to die.	Husband jobless; rumoured financial problems. Difficulty in assimilation into surrounding community and society.	22	Desmond, 6 Catherine, 5 Poisoned: carbon monoxide.	Father bludgeoned his wife to death then killed himself alongside the children.	Marital difficulty; father has affair; mother incandescent and has affair herself. Mother insults father about enjoying sex more with her new liaison.

perpetrated by fathers (all biological with the exception of two); Table 5.2 provides details of 44 filicides perpetrated by mothers, and Table 5.3, details of 22 familicides, invariably perpetrated by fathers. The total is 128. These three categories will be referred to in the remainder of this and subsequent chapters as (i) male filicide; (ii) female filicide; and (iii) familicide. Remember that though they are distinct categories, categories (i) and (iii) have the same perpetrator, that is: fathers. The fathers who commit familicide (annihilating their whole family and themselves) are also committing a filicide act for each child whom they kill. When one writes or speaks about filicide killings perpetrated by men, those *men* may belong to either category (i) (male filicide) or category (iii) (familicide). Thus the first and third categories will often be combined when calculating factors like the total number of children killed by fathers, their ages, gender, and so on.

There are three subcategories in Tables 5.1 and 5.2: those who kill their children, those who kill their children and attempt but fail to commit suicide; and those who kill their children and succeed in committing suicide. There are no such subcategories needed in the third table on familicide killings, which by definition means that the perpetrator always succeeds in killing himself after having killed all other father members. Domestic violence is a prominent feature throughout all three tables; it is abbreviated to DV. The terms **suicide**, **attempted suicide** and **DV** are shown in **bold**.

The tables have been constructed on the basis of: (i) coroner's inquests, many of which the author personally attended; (ii) coroners' reports; (iii) murder trials attended by the author; (iv) judges' sentencing and explanatory statements; (v) serious case reviews; (vi) executive summaries of serious case reviews; (vii) case management reports; (viii) public inquiry reports; (ix) confidential inquiry reports; and (x) press, television and social media reports and commentaries.

A brief comparison

Clearly these tables display the specific contexts of killings, which we have been discussing. An obvious question arises: how would this number of killings compare with the number of killings in similar or identical contexts in other countries?

Over the same period covered by this study, in Denmark, there were 18 male filicides in which 31 children were killed; four female filicides in which seven children were killed, and two familicides in which four children were killed.

In Ireland, over the same period, there were five male filicides in which eight children were killed, seven female filicides in which ten children were killed, and three familicides in which six children were killed.

The populations are substantially smaller than in the UK, approximately five million in Denmark and four million in Ireland. The numbers of filicide killings in those two countries are therefore comparatively high. As in the UK, there were of course many more filicide killings in Denmark and Ireland over this period by both mothers and fathers (through sustained abuse and neglect, and so on) but not in the context which is the focus of this study: marital break-up, fractious disputes, separations, fights over custody and deteriorating mental health. Occasionally, the contexts as well as the methods of killings in all three countries are disturbingly identical.

Acknowledging the reality

In attending inquests on many of the cases in the above tables, I have been surprised how often the word 'probably' is used regarding the cause of death. This is particularly so in cases involving fire. In the above three categories, 24 children, aged between 3 months and 16 years perished in deliberately started fires. An additional nine were attacked before the fires started, and may or may not have been dead when they did start. There were 11 fire perpetrators, 9 fathers and two mothers. There were seven innocent adult victims, five mothers, one grandmother and one grandfather.

Often a pathologist and a coroner will say words to the effect that: 'we can't be certain, though the victims *probably* died of smoke inhalation' (that is, before the flames engulfed them). This is an admirably compassionate statement to make in the presence of grieving parents. But, 'smoke inhalation' can be one of those sanitizing and misleading concepts that may not convey the reality; the reality, for example, of a child suddenly awakening to the realization that the house (or car) is alight, and will attempt to run in blind panic, with nowhere to run, choking with the fumes, seeing the flames dancing off every wall, scorched by whatever their hands and their bare feet touch, and then the sheer terror and the choking for breath mercifully causing them to collapse, to lose consciousness, and the fire burning them beyond recognition. This is not a thought conjured up in this author's over-active, worst-scenario imagination; it is actually the chilling record captured in the recorded voice of a 13-year-old victim in Northern Ireland in 2006 (Toner, 2008). The perpetrator, a convicted paedophile, when facing the prospect of his partner and five children leaving him, burnt his home to the ground. The oldest child, 13, somehow had the presence of mind to phone the emergency services and scream out that the flames were spreading all around her and her parents and younger siblings. Her faith must have been amazingly strong in the circumstances: she also somehow had the presence of mind to invoke the help of prayer. Rosary beads were clasped around her fingers when her charred remains were discovered afterwards. She is regarded by many people in Northern Ireland as a heroine.

These are the images which haunt parent survivors of fire killings. Even if friends, or the coroner, or the pathologist compassionately attempt to persuade them that the 'poor child probably knew or felt nothing', an entirely different and more realistic probability will re-emerge in their minds later, more potent, and much more difficult to get rid of. I do not know of any filicide perpetrator in history who chose fire with the express objective of ensuring that their victims died of smoke inhalation! And while victims do unarguably die of smoke inhalation, I am not aware of any pathologist who could say with absolute confidence that smoke inhalation was the cause of death in children whose bodies have been burnt well beyond recognition, and beyond any possibility of a satisfactory post-mortem examination.

Premeditation and deception

'It is beyond human comprehension.' I have heard at least three coroners say that, and undoubtedly, a good many more coroners have said something similar. This shared sense of bafflement and helplessness on hearing of a filicide killing sometimes creates a perception that the family at the centre of the tragedy is the victim of mysterious destructive and uncontrollable forces that strike without reason or provocation, hurtling the family mercilessly towards Armageddon. Nothing could be further from the truth.

Most filicide killings are preceded by, and are wholly dependent upon an exceptionally high degree of premeditation and deception on the part of the perpetrator. The manifestation of this premeditation takes many forms. Male perpetrators will often choose the day of contact visits in those cases in which the couples are separated (that is, the vast majority). Female perpetrators will often choose the hours of darkness, when fathers are absent and there are no other adults anywhere near; when they are in complete control of both the children and the environment. Many male and female perpetrators may later, justifiably, claim in their defence that they were suffering some form of mental illness (depression is the most frequently used defence). But that does not preclude them from meticulous planning and a lucidity of mind as they carry out the killings. Alder and Polk (2001) and Johnson (2005) both highlight premeditation as a significant feature in many of the cases they studied.

There is a more sinister manifestation of premeditation at play here. It is in the level and type of deception which many of the perpetrators find necessary in order to be able to kill their children in the manner and in the location in which they intend. The children are lied to repeatedly. They are lured into conveniently isolated locations. They are baited with all kinds of goodies, and they are deliberately and effectively suffused with a sense of contentment and security by the very same adult who is determined to kill them. It is another challenging aspect of filicide killings which is either greatly underplayed or ignored entirely in the research literature. Here are the details of what happened in some of the cases above.

- A father collects his children on the pretext of taking them to a particular beauty spot. The older child initially refuses to go but is bribed with the offer of £10 to purchase a toy which he had been wanting. The father tapes his final conversation on the journey; he assures his children: 'We're going to have a very good game today' (Thomson and Ross, 2011). The children are suddenly stabbed repeatedly. The father then sets the car alight. He leaves a revenge note for his former wife.
- A mother preparing to kill her two children, aged 5 and 11 months, asked the oldest child if she would prefer to live a few very happy days with her mother or a long time without her mother. The child, incapable of understanding what her mother meant, said that

she would prefer to stay with her mother. The child, along with a younger sibling, was then asphyxiated.
- A father, during contact, announces that he's taking his three very young children to the zoo. Then he kills them and himself through carbon monoxide poisoning in the car. He leaves a revenge note for his wife.
- A mother, uncharacteristically, took her two teenage children shopping before stabbing them 37 and 29 times respectively.
- A father called to take his four children on an 'access outing'. He bought them sweets. They were eating the sweets at the same time as he was poisoning them and himself with carbon monoxide.
- A mother who had been planning the killing for many months with the help of Internet sites, took a bath with her 11-year-old son, and drowned him. He tried resisting and escaping, and left bite marks on her fingers.
- A father, on the day his wife left him, persuaded his teenage son to go on an errand, to give him sufficient time to kill a much younger son and a disabled daughter.
- Food treats are a common method of assuring the victim that everything is fine. A mother treated her children to a visit to the pizza parlour, before stabbing them to death. A father bought his children fish and chips before clubbing them to death. Another called to take his two children to the Wacky Warehouse followed by a visit to Burger King. Another took his four children to a Chuck Wagon restaurant before killing all four of them.

There are at least another 34 cases in the current study with similar deceptions. The actual number, realistically, is probably much higher; in the cataclysm of a filicide killing, such details will, in many cases, be forgotten or ignored.

In our reluctance to avoid even the merest hint of judgement or criticism, we lose sight of the enormity of the multifaceted injustice to the child. Most of these killings are cruel beyond belief, but so many of them are formulated on a betrayal of trust that is equally cruel and horrifying: it is serial lying on a grand scale, during which meticulous preparation for the chosen method and location of death is being made. As many judges have rightly pointed out, this capacity for sustained lying and preparation raises questions about the entirely predictable defence of some kind of 'mental incapacity' invariably advanced by those representing the parent who has killed.

The law acknowledges the reality

If coroners in their interpretation of events bend over backwards to alleviate the suffering of the bereaved, the same cannot be said of judges who preside over those cases in which surviving perpetrators are tried and convicted of killing their children. In a number of highly publicized cases, judges have spoken at length about one particularly terrifying aspect of the killings: namely, that one child sees another child being strangled, or drowned, or suffocated, or knifed to death, and knows that he or she is about to meet the same fate. Most of the children are far too young to escape, but old enough to know precisely what is happening. When police and/or pathologists re-enact these scenarios during inquests or trials, it is often the point at which families can no longer maintain control. The testimony inescapably tells us that a child saw his brother or sister struggling in vain as they were strangled, or heard him or her screaming in terror as they were repeatedly attacked, or saw him or her futilely stretching tiny blood-drenched hands in the way of a thrusting knife. No less than 84 children in the present study endured these types of nightmares, before they themselves were killed. In one case, three children aged 15, 13 and 6 valiantly tried to prevent their father strangling their mother. They couldn't, and when she was dead, he stabbed all three to death.

Many judges not only acknowledge this particular reality, but underline it in their summing up and in their sentencing. In the most publicized and longest filicide trial in history (not included in this study), that of the murder of 17-year-old Shafilia Ahmed, for whom her parents were convicted and each sentenced to 25 years imprisonment, the trial judge dwelt upon what he regarded as one of the most aggravating circumstances of the case, namely, that the parents brutally murdered Shafilia in the presence of her sisters and brother.

Forgotten casualties

There is no mention in the above categories of the 15 children who escaped from the killings. Even in the most highly publicized cases, those children are quickly forgotten about. Here is what happened to some of them:

- One child nearly died from carbon monoxide poisoning which killed a sibling.
- Two children, 6 and 4, had their throats slit before the father slit his own throat; fortunately a quick-acting neighbour and a near-instant response from paramedics saved the children, but not the father.
- An 18-month-old child survived, while a 4-year-old sibling succumbed to the sustained attack by their father, using a lamp stand to batter them and a knife to stab them.
- A 2-year-old survived, while the 6-year-old sibling didn't, both of them having been thrown over a balcony 50 feet above the ground.
- A 14-year-old miraculously survived multiple stab wounds, many more stab wounds than the ten stabbings that killed the 4-year-old sibling.
- A 10-year-old managed to escape through a back window, leaving her mother to be subjected to what the judge referred to as a three-hour period of sadistic, sexually degrading torture in the presence of her 2-year-old child. Both mother and child were then shot dead by the father.
- A 6-year-old managed to escape being drowned, and then could do nothing but watch a 5-year-old sibling sinking to the bottom of the icy cold waters.

How have these 'surviving' children recovered? Possibly only a surviving non-offending parent or relative can tell. Many of those parents up and leave, trying to escape the unbearable memories provoked by places and routines, by expressions on the faces of family and friends, by the relentlessness of press intrusion. At least two parents emigrated. Many parents abandon not just their homes and employment, but their names too. Nearly all sever contact with the family of the perpetrator. The fate of their surviving children rests largely in their own hands, and/or in the expertise and experience of professionals to whom those children may have been referred.

Fortunate casualties

Finally, there is another group of children at the centre of these tragedies whom we might say are incredibly fortunate to be alive. They are the children whom the perpetrators (all fathers), for unknown reasons, decide not to kill. They may lie in their pram, watching in terror, as their older siblings are being stabbed to death. In one case, it was the 11-year-old child who was left to live, as the 2-year-old was taken from the home and killed by the father who held the child as he jumped from a bridge. Another father killed his wife and two oldest children, but mysteriously left his baby safely strapped in the car as he committed suicide. A 3-year-old was murdered by having his throat slit, as his baby sibling slept soundly. A 10-month-old girl was stabbed in the head after her mother had been stabbed over 30 times; the other child, two and a half years old, was left to discover the blood-stained bodies.

All of these children may indeed be fortunate to be alive, but we can be certain that the caring capacities of the surviving bereaved mothers were, in the immediate aftermath of the killings, substantially reduced.

The study results

This study has looked at 128 cases of filicide in the UK between 1994 and 2012. The cases can be divided into three specific categories: (1) 62 cases of filicide killings by fathers (or substitute fathers); (2) 44 cases of filicide killings by mothers; and (3) 22 cases of familicide (annihilation of whole families) by fathers. Some 224 children in total were killed by 84 fathers and 44 mothers.

Which day of the week?

Now we can focus on some basic findings in this study. One aspect seldom if ever addressed in previous research is the day on which the filicide killings take place. There is, I believe, an instinctive public curiosity about this, and a widely held view among public and professionals that many of these incidents take place at the weekend (Yardley, 2013). This was not the case in any of the three categories (Table 5.4). More incidents took place on Tuesday, and the combined total for the beginning three days Monday, Tuesday and Wednesday (60) was higher than the final three days Friday, Saturday and Sunday (54) (Figure 5.1). Nearly half of the killings by mothers took place on Tuesdays and Wednesdays, and the least number (less than a quarter) took place on Saturday and Sunday. It reinforces the premeditation factor, indicating that rather than the unplanned, proverbial weekend family crisis, many perpetrators choose the day that either facilitates the killing (convenience) or advances their cause (often revenge or retaliation). Thus they may choose a day on which they are making a contact visit, or collecting the child from school; or minding the child(ren) while the partner is socializing, or caring for the child(ren) while the partner is on a business trip. Anniversaries of key events may also be chosen, particularly the wedding day (underlining a revenge motive) or a special day, such as father's day, or a birthday.

Table 5.4 No. of filicides and familicides per day of the week, 1994–2012

Days of the week	Mothers	Fathers	Familicide (fathers)	Fathers total	Mother and father totals
Monday	2	11	4	15	17
Tuesday	9	7	7	14	23
Wednesday	10	6	4	10	20
Thursday	6	7	1	8	14
Friday	6	5	3	8	14
Saturday	6	15	–	15	21
Sunday	5	11	3	14	19

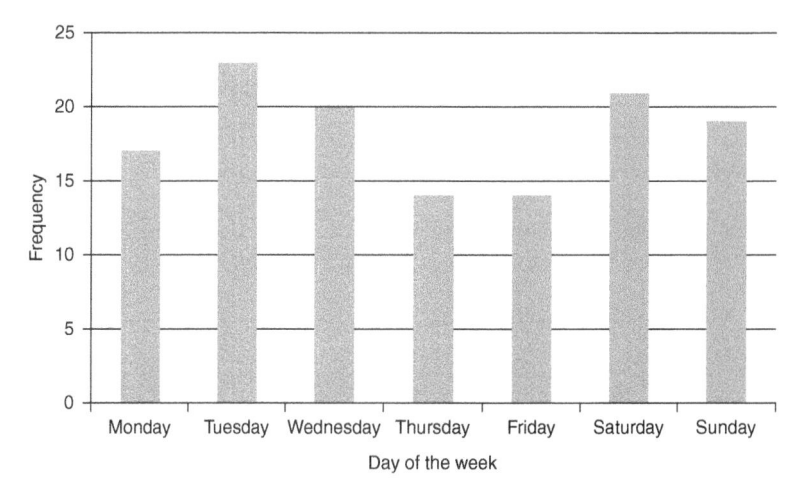

Figure 5.1 Days on which killings occurred

Gender and age of perpetrator

There was enormous diversity in Chapter 4 on the issue of the gender of perpetrators, easily explained in either the selection of target groups or by the inclusion of every category of filicide killing, including the largest category of all, child abuse and neglect fatalities. In this study, which does not include that category, the preponderance of men as perpetrators is very clear.

Eighty-four fathers (all biological fathers except two) killed 155 children (including two unborn). Thirty-seven of those fathers also killed their wives/partners. Six relatives or friends visiting at the time were also killed. Two mothers were seriously injured.

Forty-four mothers killed 69 children, including three unborn (the total of five unborn is included, because the foetuses were so far advanced that the perpetrators, had they lived, could have been prosecuted for 'child destruction' under existing UK law). No mother attempted to kill a male partner.

The age range of the perpetrators contrasts with many of the finding in Chapter 4. It is a much narrower range, with the distribution mode clearly centring between 30 and 40 years of age for both male and female perpetrators (Figure 5.2). Considering the context for the

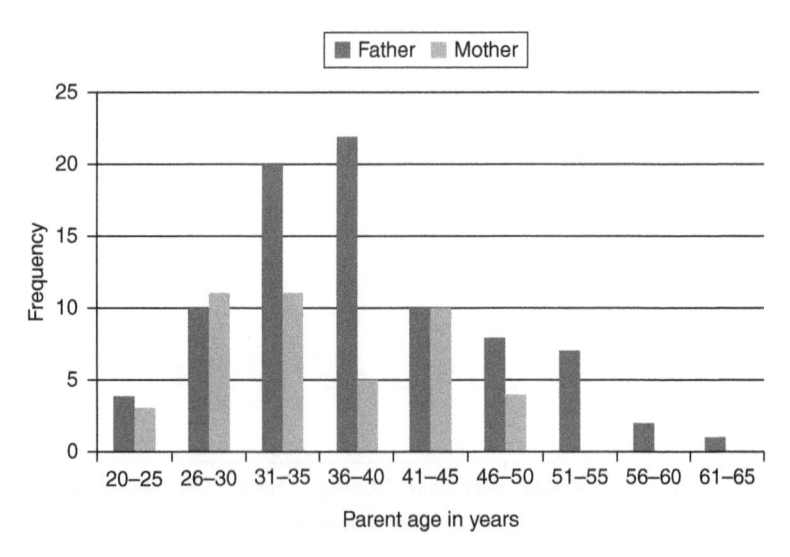

Figure 5.2 Age of parent at the time of killing

vast majority of cases, marital break-up, separation and fractious disputes over children, that finding is hardly surprising.

Age of the victims

The ages of the victims are largely consistent with previous findings. The number of children killed aged between 0 and 7 is substantially greater than those aged between 8 and 18. The killings of children aged 2, 3, 6 and 7 have the greatest frequency in this study. Figure 5.3 looks at the number of victims of male and female perpetrators combined. Figures 5.4 and 5.5 look at the number of victims of male and female perpetrators separately. Table 5.5 provides the precise ages of all children killed.

Is age a risk factor?

The number of killings by male and female perpetrators of children between the ages of 2 and 7 is significantly higher than in any other age band. Age 5 is the only age category in which mothers killed (13 children) more than fathers (9 children).

Figure 5.3 Age of victims

108 *Filicide-Suicide*

Figure 5.4 Age and gender of victims killed by fathers

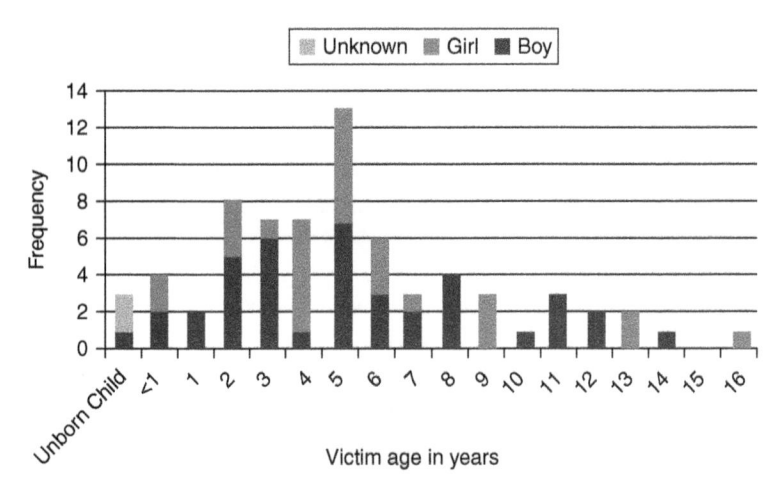

Figure 5.5 Age and gender of victims killed by mothers

Why are significantly more 5- and 6-year-olds killed? Is it something as basic as the preponderance of this age group among marital and cohabiting couples divorcing and/or separating? Or is it more complex than that? Is it the 6-year-old's burgeoning emotional and psychological development, enabling them to speak, understand, express their views and feelings, and visibly and audibly take sides in

Table 5.5 Age and number of victims

Age of victim in years	Killed by mother (44 mothers)	Killed by father (84 fathers)	Totals
0–12 months	4	7	11
1	2	5	7
2	8	18	26
3	7	21	28
4	6	12	18
5	13	9	22
6	6	25	31
7	3	16	19
8	4	8	12
9	3	7	10
10	1	7	8
11	3	3	6
12	2	3	5
13	2	2	4
14	1	2	3
15	–	3	3
16	1	2	3
17	–	1	1
18	–	2	2
Unborn child	3	2	5
Totals	69	155	224

the dispute? Whatever the reason, this study supports much previous research findings across the whole spectrum of filicide that many more under-7s are killed than 7-plus, and that 5- and 6-year-olds constitute particularly vulnerable age groups.

Filicide-suicide

More mothers committed suicide (48 per cent = 21) and more mothers attempted suicide (25 per cent = 11) (Figure 5.6). This frequency is significantly higher than in many of the findings in Chapter 4. The prevalence of mental illness among the mothers (75 per cent) may have some bearing on this finding (metal illness will be discussed in more detail in Chapter 6).

Method of killing

Carbon monoxide poisoning in a vehicle, and death through fire (that is, burnt to death or died because of smoke inhalation) both occurred more frequently (53 children in total) than in many other

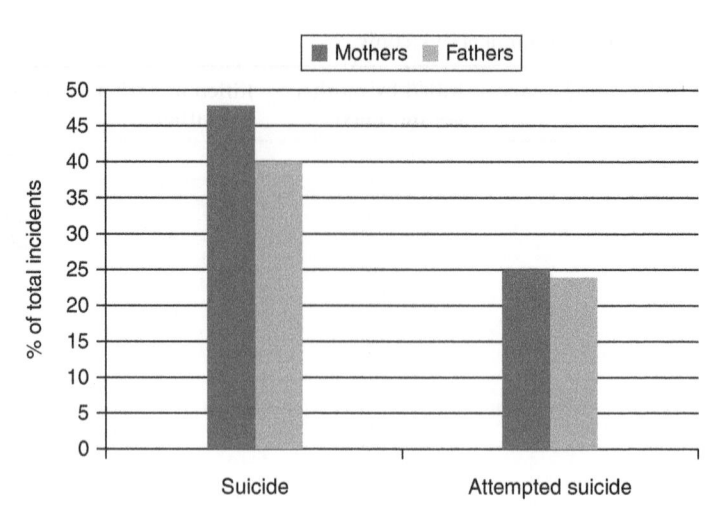

Figure 5.6 Suicides and attempted suicides by mothers and fathers (%)

research studies on the method of killing. Even more significant is the unusually high numbers of stabbings by both fathers and mothers. Thirty-five children (16 per cent, mean age, 6 years, 3 months) were stabbed to death by their fathers, and 16 (7 per cent, mean age, 8 years 10 months) by mothers (Figure 5.7). There may be some symbolic significance in this choice of killing method which to date, researchers have not considered. They are nearly always multiple killings followed by suicide. The question arises as to whether or not in their planning, they have contemplated and been more strongly motivated by the unavoidable fact that not just the dead bodies of their children, but also the floor, bedclothes, walls, windows, and furniture pieces will be awash with blood, as they (then invariably) subject their own bodies to the same fate. It is unimaginable what children see, hear, and suffer during these types of killings.

Revenge-retaliation as a motivator

Resnick (1969) used the term *revenge* and both d'Orbán (1979) and Cheung (1986) used the word *retaliatory*. I prefer to use both terms together, as the dividing line between the two is seldom clear. Revenge-retaliation of course cannot be proven, but the suggestion that it was the motivating factor is based upon at least two of the

Killed by Mother ■ Killed by Father

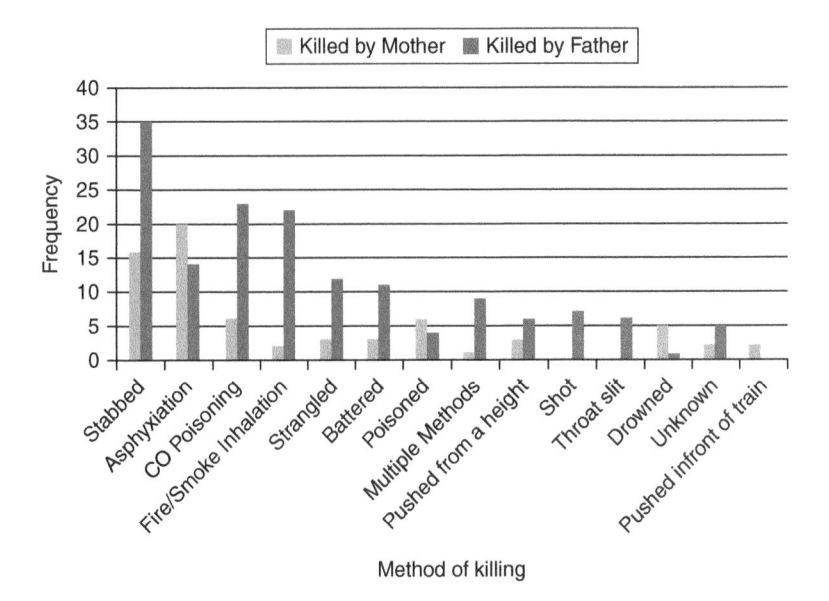

Figure 5.7 Method of killing

Table 5.6 Revenge-retaliation

	Filicide fathers (N = 62)	Familicide fathers (N = 22)	Filicide mothers (N = 44)	Cumulative total (N = 128)
Revenge/Retaliation	52	8	13	73
%	84	36	30	57

following: (i) the context of the killings, particularly if they occurred immediately after the revelation of an affair; (ii) the perpetrators' own words, heard by witnesses, or spoken or written in suicide notes; (iii) interpretations by coroners; (iv) interpretations by judges; (v) publicized opinions of forensic psychiatrists and/or psychologists; and (vi) views and feelings of surviving relatives.

Killing as an expression of revenge and/or retaliation is significantly higher in this study than in any other (Table 5.6), but given the context of so many of these cases, that is, relationship break-up, third party involvement, bitter custody and access disputes, domestic violence, threats of violence, deteriorating mental health, and so on, the frequency of revenge-retaliation is unsurprising.

Summary

This study has looked at 128 cases of filicide in the UK between 1994 and 2012. The cases can be divided into three specific categories: (i) 62 cases of filicide killings by fathers (or substitute fathers); (ii) 44 cases of filicide killings by mothers; and (iii) 22 cases of familicide (annihilation of whole families) by fathers. 224 children in total were killed by 84 fathers and 44 mothers.

The circumstances of filicide cases are never identical, but the similarities in these 128 cases are significant. The vast majority of them are about relationships disintegrating, and about mutual animosities and recriminations between parents.

This chapter departs from the convention of registering these deaths purely in the form of statistics, and presents them in such a manner that the reader can appreciate (i) the true nature and extent of the killings; (ii) the profoundly unhappy, often violent contexts in which the idea of murdering one's child(ren) may have taken root; and, not least, (iii) the chosen method of killing, and the likely cause of death.

From the three basic categories of filicide killings, there emerge five categories of child victims: (i) those who are killed; (ii) their sibling who watch them being killed, knowing they are about to be killed themselves; (iii) their siblings who are attacked and injured (often seriously) but who survive; (iv) those who manage to escape; and (v) those whom the perpetrator decides to leave alone with the devastated parent and who may or may not have witnessed their siblings being killed.

Apart from their suffering, the children are often the victims of perpetrators' fiendish deceptions. They are lied to repeatedly to facilitate the killings; they are usually promised some kind of treat such as a visit to the zoo, or to the seaside, or some well-known beauty spot, or a pizza restaurant. The primary purpose is to ensure the 'right' timing and location for the killings, and the absence of the other parent or the public who might intervene. Surprisingly, these kinds of deceptions are used as much by parents who are designated mentally ill, as by those who are not.

The main findings of the study are as follows:

- The days on which the killings take place, are not, as many are inclined to believe, predominantly at weekends. More killings took place on Tuesday and Wednesday than on any other two days.
- Eighty-four men killed 155 children, including 2 unborn, and 44 women killed 69 children, including three unborn.
- The ages of the victims are largely consistent with previous findings, showing that the 2–7 age group is particularly vulnerable, with 6 being the age at which most children were killed. Research has not yet established why this may be so. It could be the children's burgeoning emotional and psychological development, enabling them to speak, understand, and express their views and feelings; more ominously, it could be their ability to take side in the dispute.
- More mothers than fathers committed suicide and more mothers than fathers attempted suicide.
- The method of killing is largely consistent with previous research, with the exception of a high frequency of deaths caused by multiple stab wounds.
- The frequency of revenge as a motivator is exceptionally high, but given the context in which the killings take place, that may not be surprising.

The nature and extent of UK filicide killings in the context of relationship breakdowns, and all that ensue from them, have not been officially recognized by government or by relevant agencies. It is hoped that this study may help to rectify that. As will become clear in subsequent chapters, these findings contain the seeds of a new knowledge base which may be instrumental in evolving a different attitude and approach to cases which have the potential for filicide.

6
Mental illness and filicide killings

Introduction

Mental illness looms large in filicide literature and research. It often dominates discussion in trials, inquests and inquiry reports on filicide killings. It is the factor more often referred to than any other, to explain the inexplicable, to alleviate us of a terrible burden of helplessness and incomprehensibility. The mental illness of filicide perpetrators is often the motivating factor that encourages coroners to declare that filicide killings are neither predictable nor preventable. Many professionals and the wider public are inclined to believe that.

But not all filicide killings are caused by mental illness. Nor indeed, are all perpetrators mentally ill. This chapter will critically review research on: (1) the prevalence of mental illness; (2) the populations from which sample groups are drawn for research; and, (3) most critically, the information sources upon which much of the research is based. Serious questions arise about the reliability of these sources, and the validity of the diverse findings.

Very little has been written about how *mental health* is affected by the multiple processes and factors in operation preceding filicide killings, and even less about how *mental illness* itself impacts upon those processes and factors. Our knowledge and understanding of such matters are not likely to be advanced by the empirical nature of much of the research, but rather, by in-depth study of case histories. Three separate official inquiry reports on young mothers who killed their children and committed suicide have recently been published.

Mental illness and/or family-marital strains were characteristics in all three cases. The mothers' predicaments were exacerbated by the responses (or lack of them) of mental health and child protection services. One of these reports will be examined in detail. The findings in all three reports do not support the view that filicide killings are unpredictable and unpreventable.

A journey unforeseen

The perpetrators of filicide and their devastated partners and families had something in common with the general population. They began their partnerships in happier times. Probably they were in a loving relationship (or in 'total bliss' as one mother told me). They would certainly have wanted that relationship to last, and they probably would have worked and saved and planned with that objective in mind. Perhaps there may have been some justifiable apprehensions and doubts, but generally speaking, there was likely to have been more joy and hope and optimism. Many of the bereaved mothers or fathers, and family members, testify to this idyll.

Something else that we share in common with parents who will be engulfed in filicide tragedies is that we cannot possibly imagine killing our own children under any circumstances, exactly as they thought a mere two, three or four years before they actually did kill their children. There is, however, an additional fate that befalls some of the perpetrators of filicide, and which makes their journey and their actions, certainly no more acceptable, but less incomprehensible: mental illness.

Mental illness: a predominant characteristic?

Resnick (1969) gave a psychiatric diagnosis to 92 per cent (121) of his study group of 131 filicide offenders. It included psychosis, neurosis, personality disorder, delirium, manic depressive and 'retarded'. For decades after, filicide research would reaffirm this predominance of mental illness in filicide killings. It could hardly do otherwise, since the vast majority of its subjects were all filicide offenders held in specialist hospital settings, prisons, and in large psychiatric institutions. Marleau *et al.* (1999), for example, were certain to find that 100 per cent of their subjects were diagnosed with mental illness of some kind, since they were all male perpetrators resident in a maximum security psychiatric hospital.

Spinelli (2001) studied 16 cases of neonaticide and found all the women displaying an array of symptoms: denial, depersonalization and dissociative hallucinations. Fourteen of the women experienced brief periods of amnesia. Spinelli cautions, however, that all the subjects were charged with homicide, and the research was the product of interviews conducted by psychiatrists on behalf of the defence. Spinelli repeatedly raises the possibility of what she called 'malingerers' attempting to manipulate assessment.

McKee and Shea (1998) found that 80 per cent (16) of their sample of 20 maternal perpetrators had diagnosable mental disorders; 40 per cent (8) had been diagnosed with psychotic or paranoid disorders, and 25 per cent (5) were suffering major depression at the time of the offence. Lewis and Bunce (2003) examined the records of 55 female perpetrators and found that more than 52 per cent had psychotic symptoms at the time of the filicide. Like Spinelli's group and that of McKee and Shea, all the women had been referred for pre-trial psychiatric evaluation.

Contrasting views and variations on prevalence of mental illness

Flynn *et al.* (2013) examined 297 cases of convicted filicide perpetrators and 45 filicide-suicides. Forty per cent of convicted perpetrators had a history of mental health problems. Of these, 66 per cent (67) were women and 27 per cent (52) men. The most common diagnosis was affective disorder (43 = 14 per cent) Severe mental illness occurred in 23 per cent (68) of the cases.

In the current research of 128 cases of filicide (84 men and 44 women), 38 per cent (49) of the perpetrators had been diagnosed at some point with mental illness. The prevalence of mental illness among female perpetrators is significantly higher: 75 per cent (33) in contrast to 19 per cent (16) of men. Fifty-two per cent (23) of the total number of female perpetrators suffered depression, and 8 per cent (7) of the total number of men. Nine per cent (4) of females were known cannabis users, two of whom suffered depression and two of whom were diagnosed with psychotic illnesses; two other women were diagnosed with paranoid schizophrenia. Three per cent of men

(2) were addicted to alcohol, and one was diagnosed with bipolar disorder. Two mothers were diagnosed with narcissistic personality disorders, and two had multiple diagnoses.

d'Orbán's research on filicide mothers in Holloway Prison is somewhat at variance with the high frequency of mental illness among women. She classified 24 women out of a total of 89 as mentally ill (29 per cent); 40 (35per cent) of the women had previously had psychiatric treatment, but for what, and when, and its relevance to the killing of their children, are not stated. Cheung (1986) gave 14 (40 per cent) of 35 filicide mothers a diagnosis of mental illness. Forty-three per cent of d'Orbán's group were diagnosed with personality disorder, but only 11 per cent of Cheung's were given the same diagnosis.

Putkonen *et al.* (2009) compared 20 filicide perpetrators with a control group of 20 homicide offenders (5 charged with murder, and 15 charged with manslaughter). Putkonen *et al.* found that: (i) more than twice as many (13 = 65 per cent) of the control group had received psychiatric treatment than the filicide group (6 = 30 per cent): (ii) 15 (75 per cent) of the control group had personality disorders, compared to 11 (55 per cent) of the filicide group; and (iii) 14 (70 per cent) of the control group were alcohol-dependent, compared to 4 (20 per cent) of the latter. The authors sum up that the filicide offenders scored significantly lower than the homicide group on psychopathy testing. They conclude: 'Contrary to previous conclusions, we did not find that the filicide offenders had significantly more mental illness and more serious psychopathology than the other homicide offenders.'

Mouzos and Rushforth (2003) looked at 325 filicides which occurred over a 13-year period. There were nearly twice as many male perpetrators (205 = 63 per cent) as female (120 = 37 per cent). They found that 15 per cent (50) of parents were suffering from an unspecified mental disorder at the time of the killing. Thirty-three per cent (40) of the female filicide offenders and 9 per cent (19) of males were found to be mentally ill. To complete the widely (or is it wildly) diverse findings, Gilbert's (2008) examination of serious case reviews disclosed that only 28 per cent of perpetrators of serious abuse, filicide and homicide, had mental health problems, while Scott (1973a) did not detect any mental illness at all in the cases of 29 male perpetrators who battered their babies to death.

Why such disparity?

There are many questions arising from such diverse findings. Flynn *et al.* (2013) caution about the association of filicide with mental illness because of: (i) the relatively small samples that researchers have used; (ii) the length of time necessary to accumulate sufficient cases; and (iii) the bias of psychiatric and/or forensic facilities. They predict that such studies inevitably show a higher frequency of mental illness, and contrast them with the findings of studies of other filicide populations, such as parents who have killed their children through abuse and neglect (which makes Scott's (1973a) finding above less surprising). Another caution they could have mentioned is about the age range when researchers find a high prevalence of mental illness. In Kauppi *et al.*'s (2010) study, the age range of perpetrators was 20–76. Liem and Koenraadt (2008) had a similarly high age range for their 161 perpetrators, that is, 18–58 for the female perpetrators and 19–72 for males, as did Flynn *et al.* (2013) with a 15–70 age range for males and 14–50 for females. In the current study of 128 perpetrators, the age range was 21–62, with 118 of them under the age of 50. The frequency of mental illness increases as we get older (Pilgrim and Rogers, 1993) so one would expect that where the age range of perpetrators stretches into the seventies and beyond, more mental illness will be recorded. That does not, however, shed light on the figure of 75 per cent of mothers suffering mental illness in the current study; the context of marital breakdown and separation is probably more pertinent than age.

The prevalence of mental illness in filicide will always be highly problematic given the number of perpetrators who commit suicide, and the number of male perpetrators in particular who have never been clinically assessed. Flynn *et al.* (2013) state that 102 perpetrators in their research did not have clinical assessment reports. Designating a perpetrator as mentally ill can only be based upon clinical assessment when he or she was alive; but, just because a dead perpetrator may never have had contact with mental health services does not mean that he or she did not suffer from mental illness.

What are the sources upon which the research depends?

The sources upon which the researchers have depended are as diverse as the subjects. They include: (i) psychiatric evaluation and tests (e.g., Spinelli, 2001); (ii) retrospective examination of clinical records over a 50-year period in a forensic psychiatric observation hospital (Liem *et al.*, 2009); (iii) coroners' files on domestic homicide over 10–37-year-periods (Bourget and Gagne, 2005; Friedman *et al.*, 2008); (iv) peer-reviewed articles on filicide during the last 50 years (West *et al.*, 2009); (v) database searches for studies of maternal filicide and neonaticide (Friedman, Hrouda *et al.*, 2005); (vi) databases and newspaper analysis (Liem et al., 2009); (vii) statistics obtained from government departments for filicide in general and from death certificates for neonaticides in particular (Kauppi *et al.*, 2010); (viii) clinical files, recorded interviews, filicide articles, newspaper reports on filicide cases over a 200-year period (Resnick, 1969); and (ix) recorded interviews with partners and family members of perpetrators, male and female, who committed suicide (Johnson, 2005; Kirkwood, 2012).

Not just inconsistencies and contradictions

Researchers often mention the limitations of these sources of information. Spinelli (2001) regrets 'the selection of cases by court referral and the absence of a comparison group' (p. 812). Kauppi *et al.* (2010, p. 235) write:

> Despite the many sources of information used in the forensic psychiatric examinations, we have only the information that people were willing and able to provide, and the records also varied in quality and quantity, including more or less imprecise data and reported experiences about the victims and perpetrators' lives.

In Resnick's (1969) pioneering work, he was unable to establish the ages of 54 (41 per cent) of his subjects. Johnson (2005, p. 22) writes of her long wait for approval to access official records, 'which subsequently yielded little or no useful data'. The reality is that tragedy after tragedy (other than filicides), in the fields of medicine, psychiatry, social work and social welfare, have been influenced in no small measure by appalling record keeping, illegible writing, half-baked files, mistaken assessment and diagnosis, and even that most basic of all errors, spelling the names of patients and clients wrongly, or getting their ages wrong. Most of these errors were noted in two cited reports into filicide killings perpetrated by mothers suffering from depression (Boyd, 2008; NHS London Strategic Health Authority, 2010). They are repeatedly cited in serious case reviews, for example, as in Hampshire Safeguarding Children Board (2009, p. 6): 'It is extremely unfortunate that ... the wrong spelling of mother's name prevented the tying up of records.' Singly, such mistakes may amount to little, but cumulatively, they can have major impact on the quality and consistency of service.

Coroners' reports

Bennewith *et al.* (2005) attempted to establish the usefulness of coroner's data on 492 suicides, and concluded that there was 'wide variation ... in information relevant to specific methods'; they found, for example, that: (i) information on the source ligature in suicides by hanging was frequently missing; (ii) information about licensing and storage in cases of suicides by firearms were not routinely recorded; and (iii) information on treatment and blood levels of those who had poisoned themselves and died in hospital, was not routinely available. Christiansen *et al.* (2007) tell of autopsy reports lost in Danish filicide research. Flynn *et al.* (2013) reveal that entire court files were missing in 16 cases. Friedman, Hrouda *et al.* (2005, p. 501) provide a more detailed scrutiny of the limitations of a retrospective study of coroners' records:

> We were not able to obtain significant data regarding length of symptoms, last psychiatric visit, length of psychiatric symptoms, presence of hallucinations or manic symptoms, abuse or abandonment of offenders during their own childhoods, history of head trauma, and history of postpartum depression or psychosis.

A battleground

Mental ill-health has undoubtedly contributed to filicide killings, and, as will be seen later in this chapter, depression has unquestionably been a major factor in many maternal filicides. But the research and literature that seek to enlighten us about the prevalence of mental illness among both maternal and paternal filicide perpetrators, and more importantly, about how mental illness may influence the motivation to kill, are seriously flawed. It is little wonder that so many filicide cases today, both in the UK and elsewhere, end up in criminal courts as battlegrounds for the diametrically opposing psychiatric sides arguing that the killer was perfectly sane or seriously mentally ill. As part of this study, I recently attended a murder trial in which three psychiatrists for the defence and three for the prosecution spent a total of six days testifying, each being cross-examined by the opposing sides.

Depression, maternal filicide and suicide

There is as yet no research to tell us which mental illness poses the greatest risk of filicide killings. But there can be little dispute that many maternal filicides are perpetrated by mothers suffering from depression. In cases of depressed young mothers with very young children, it is highly likely that many professionals, such as mental health workers, GPs, social workers and health visitors are involved. The remainder of this chapter will look at three such cases. One in particular has been subject to intense media scrutiny (Honigsbaum and Barton, 2005) and an official investigation (NHS London Strategic Health Authority, 2010). The names of all the family members have been altered.

Case study 1

Background

Raveena was born and brought up in England, a daughter of Indian parents. Her parents separated when she was a very young child, a highly unusual occurrence at that time. She met her husband during her late teens, on a visit to India, and their arranged marriage took place there. The couple immediately returned and settled in Britain. Their first child, Simar, was born two years later, and the second, Arjan, four years after that. Friends and neighbours quickly noted that all was not well in the relationship. Raveena, educated in every sense in the British way of life, socially active, attending school until she was 18, gaining qualification in business and computer studies, and later employed in a local media outlet where she was much loved and respected, found her life transformed after marriage. She and her husband perceived marriage and motherhood differently. Her husband, brought up in an entirely different environment, not nearly as fluent in English, faced the task of integrating into a society that was in some respects quite alien to him. He also had to gain and hold on to a job, and establish himself as father and husband in a domestic situation in which the mother of his wife still played a prominent role. A persistent theme in the case was Raveena's complaint that she couldn't communicate with her husband. She wasn't referring only to the language.

Multiple diagnoses

After the birth of her first child, a girl (a source of disappointment to her and her husband), Raveena was diagnosed with postnatal depression. She was referred to a community mental health team (CMHT) and a health visitor was assigned to her. She eventually recovered, though not for a lengthy period. She would relapse numerous times over the next five years, and would be diagnosed as suffering from obsessive compulsive disorder, adjustment disorder, moderate depression, and recurrent depressive disorder with somatic symptoms. The inquiry revealed that no proven diagnostic tool (such as the Edinburgh Postnatal Depression Scale (Cox *et al.*, 1987)) was used to confirm any of these diagnoses, made by three different psychiatrists, an obstetrician and her GP. The inquiry report provides much evidence of increasing concern over the next 4–5 years, among professionals, of numerous phone calls and visits; of discussions, and commitment to more discussions, and of 'plans' which amounted to nothing more than additional discussions and visits.

Domestic violence

Some years later, the police Domestic Violence Unit went to the home after a call by Raveena. A row had apparently degenerated into a physical assault by her husband. He was arrested. This incident had major implications for both husband and wife and the extended family. Raveena refused to pursue a prosecution, and she temporarily moved to the home of her mother and grandmother. Her husband went abroad. He refused to take telephone calls from his wife. He told her he wouldn't return. She reacted with panic and despair, and was seen repeatedly banging her head against the wall. Eventually, she made a penitentiary visit to India, and was subjected to a sustained confrontation with the large extended family of her husband, during which she was repeatedly harangued about summoning the police and bringing shame on the family. She had to reassure them that it would never happen again, which was certainly no guarantee that her husband would not attack her again.

The police referred the domestic violence incident to social services, who responded by sending a letter to Raveena and her husband telling them of the adverse affects on small children witnessing violence. No visit or assessment were made.

Acknowledging the core problem

Raveena eventually had her consultation with a psychiatrist. In it she gives a complete history of her situation, revealing that her problems with her husband, her children (whose illnesses and visits to accident and emergency (A&E) had increased alarmingly), her in-laws, and not least, her own physical and mental health, were all much worse than had been previously realized. The psychiatrist saw her relationship with her husband as the core problem. He recommended that she contact Relate. She knew that her husband would strongly object to such a proposal.

Raveena's situation worsened further. Professionals, including the GP, were in frequent contact, all sharing their observations about a situation apparently getting beyond their control. Raveena was losing weight; she was crying for long periods, she was incapable of caring for her children as she would have liked (they were still attending A&E and the GP at a worrying rate); she had no energy; she was becoming increasingly withdrawn. Another psychiatrist diagnosed her condition as moderate depression with obsessive compulsive disorder against a backdrop of marital strains. She was seen by three different psychiatrists inside ten months. One of them again alluded to the marital discord as the main problem, and he was the first professional to observe and record that the oldest child may have been at risk of neglect. He referred the case to the Children and Families Team.

Child protection, 'no concerns'

The Children and Families Team allocated a social worker. The social worker visited two weeks later and reported that there were no concerns regarding the children's welfare. There is no indication or record of a comprehensive assessment being made, nor do we know how long the visit lasted and precisely what the social worker observed. It is not entirely clear whether or not the worker observed the children's interactions with the mother.

Within the next two to three weeks, more professionals became involved; more medication was prescribed, and there were more and more conversations with Raveena who was consistently telling them of her helplessness, her suicidal thoughts, and her overall worsening situation. She repeatedly recited the same list of woes, expressed the same despair and helplessness, and said she was a bad mother, and, worst of all, a failure in the eyes of her husband's family.

Her husband, who has been perceived by many professionals as central to Raveena's predicament, now figured even less in the *planning* and activities on her behalf. Interviews with Raveena, were, at her request, conducted at her mother's home. On one occasion, a Friday afternoon, professionals record in their files that they are *not* concerned about how Raveena may cope over that particular weekend, because, they say, her husband will be there to help with the children.

A twice-cancelled visit by a social worker from children and families Social Work Team took place 24 hours before Raveena killed the children and herself. The worker once again recorded that there were no concerns in respect of the children's welfare.

Analysis

The above narrative may appear too selective and over-critical, but the inquiry report itself (253 pages long) is a damning critique of the services provided to this young mother and her two children over many years. The occurrences of practice that was ineffective, or incompetent, or confusing, are too numerous to mention, but the most serious shortcomings included the following:

- Despite intensive involvement by many mental health professionals over a seven-year period, there was no recognizable assessment or care plan in the CMHT records.
- Given (i) the rapid deterioration in the mental health of the mother during the latter stages of that period; (ii) her disclosure of suicidal thoughts on three occasions; and (iii) the fact that she was the primary carer of two small children, there was no evidence of a comprehensive risk assessment being made, either in respect of the mother or the children.
- The prescribing of too many types of anti-depressants, sometimes changed on the basis of a phone call without the patient being seen.

- Raveena was subject to countless referrals, many of them self-made, mainly to mental health services. Proper assessment of Raveena's needs could not be made on the basis of the poor quality of referral taking.
- As is evident in every mental health and child abuse inquiry report, and alluded to earlier in this chapter, the records were sometimes non-existent, inaccurate, sloppy, illegible and misleading.

There are two areas of particular interest in the inquiry, pertinent to this present study, namely, cultural diversity and child protection.

Cultural diversity

This section of the report begins by providing an important context: many South Asian women in the UK (particularly in the 16–24 age group) are at much greater risk of committing suicide than those in other identifiable groups. This phenomenon has been extensively researched (e.g., Bhugra *et al.*, 1999; Chew-Graham *et al.*, 2002; Cooper *et al.*, 2006; Merril and Owens, 2006). The research has identified marital problems stemming from cultural conflict as the most common underlying characteristic in many of these suicides. The concept of *Izzat* (honour) dominates the lives of many young Asian women, imposing strictures and dictating acceptable and unacceptable behaviour, in relationships, in families, and in society as a whole. The *Issat* framework can generate enormous stress for young Asian women, particularly for those born and educated in the UK. The inquiry report finds much vindication of this research in the life of Raveena. It is particularly struck by Raveena's final words, spoken to her husband in a telephone call moments before her death, and widely reported when they were read out at the inquest: 'I am sorry, I am sorry for everything, say sorry to everyone. I always loved you and I am going.' The inquiry report team believed that this utterance revealed the level of responsibility that Raveena had taken on board because of an honour code, which, they thought, had governed her life. The inquiry team concluded that because of these stresses and pressures, she was, to some extent, driven to suicide and filicide.

Apart from attaching such cultural significance to an utterance that is almost identical to those made by many indigenous white female perpetrators, the conclusion raises numerous questions: first, could she not have been driven to suicide to an equal extent, because she increasingly realized that so many professionals were unable to confront the core problem which they appeared to recognise, that is, the marital, family and cultural pressures bearing down upon her, and which were undermining all their medical, social, therapeutic and psychiatric attempts, to enable her to cope? Second, as the inquiry report makes clear, the standard of work overall was poor. The most damning criticisms are: the lack of comprehensive assessment in general, and the lack of risk assessment in particular. Third, was Raveena conscious of the fact that her illness, its causes and its consequences were not being adequately assessed? Did she sense a lack of competence and control in the people who were entrusted with her care? As her condition deteriorated, and her sense of helplessness and hopelessness intensified, was her perception of the service she was receiving so understandably negative that it made her condition worse? Looking at these questions as a whole, it is not unreasonable to suggest that Raveena's deterioration and her eventual suicide were driven as much by the poor quality of service she received as by the perceived oppressive cultural and family pressures which so preoccupied the inquiry panel.

Child protection

Although Raveena had alluded to suicidal thoughts and consistently said that she would not harm her children, there is no record available in the report, indicating that any professional discussed this matter with her in depth. Visits by social workers from the Children and Families Team are invariably summed up by phrases like: 'no concerns were noted; no concerns were reported; no concerns were raised; there were no health concerns; there were no child protection concerns ... there was nothing to support the psychiatrist's concern about the children'.

Given the knowledge of Raveena's situation, which literally dozens of professionals were aware of before the Children and Families Team got involved, such 'reassurances' are perplexing. Family and childcare workers must know of the risks of serious harm to children in a home and environment, the main characteristics of which are:

- A mother, the principal carer, profoundly unhappy, and suffering periodic bouts of severe depression. In the earlier stages of her illness, a worker observed that there was no facial responsiveness

to her children, that she tried to force-feed one of them and prevented another from crawling on the floor.
- Parents in strife, constantly arguing over rights and duties.
- Domestic violence and separation; threats of permanent separation.
- Sustained involvement of visiting in-laws (which the mother has always dreaded); this was undermining and destabilizing, and generated an atmosphere not conducive to the children's welfare.
- A quite staggering number of hospital and GP visits, many of them warranted and some unwarranted, initiated by an over-anxious mother.

Raveena's children must have been adversely affected by some or all of these factors. If a mother, for whatever reason, is unable to emotionally respond to very young children, and if that lack of emotional responsiveness is sustained and repetitive, the children are being emotionally abused (O'Hagan, 2006). If social workers did not realize this, it raises questions about the accuracy and quality of their observations.

Finally, the response of social services to the incident of domestic violence was totally inadequate: the couple were sent a letter telling them of the risks of children witnessing domestic violence. This is a standard procedure adopted by many social services departments throughout the UK, It prompted Women's Aid (2000) to say:

> At its worst, we have seen the development of the 'cover your back' letter. Such letters ... are usually written by social workers to the parents in a household where domestic violence has come to their attention. They warn that the family has come to the notice of social services and, while often 'offering support', also point out that domestic violence is a form of child abuse. Such a response tends to confirm all the worst stereotypes of the ineffectiveness of social work practice in this area. It fails to differentiate between domestic violence offenders and their victims.

The inquiry report compounds the problem when it describes the domestic violence incident, and emphasizes 'No evidence of violence against the children was recorded.' If professionals know that very young children witness violent attacks against their mother, the principal carer, that is evidence in itself of emotional and psychological abuse (O'Hagan, 1993, 2006). Such inescapable logic is now enshrined in legislation.

Let's very briefly look at the findings of two other inquiry reports on young mothers who killed their children and themselves, while suffering from depression:

Similar failings, same outcome: case study 2

Only six weeks before Raveena killed herself and her two children, a 40-year-old mother in another part of the UK took her own life after killing her 9-year-old daughter. She and her husband had separated a few months earlier, an event which triggered a major crisis in her life, in which she made a serious but failed attempt to kill herself. In the few remaining months of her life, she suffered a worsening depression. Unlike the secrecy and anonymity surrounding the inquiry about Raveena, the report on Madeleine O'Neill and her daughter Lauren (Boyd, 2008) is a totally transparent and highly critical account of how mental health and child protection agencies failed mother and daughter. It identified the following:

- poor communication between the professionals of differing agencies, and between professionals and family members;
- professionals not being alert to obvious indicators of risk, and more specifically, making no attempt to assess risk to the child in particular;
- a lack of understanding of mental illness and the significance of deliberate self-harm;
- inadequate supervision of frontline staff;
- incomplete care planning;
- inaccurate recording of information;
- the loss of vital documentation when she was being transferred from one psychiatric setting to another.

Case study 3

The third case was, and remains, the most widely publicized, probably because the mother was a psychiatrist of Indian origin, for whom many of her senior colleagues in the NHS had predicted a highly successful future. Her husband recently chose to speak openly about their tragedy (Rogers, 2013). Suffering bouts of severe depression since her teenage years (which her colleagues were not aware of), she stabbed her 3-month-old baby to death and set his body alight; she attempted to do the same to herself, but died of burns in hospital two weeks later. As well as many of the failings listed above in the previous two cases, North East London Strategic Health Authority (2002) identified the following;

- The Royal College of Psychiatrists' guidelines on perinatal mental illness were not communicated to all the professionals involved and were not adhered to.
- Involved professionals seemingly were not aware that following a birth where the mother has a history of severe depression, the risk of relapse is virtually inevitable and that preparedness to intervene in the relapse is the key to effective care planning.
- There was never a fully informed risk assessment made of mother and child, despite a long history of depression and attempted suicide.
- A general ignorance of the most pertinent literature and research.
- Services were not sufficiently child-centred. As children of severely mentally ill parents may be at risk of significant harm, services need to be child protection-proofed by the appropriate Area Child Protection Board (later replaced by Safeguarding Children Boards).
- Lack of consultation and communication between Community Mental Health Team and Child Protection Service.
- The mother's parents and her husband were never contacted or consulted by professionals. Yet they were a potentially invaluable resource that could have greatly augmented the quality of service provision.
- There was no formal care plan in accordance with the Care Program Approach.

Lessons we unlearnt

In this current study of 44 maternal filicides (listed in Chapter 5) in which 75 per cent of the mothers were designated mentally ill, six of those cases were subject to serious case reviews (Birmingham SCB, 2012; Derbyshire Safeguarding Children Board, 2008; Hackney SCB 2008; Leicester Safeguarding Children Board, 2012; Manchester SCB, 2013; Warwickshire SCB, 2012). All six reports combined expose similar and identical failings, the most prominent of which in each of the three is the absence of comprehensive mental health and child protection risk assessments; there were also (i) contrasting diagnoses; (ii) important documentation lost (including a referral to social services expressing concern about the welfare of the child and mother's capacity to cope); (iii) injuries to a child not robustly investigated because the family were highly regarded by the GP, and (iv) illegible handwritten notes sent from one professional to another. The date of these reviews implies that the previous three reports were not read, or that the lessons were not learnt.

Unpredictable and unpreventable?

These cases may not be typical. Professionals do succeed more often than not. But what all the listed failings suggest is that, if the work, knowledge, and professionalism had been of a markedly higher standard, it would have lessened the likelihood of such catastrophic endings. This view is occasionally expressed in inquiry reports, and none more so than in the North East London Strategic Health Authority (2002) report.

The inquiry report panel examining the circumstances of Raveena's death said that it was 'remarkable' that so many of the professionals stated that they had learnt nothing from the case, an attitude of mind which the panel attributed to an assertion on their part that the deaths of Raveena and her children were unpredictable and unpreventable. This is, in my opinion, the most depressing revelation to emerge from any inquiry report in any discipline during the past 60 years. The workers' assertion in relation to some historic family and childcare tragedies may have validity, but in the particular circumstances of Raveena and her children, and what we now know of the quality of service that was provided to them, it is a hugely ironical assertion bordering on the incredulous.

Summary

Mental illness is a prominent feature in filicide cases, but there is great diversity in the findings of research linking the two. This diversity can be traced to two important sources: the status and location of the subjects of the research, and the documentary information on which much of the research is based.

Researchers themselves are the first to acknowledge the limitations of many of their sample groups and the unreliability of some of their information sources. Resnick (1969), for example, was unable to establish the ages of no less than 41 per cent of the perpetrators in his exceptionally large subject group. Regrettably, contemporary record-keeping and official documentation on filicide deaths are exposed as no less prone to inaccuracy and inadequacy, and worse, the disappearance of files!

Recent inquiry reports on filicide killings have been instructive in charting the intensifying helplessness experienced by young mothers in the throes of severe depression and/or marital problems, and the inadequacy of response by numerous agencies. One exhaustive inquiry exposed 58 areas of concern arising out of ineffective, incompetent, working practice which may, on occasions, have contributed to and accelerated the downward spiral in which a young mother was trapped. Despite these deficiencies and the inexplicable failure to carry out comprehensive risk assessment on behalf of both the mother and her children, many of the workers stated that they had not learnt anything from the case, an attitude of mind stemming from the assertion that the deaths of the children and the suicide of the mother were both unpredictable and unpreventable. The irony of this particular stance coming after a catalogue of failings over a seven-year period has obviously been lost on those workers, who must have believed that good or bad practice can make no difference.

This encapsulates the enormity of the task facing managers and trainers in all agencies that seek to prevent filicide killings. They should know that many inquiry reports, similar to those referred to in this chapter, and much research literature (for example, Johnson, 2005; Kirkwood, 2012; Saunders, 2004) contend that filicide killings, particularly in the context of marital strife and domestic violence, *are* most certainly predictable and preventable. The very act of a good quality assessment of risk can reveal children's vulnerability in entirely different family situations: becoming, for example, the ultimate pawns in domestic violence situations, or, the principal tool of revenge when an affair is revealed, or, as in the tragedies recounted in this chapter, the object of murderous delusions in the minds of profoundly unhappy and sick parents.

Part III
Dispelling the Myths, Working Towards Prevention

Part III

7
To kill out of love...?

Introduction

A recurrent theme in previous chapters is the difficulty experienced by the bereaved and society at large in responding to filicide killings. They are too shocking, always painful to read about, and devastating to anyone related or close to the family involved. For the vast majority of people, the motivation behind filicide killings is inexplicable. One of the earliest categories of motivation which researchers identified is that of love: parents kill their children out of altruism or love. This chapter will critically explore the origins and development of this explanation. It is frequently advanced today by psychiatrists and commentators, by coroners and not least by clergy conducting funeral services for the victims. The language used is often confusing and contradictory, but few listeners or readers would deny its alleviating effects for a grateful public who have no alternative explanation, and particularly for those who are caught up in the terrible consequences of the tragedy. Apart from the ambiguity with which it is expressed, this explanation that love is the principal motivating force may have adverse effects which the pioneers who advanced it did not anticipate. It is time to reaffirm the meaning of love, even in the context of filicide killings.

Origins

The concept of love as a motivating force in filicide originated in Resnick's (1969) categorization, often repeated in subsequent collaborative efforts with his colleagues (Friedman, Hrouda et al., 2005; Friedman, McCue-Horowitz et al., 2005; Friedman et al., 2008). No subsequent filicide research has failed to acknowledge this categorization, nor has anyone ever questioned it.

There are three significant features in Resnick's (1969) lengthy section on love as a motivator. First, he uses the words 'love' and 'altruism' synonymously. In Friedman and Resnick, it is stated that: 'in an altruistic filicide, a mother kills her child out of love' (2007, p. 137). Second, although the word 'love' is used repeatedly, it is never defined. Third, Resnick calculated that 38 per cent of the killings in his study of 131 cases were perpetrated 'out of love', convincing him that this motivation is what 'distinguishes filicide from other homicides' (1969, p. 329). In later research, Friedman, Hrouda et al. (2005) find that over 70 per cent of the killings were altruistic.

Resnick acknowledges the difficulty readers may have in understanding love as the motivating force:

> At first glance it may be difficult to see how the term 'altruistic' could be applied to a mother beating her daughter to death. However, the depressive murderer usually picks an 'overloved' individual for his victim. The suicidal mother may identify her child with herself and project her own unacceptable symptoms onto the victim. By this mechanism Mrs. A. viewed Betty as a 'ruined monster' that had to be destroyed.
>
> (ibid., p. 331)

Clearly, Mrs A is very seriously mentally ill. The final diagnosis Resnick gave her was 'schizophrenic reaction, schizo-affective type'.

In Resnick's typical psychoanalytical interpretation of events, there does not appear to be the slightest manifestation of love in Mrs A's actions or in the actions of the many more cases he cited. Whatever their thought processes, and whatever the degree of mental illness they are experiencing, they are all perpetrating actions which are the antithesis of 'love' as that word is generally understood. The question then arises, why did Resnick and his colleagues interpret and apply their construct, 'altruistic' or 'love' killings, so liberally? And why have subsequent researchers given Resnick's altruism-love categorization such uncritical, unquestioning prominence, and still apply it equally assiduously today?

Searching for the meaning of love

Despite being the most written-about subject in human history, and, in our internet age, the most Googled, love lacks a universal definition that everyone can respect. Which is probably the reason why, when the *Guardian* recently commissioned a physicist, a psychotherapist, a philosopher, a romantic novelist, and a Catholic nun to write about love, all of them wisely refrained from giving a definition. The elusiveness of the subject is apparent in their opening remarks: 'Love is more easily experienced than defined ... it depends on where you're at in relation to it ... it is not just one thing ... there are several variations ... basically, love is just chemistry' (al-Khalili *et al.* 2012).

We are so conditioned in our modern Western culture to think of love as the ultimate and desirable objective in human relationships, that we may forget that since time immemorial, perceptions of love have varied widely. For example, Plato's discussion in the *Symposium* between Socrates and Phaedrus (Leslie, 1932) gives us perhaps the most famous in-depth discussion on love, but it is, in the core tradition of ancient Greece, centred on youth, the love of men for youths, not women! Houghton's (1970) treatise on love dismisses the 'high-flown portentous silliness of much of the *Symposium*' (p. 1); she was obviously not impressed when Socrates proclaims: 'human nature ... cannot easily find a better helper than Love. I hold therefore, that all men should honour Love ... as I myself honour it' (Leslie, 1932, p. 91).

Hamilton's (2006) modern perspective is much more ambivalent. He argues cogently that the idealized version of love should not preclude the possibility of love in relationships which are vulnerable, messy, and, yes, capable of violence. He says we cannot claim, as does Wybourne (2012) (and Saint Paul) that love is the one thing that can never hurt anyone. Hamilton reminds us that, people do harm their loved ones. He adds: 'The more intimate the relationship, the greater the capacity for harm' (p. 244). He quotes Neu (2002): 'Love makes us vulnerable in ways that enhance the possibilities of pain' (2012, p. 88). This is undoubtedly true, but neither Hamilton or Neu address the question: can we harm and love simultaneously?

Of course we can hurt and harm the people we love, unintentionally, or deliberately. We can harm and hurt them, emotionally and psychologically, by action or words; and if love still binds us, it usually then manifests itself in feelings such as guilt and remorse, or reconciliatory gestures such as an embrace or flowers! These hurt-harm scenarios are in truth light years away from filicide killings, in which the predominant features are the imbalance of power, between an almighty life-over-death parental power and a child's utter helplessness and total dependency, between absolute choice and no choice. When one extinguishes the other, can that be love?

Who said it was 'love'?

Resnick never attributes the claim about killing for love to the voice of the perpetrator. It is his own conceptualization, for which there is no theoretical underpinning, and certainly no supportive research. Possibly some patient or patients did say to him: 'I did it out of love' but there are no such quotes in his pioneering work. One mother who shot dead her son was recorded as saying 'How could I do such a thing to a boy I loved?' (Resnick, 1969, p. 327), which, in the circumstances, is a rather detached, unloving maternal response (its significance is in the words: 'a boy' and in the past tense, 'loved'). We do not know whether or not she answered the question; but Resnick certainly answered it for her; she is another of his many respondents attributed with killing out of love.

The more one looks at the earliest filicide research, the clearer it becomes that it is not the perpetrators who claim that their killings stemmed from love or altruistic motives. It is the researchers themselves who have done so, particularly psychiatrists. Altruism-love in the context of filicide killings appears to be a psychiatric construct. In many ways it is also a typically 1960s construct. That is not to suggest that it can never apply – there are some 'mercy' killings that come to mind in which one may argue that it does apply – but merely that it has been applied too liberally. Even the statistic of 38 per cent of 131 cases being altruistic is surprisingly high (Resnick, 1969), in stark contrast to the findings in this current study: 84 per cent of male filicide perpetrators and 30 per cent female were motivated by revenge-retaliation.

From whose perspective?

In advancing this conviction that perpetrators kill out of love, psychiatric researchers and commentators often give the impression that the perpetrator's world is one of reason and logic, and that the altruistic killing is executed accordingly; it is both inevitable and commonsensical within the context of that world. In other words, psychiatrists conjecture and attempt to recreate the perpetrator's world, and speak authoritatively and lucidly on behalf of the perpetrator. Unlike forensic psychologist Gerald Bailes (Neustatter, 2001), who certainly does succeed in recreating that world, but ensures his opinions are unaffected by it: 'he (the perpetrator) may be driven by delusions that *make him think* he is acting out of love'. As Stanton and Simpson state: 'The murder would be seen as a rational act in the context of the mother's delusional perception of the world' (2002, p. 10). The case of Mrs A and Betty above is a good example of this (Resnick, 1969).

Emotional interactions which preclude love

But no filicide researcher, psychiatrist or otherwise, has raised the question of what precisely the 'loving' perpetrator is experiencing during the killing. In particular, what emotions are being felt and expressed? Looking at the case of Mrs A again, she first tried to choke her 5-year-old daughter, and failing that, lifted a rock and kept striking her on the head until she was dead. As always in filicide literature, there is no attempt to recreate what was happening to the child during these attacks. The pain and terror of choking, and then having her skull pulped with a rock by the mother she was totally dependent upon, can barely be contemplated. The physical, emotional and psychological torment defies description. The reason for highlighting this suffering is to consider what it means for the quality of interaction between the two sets of emotions, of perpetrator and victim. We can well imagine what emotions were being felt and expressed by the child: shock, submission, pleas, panic, fear, terror, anguish and unimaginable agony before unconsciousness. But for the very sick patient, the mother, what emotions is she feeling? No one knows; no one was there; no one has ever written about it; but it is reasonable to assume that, even though Mrs A was seriously ill and delusional, she could not have carried out these sustained attacks on her 5-year-old daughter without feeling powerful negative emotions like aggression, determined domination, hatred and/or self-hatred, anger, fear and loathing. The conviction of the delusion, the determination of the action, and the achievement of the murderous objective may also have generated and fuelled some sense of fulfilment. All of these emotions, combined with her ability to see and hear the intensification of the suffering she was inflicting on her daughter, are undoubtedly testimony to the severity of her illness. What she is experiencing physically, emotionally and psychologically, is symptomatic of a delusion; it is not a manifestation of love.

Categories in which love is attributed to filicide killings

In the current study undertaken for this text, love is knowingly attributed to the perpetrator's actions in 22 cases, by numerous individuals involved in some aspects of the tragedy (for example, the perpetrators themselves, partners, other family members and/or friends, barristers defending them, coroners, psychiatrists, clergy). Some of the cases are very similar to those in earlier studies. All of them belong to a specific category; two of the most prominent categories are:

'Love' combined with fear

These perpetrators are predominantly female and commit or attempt to commit suicide. They fear that their children will end up with someone totally unacceptable to them: their partner or former partner, in a foster or residential home. They must take the children they 'love' with them. Here are three examples:

1. The mother of Jason, 5, suffered repetitive bouts of mental illness during and after the break-up of her marriage. She developed irrational fears about access between her former husband and Jason, and eventually moved to another part of the country to ensure there was no contact whatsoever. Her mental health deteriorated. She poisoned Jason with prescriptive pills, then attempted suicide. She was convicted of manslaughter. Her defence barrister argued that 'this happened out of misguided love and not malice'.
2. The mother of 3-year-old Bell concealed the child's paternity from two men with whom she was having a relationship while married to a third. When one acquired evidence that he was the father, she smothered Bell and attempted suicide. Her husband claimed that she and the child were inseparable, and that she loved Bell

more than anything else in the world. Although her depression was acknowledged, she was convicted of murder.
3. The mother of Rose, 5 and David, 11 months, smothered them while on the run from the authorities. She wrote to them in a suicide note just before she killed them: 'I love you very much. I haven't been able to give you a marvellous life together. I am so sorry.' Her defence barrister said: 'She believed the children would be taken away from her and institutionalised. For her, this was worse than death. She killed them out of love. She loved the children.' This mother failed in her suicide attempt and received a life sentence.

These are three of eight cases in which a mother states or implies she is killing out of love, or, someone else is attributing to her love as the motivator underpinning her actions. Seven of the mothers were diagnosed mentally ill, including severe depression, psychotic episodes or schizophrenia. In four of the eight cases the fear of losing the children to social services was delusional. Social services were not involved, and, even if they had been involved, there was a remaining parent to care for the children, plus locally based, heavily involved, extended family members, particularly grandparents. One of the eight mothers told police *after* killing her child, that it was the 'social workers who had taken her', indicative of the delusions and obsessive fears she had about losing her child.

The antithesis of love

In considering this professed love, we have to return to the actual killings, and specifically, the emotional interactions between child(ren) and parent at the precise moment the killings were carried out. The eight mothers killed 14 children. Four of the children, aged 6 months, 2, 11 and 14 were stabbed to death; 7 were asphyxiated; 2 were drowned, and 1, aged 12, was poisoned. At the precise moment of stabbing, asphyxiating, drowning or poisoning, the mothers could not have been experiencing the core emotions and features of parental love, such as joy, pride, happiness, protectiveness, concern and compassion. Whatever mental illnesses these mothers were suffering, the emotional interactions between them and their children were the antithesis of love.

Whenever a mother kills her child, whatever love she once had for the child, metamorphoses into a murderous aggression. The terror, panic and resistance of the victim may only serve to fuel and intensify this aggression. *Murderous aggression* may not seem to be an appropriate term to apply to a *loving* mother, but it is precisely what the action of a filicide perpetrator is, in intent and outcome, irrespective of any alternative delusory idea they may have. The word *aggression* is unavoidable. Geen's (2001) classic text defines aggression as 'the delivery of an aversive stimulus [such as the killing actions we are looking at] with an intent to harm and with an expectation of causing such harm, when the other person (the victim) is motivated to escape or avoid the stimulus' (p. 3.)

Some may contest the use of the term by reminding us that in some instances, parents go to great lengths, and plan meticulously, to enable them to kill quietly, to snuff out the life of the child without any messy, inconvenient, noisy *aggression*. Such an interpretation is generous but misguided. The principal features of the killing scenario are strength and power pitted against helplessness and fragility; the desire and need to extinguish life and the child's terror-stricken but futile attempts to hold onto life; absolute choice verses no choice. These three enormous imbalances predominate, even in so-called mercy killings, where a parent believes that a child's disability, or their suffering, or their terminal illness, makes the life of the child (and perhaps the life of the parent too) not worth preserving.

We know from the perpetrators themselves, from those who lived and testified, and from those who died and left suicide notes, precisely what other emotions they were experiencing. They were also, as a consequence of their illness, and/or social isolation, and/or marital difficulties, in the throes of *despair, hopelessness, guilt, fear* and *misery*. A young mother repeated nine times in her suicide note the words in capital letters 'THIS IS HELL' before killing her two children (MacLaughlin, 2000). Another mother, single and unsupported, addicted to cannabis, stabbed her two infants to death. She gave graphic heart-rending testimony to the inquest. She said that she had loved her children with all her heart, but: 'I was scared ... I was confused ... and I was psychotic. I didn't know what was going on. I thought everyone was after me ... I wanted to kill myself.' When one's life becomes dominated by such negative destructive emotions, perceptions and delusions, that is the time when one's capacity for loving is drastically limited, if not extinguished.

Revenge disguised as love

In this second category, the perpetrators profess their love for the victims at the same time as they directly or indirectly blame their partners for the killings. Here are three of them.

1. Yvonne, 4, and Terry, 2, were strangled with internet cables, a cruel ironic twist, by their father, on learning that his estranged wife was surfing dating sites and suspecting she was in a relationship with another man. He left a suicide note read out in court, in which he spoke directly to the children he'd strangled: 'Sorry my lovely [children's actual names]… I love you. Sorry mummy decided to leave us for new boyfriend' (in reality of course, this was a note to his wife, which, combined with a video recording he made of the children waving goodbye to her, was certain to torment her thereafter. He failed in his attempt to kill himself.
2. The father of 4-year-old Barry stabbed and battered him to death with a knife and lampstand. (He also stabbed and battered his 18-month-old daughter, but she survived.) He left a suicide note read out at the inquest, which included these words addressed to his children: 'I have loved you ever since the moment you were born. I have never stopped loving you.' A psychiatrist at the inquest said that he was 'mentally abnormal' at the time of the killing. His wife had left him and was in a relationship with his best friend.
3. The father of 4-year-old Maisie gave her anti-depressant pills, then chloroformed and strangled her. He left a suicide note for his wife in which he said that he had 'taken' Maisie so that she could be 'loved, cherished and adored'. He had discovered his wife's affair with another man.

Not love, but the tools of revenge

These case examples are less complex than those in the first category, but on the issue of 'love', the same question arises: what was happening emotionally precisely at the moment of killing? These fathers were not feeling parental love; they were not looking down on their children with pride, joy, happiness, protectiveness, concern and compassion. They were consumed with and driven by hatred, revenge, spite and murderous aggression; and they were somehow able to insulate themselves from the visible and audible suffering they were inflicting on the children they professed to love. They were using their children as pawns, as tools of revenge, exploiting them with hideous cruelty.

In the third case, the use of anti-depressants and chloroform might suggest a modicum of concern about limiting the pain the child would endure. But, as was explored in the first category, it could also indicate detailed planning aimed towards killing with as much inconvenience and silence as possible (Maisie's mother was sleeping in the bedroom above as she was being murdered). Any notion of a residual compassion or pity in the killer should be eliminated, however, in the knowledge revealed during his trial. He had to use so much force in subduing her resistance to the chloroform that his finger nails left scratch marks on her cheeks. The skin around her eyes and mouth were burnt by the chemical. He admitted strangling her with his left hand as she lay dying in his right. Despite all the protestations about the father's 'love' for Maisie, the judge was having none of it. The child was murdered, he said in 'a planned and premeditated attack', because the father had discovered 'sexually explicit e-mails' between his wife and her lover. In short, a revenge killing, and the daughter he 'loved' being chosen as the principal tool of that revenge.

Not having the capacity to love

'Killed out of love' makes great headline-grabbing news. Anyone who make this claim, be they academic, psychiatrist or criminologist will be prominently reported. In response to the highly publicized familicide killings perpetrated by Robert Mochrie (Neustatter, 2001), a forensic psychologist identified two categories of men who killed their children (BBC News Online, 2001). In the first category, the men are motivated by love, but are also driven by suicidal tendencies. Whatever complex reasons lie beneath this type of psyche, the contributor believed they always relate to depression and low self-esteem arising out of the men's position in work and in the family. They always have a fear of losing their children and their partners. They see no future for themselves and they have all kinds of cognitive distortions combined with an overwhelming feeling of hopelessness. The contributor stressed that the killings perpetrated by these men have 'nothing whatsoever to do with evil; they are all to do with love.'

In identifying all the burdens and misfortunes of these men, that contributor was treading precisely along the same path as this author, but arriving at an entirely different conclusion. Depression, low self-esteem, suicidal tendencies, an overwhelming sense of hopelessness, and above all else, having 'all kinds of cognitive distortions', are not exactly conducive to feeling and expressing paternal love. In fact, it is difficult to imagine that any human being, suffering such a totality of debilitating emotional and psychological misery and malfunctioning, and the social isolation or marginalization which would be its consequence, could simultaneously be capable of feeling and expressing love for another fellow human being.

Distorting language to alleviate the pain

The concept of the 'loving' parent is so embedded in our culture, history and upbringing that some commentators, though readily acknowledging that filicide killings cannot be an expression of 'love' as we normally understand the word, are nevertheless reluctant to explicitly say so. The word and the idea need somehow to be retained. Thus a new terminology may be born enabling us to do just that, at the same time as attempting to shed additional light on the horrors of filicide. For example, Orr (2002) believes that men commit these 'appalling deeds' because they are motivated not by love, but by a 'frightening pathological love'. Sophie Hannah (2008), a novelist who has written a fictional account of a suspected filicide killing, wrote of finding during her research the term 'pathological altruism' which she then applied to a number of cases included in this study. Neither term is defined.

The problems with 'love'

There are three potential problems areas arising from the attribution of love as a motivator for killing one's children. First, the promotion of 'love' on behalf of the perpetrator can also reaffirm for so many that conviction of despair and helplessness that these killings were neither predictable nor preventable: what can you do when a 'loving father' goes off the rails, believing he is 'loving' when he is killing?

The second is that the love-motivation idea is always given maximum publicity and detracts from the nature and extent of the suffering inflicted on the children. Coroners' inquests, pathologists' reports, homilies in church services for the deceased, serious case reviews, all avoid, as of necessity, any suggestion or indication that the children may have suffered unbearably, may have been simply terrified into submission and resignation to their fate, may have repeatedly begged their mother or their father to stop knifing them, or bludgeoning them, or strangling them, or poisoning them, or burning them to death. No one wants to hear of this. For a mourning community, and for the relatives of the perpetrator in particular, it is more tolerable and reassuring to hear that he or she killed out of love, irrespective of the method he or she employed. It is not therefore, just a diversionary opportunity; it is also, potentially, a balm, and, an explanation where perhaps none existed before.

But it will be of no comfort at all to a surviving parent tormented by questions like: what exactly did happen to my child? How much violence was used? How much pain did they endure? Did they see each other being killed? Did they try to help each other? How long did it take them to die (Thomson and Ross, 2011)? When the inquests and funerals are over, the same questions will return with debilitating frequency and force.

There are many examples of this sequence of events and the surviving parent's response, in the current study. One in particular paradoxically proves that parents can actually envisage themselves killing out of *genuine* love. The mother of Kevin, aged 6, and Lois, aged 4, knew that they had been killed with excessive violence by their father. But she did not know the precise details. Nor did the police or coroner. The questions above haunted her for years. In a radio interview, she said this:

> What really upset me – and still does – is the way they must have felt, the fear, and if I knew that they had to die, I could, and this is going to sound very bizarre, but I could, I could go back in time and I could kill them myself, but I'd make sure that they didn't know anything about it, that they didn't suffer any pain, they

didn't know it was me, they would just go to sleep like any other night.

(BBC4, 2012)

This is probably the most common natural response among surviving parents in similar tragedies, an unfathomable genuine love that exposes the perversions of its imitators.

A case example

In 2000, a father kidnapped his 4-year-old child after the break-up of his marriage. He kept the child imprisoned for nearly two years, obviously not realizing that he was, in effect, inflicting on her two years of social deprivation and emotional and psychological abuse, preventing her from seeing, hearing or knowing about the mother from whom she had been severed, and for whom she pined. She never saw the light of day throughout her captivity. The father relied on his lover-accomplice to sustain the kidnap and to feed the child. When police eventually found the location and were about to arrest him, he raised his shotgun and shot his daughter point blank in the face. Half her head was blown off, so much so that the inquest had to be adjourned because forensics could not complete the necessary identification tests. He then shot himself. The child was still wearing the same clothes, now ragged, that she wore when she was first taken. She wore the same shoes, with toecaps cut away to allow space for her lengthening toes (Tallant, 2011).

As expected, there was no reference during the two separate funeral services for victim and perpetrator, to the suffering the child must have endured. Much was said about the 'illness', the 'pain', and 'burdens' carried by the perpetrator. On the day of the perpetrator's funeral, there was a sensational interruption to a local radio chat show discussing the case. The sister of the perpetrator rang in to angrily complain about what was being said about her brother and her family. She said that: 'What he did … he did out of love and nothing else … that's our interpretation of it and we know the full story' (Tallant, 2011). At the service itself, the priest said: 'It was obvious that [the father] did what he did out of a tremendous love' (Hogan, 2001; Tallant; 2011). When the father's accomplice was eventually apprehended and tried, it was once again, a judge, who got to the core of the matter. The child, he said, had been 'deprived of a basic human right, the right to a childhood over the two-year period. The right to go to school, the right to play with other children; and the love, affection and guidance of her mother were also denied her' (Duffy, 2003; Tallant, 2011).

Emulating the killing perpetrated out of 'love'

That case appropriately brings us to the third problem area. It may well be that the priest had listened to the killer's sister on the radio and decided to repeat the explanation about love, or, he could well have decided to do so long beforehand. But the dual pronouncements on the same day do raise the spectre of contagion. The feminist filicide researcher Johnson lays some responsibility on the press, who, occasionally, depict these type of killings 'as an act of love rather than an act of extreme and premeditated violence' (2005, p. 133).

Whoever is responsible is not the point; it is the potential consequences. When this patently obvious misinterpretation of the cold-blooded killing of a child reaches the wider audience, there may well be another individual out there, whose marriage is fractiously crumbling, whose wife and children are leaving, who finds himself peering over the filicide-suicide precipice, and for whom headlines about 'killing out of love' have a much deeper and sinister resonance. Copying, emulating, aspiring to ... these are all credible possibilities which have been advanced by practitioners and researchers in response to increased frequencies of filicide and familicide killings (Health Service Executive, 2011; Tallant, 2011).

A disturbing revelation for this author has been to learn about the number of perpetrators who, having determined to kill themselves after killing their children, were found to have spent weeks and months surfing suicide internet sites. There is no research available, to tell us why. But it is reasonable to assume that in their profound misery, desperation and despair, about which there is universal consensus, there must have been some solace in this virtual-world companionship; a sense of belonging, a sharing in the conviction about the 'rightness', the 'goodness', the inevitability of action that is unmentionable in the real world.

Therein lies the danger of pronouncing and publicizing a belief that parents kill out of love. A prospective killer, then, need not think that he is alone; and he knows that the killings he intends to execute have repeatedly been identified by well-meaning psychiatrists, psychologists and ministers of God as an expression of love. Apart from its danger, this view is baseless.

Summary

The categorization 'altruistic killings', also referred to as 'killing out of love' was first established in the 1960s by the psychiatric pioneers of filicide research. It is a construct without theoretical underpinning, and applied inappropriately to many cases. There are three possible reasons for this misleading categorization. One is the definition or understanding of 'love' which the pioneers were using. It could not have been a universally accepted definition, and it is abundantly clear that they never addressed the question: can a parent simultaneously love a child and subject that child to unspeakable barbarity with the sole purpose of ending the child's life? The answer is inescapably 'no', but the implication of the widespread application of this altruism-love categorization is that many believe the answer is 'yes'. A second possible reason is that the majority of patients on whom the work of the pioneers is based were designated seriously mentally ill, many of them suffering psychotic delusions. The pioneers often give the impression when they speak about a 'love' motive that they are writing, thinking and perceiving from the perspective of the deluded patient, and not from the basis of reality. A third reason is that the pioneers never at any time considered the quality of emotional interactions at the moment of killing. Maternal and paternal love is strongly characterized and expressed in the company of and in interaction with the child by the emotions of pleasure, joy, pride, happiness, humour and curiosity. In contrast, filicide perpetrators at the time of the killings are more likely to be in the throes of despair, hopelessness, guilt, fear and misery, and some driven by hatred, revenge, spite, murderous aggression and delusion. When they commence the killing, and generate panic, terror and agony in the child, they cannot be 'loving' the child.

Apart from it having no basis in truth, the concept of 'killing out of love' has had numerous unforeseen consequences. It is a compelling concept which detracts from the terror and suffering inflicted upon the child. For the remaining parent, that is the tormenting question: what precisely happened to my child ... how did they cope? There is a kind of superior detachment and finality about the concept, giving credence to that conviction of despair, that if a 'loving' parent chooses to kill their child, then such killings are definitely neither predictable nor preventable.

Finally, the huge publicity given to 'expert' opinion that a killing was perpetrated 'out of love', may be precisely what persuades other parents, teetering on the filicide-suicide precipice, to commit a similar act. Knowing that, in death, not only their loyal relatives and friends, but also, reputable opinion in the fields of psychiatry and psychology, will be identifying their killings as an expression of their 'love', may be, for some would-be perpetrators, an incentive that encourages them to take that final leap.

8
The legislative context

Introduction

UK governments have enacted more family, childcare and mental health legislation during the past 50 years than all of their predecessors combined. Much of that recent legislation is relevant to the cases listed in Chapter 5. This chapter will focus on the three categories of legislation most pertinent to filicide and familicide killings: (i) legislation to combat domestic violence; (ii) legislation to improve mental health services, particularly in respect of mentally ill parents and their vulnerable children, and (iii) legislation to safeguard and promote the welfare and protection of children.

The new legislative frameworks are broadly welcome, and must inevitably improve the quality of services to children and families. With new laws should come changing attitude and culture. This is particularly evident in respect of the current more robust response by police to domestic violence. Yet, ironically, it is the law itself, more specifically, childcare law, and the timing and the means by which it is implemented in bitter, residence and contact disputes, which can pose the greatest risk to children. As this chapter will demonstrate, a good many filicide victims are killed before, during, or immediately after courts make decisions on these matters. It is a dangerous time, to be explored with reference to cases from the current study.

Domestic violence

A different culture in tackling domestic violence

Table 5.1 on p. 74 on male filicides revealed that 44 per cent (27) of 62 cases had incidents of domestic violence preceding the killings. Other researchers reveal even higher frequencies of domestic violence (johnson, 2005; Kirkwood, 2012; Saunders, 2004). Nearly one million incidents of domestic violence perpetrated against women were recorded in the year 2009–10 (Home Office, 2010). There has been a flurry of legislative activity to deal with this situation. A decade ago, the Crown Prosecution Service (CPS) did not even monitor domestic violence cases, and common assault in a domestic violence situation was not even an arrestable offence. Yet in 2009–10, the CPS prosecuted over 74,000 perpetrators (Starmer, 2011). It was able to do so primarily because of new legislation and a fundamental change of attitude in the agencies at the forefront of tackling domestic violence: the Home Office and the police.

Police Domestic Violence Units were introduced in the 1990s, the beginning of a culture change within the most important agency dealing with the problem. In 2000, the police were advised by the Home Office to consider arrest whenever they responded to domestic violence incidents. This pro-arrest view was immensely challenging to those police officers more accustomed to delivering pep talks to an aggressive parent and then walking away. A White Paper, *Safety and Justice* (Home Office, 2003), further refined government thinking on the matter. There would be more focus on prevention through education and awareness training, and assessment of risk factors like alcohol and drugs. Most significantly, breaching civil orders such as the Non-molestation Order would be made a criminal offence. Police would be able to check for previous breaches and act accordingly, for example, by invoking the pro-arrest facility then available to them and increasingly being used. The government ear-marked £19 million of new funding which greatly facilitated the expansion of women's refuges.

A professional, systematic and rigorous approach

The changes in police culture and in their frontline responses to domestic violence occurred at different speeds in different locations. In police forces leading the field, much progress was made in formulating, structuring and implementing anti-domestic violence programmes that incorporated the dual aims of assessment and safety. The Domestic Abuse Stalking and Harassment Model (DASH) and the Domestic Violence Risk Indicator Model (DVRIM) are two of the assessment tools which came into use, enabling officers to ascertain the level of seriousness and the degree of risk in each case. Risk levels are graded, for example, *standard*, *medium*, *high* and *very high*. If there are children present, or, if the mother is known to be in an advanced state of pregnancy, an additional assessment on the impact of the violence and the risk to the children (and unborn) is necessary. Basic facts must be recorded: the names, ages and relationship of children to the perpetrator (biological or substitute parent?); the time of the incident (were they abruptly wakened by the violence against their mother?); did they witness further violence? Is this a recurring experience for them? The police must also explore the possibility of the children having been assaulted themselves, perhaps through trying to protect their mother. They must explore the adults' perception and awareness (if there is any) of the impact of the violence upon the children. If the children are present during their investigation, the police should take note of behaviour and expression, for example, persistent crying or withdrawal, apathy or aggression. It is upon the answers to all of these questions and observations that a decision to refer to Children's Services may be made. If the police judge the risk to the children to be unacceptably high, they can request an immediate response from a social services emergency duty team, or, they can themselves remove the children with a *Police Protection Order*.

The new legislation

These developments were consolidated by legislation. The Domestic Violence, Crime and Victims Act 2004 gave police substantially more powers to intervene effectively. The Serious and Organised Crime and Police Act of 2005 removed the distinction between arrestable and non-arrestable offences. The 2004 Act introduced the concept of *Domestic Homicide Reviews*, critical analyses of domestic conflict situations culminating in fatalities in which police and other agencies have been involved. Another significant development came in 2009, with the amendment of Section 5 of the Protection from Harassment Act 1997. The Restraining Orders of that Act could only be issued by a court when sentencing a defendant convicted of harassment or a similar offence. The 2009 amendment enabled courts to impose Restraining Orders in a much wider range of circumstances. It also gave victims the right to representation in court if the subject of the Restraining Order was seeking to vary or discharge that Order. *Violent Offender Orders* were introduced in the 2008 Criminal Justice Act, and they can be imposed on anyone who has been convicted of violent offences, forbidding them to have contact with named persons.

Third party witnesses to the violence, such as neighbours, relatives and friends, were to be given more credibility in helping to construct a prosecution case against offenders. A very practical user-friendly innovation from the US, greatly appreciated by the victims of domestic violence, was the Specialist Domestic Violence Courts (SDVCs). Those who serve in them, magistrates, lawyers, police and 'specialist support services' personnel for victims, all combine to provide an holistic, judicial approach to the problem. There are now 141 SDVCs operating in England and Wales, favourably evaluated (Cook et al., 2004) and certain to expand (Home Office, 2011). No more are victims expected to share the same waiting room with the partner who attacked them.

Advisers

Independent Domestic Violence Advisers (IDVAs) serve as the victim's primary point of reference, from the outset of a domestic violence incident. They assess the level of risk to both mother and children, and, given the trauma a victim may be enduring, they can take the initiative and rapidly implement safety measures. They represent victims at the new Multi Agency Risk Assessment Conference (MARAC), of which they are key members. Multi Agency Public Protection Arrangements (MAPPA) is another initiative but with the wider brief of managing violent offenders in the community (including known domestic violence offenders).

Procedures ignored; lessons unlearnt

A government-driven crusade with all the necessary expenditure and legislation, however, is no guarantee that domestic violence incidents will not end in tragedy. The 2003 White Paper coincided with a highly publicized familicide case in which a husband, Alan

Pemberton, shot his wife and his 17-year-old son; he then committed suicide (Abrams, 2005). He had subjected his wife to vicious verbal assaults and threats to kill, ever since she announced her intention to leave him. Despite an injunction, he contacted his wife numerous times, terrifying her in repeating his intention to kill her. She and her family visited and/or phoned the police when these threats were made. The police made no attempt to interview or arrest him. On the day he arrived to carry out the killings, the terrified woman made her last desperate phone call to the police. Despite all the previous contacts she had made with them, they did not even know her address. By the time they found it, all three family members were dead. The very first *Domestic Homicide Review* mentioned earlier in this chapter was carried out in respect of the Pemberton case (Walker *et al.*, 2008). It exposed 'serious operational failure by Thames Valley police' (bureaucratic speak for incompetence, negligence and a pervasive male-dominated culture in which wife-battering was still perceived as an irksome-but-can't-do-anything-about-it status quo).

Police uncertainty, deviation from procedures, and in the end simply doing nothing create a scenario repeatedly brought into sharp focus in an increasing number of Independent Police Complaints Commission (IPCC) reports on domestic violence cases that have ended in the murders of the victims. All these IPCC reports are available on their website. They confirm the views of two experienced members of a Domestic Violence team whom I interviewed for this text: the enormous variations in progress among police forces, and within each force itself. They stressed just how difficult it was within their own force, changing the attitude and approach of every police officer called upon to respond to a domestic violence incident.

Oblivious to the changing culture and its demands

Recent IPCC reports on filicide killings reveal that many police officers seem to be unaware of: (i) the lessons learnt from previous cases; and (ii) developments in law, procedure and guidelines devised specifically to avoid the same mistakes. For example, in the more recent Independent Police Complaints Commission (2012) report on 2-year-old Sonya and her mother (see Table 5.1, on p. 82), whose deaths were preceded by six years of domestic violence, the officers involved did not know about their powers of arrest in many of the incidents to which they had been summoned; nor about the need for assessment in respect of the victim and her children, nor about the existence of Independent Domestic Violence Advisors and Multi Agency Risk Assessment Conferences, to which, as the IPCC report states, this case, more than any other, should have been referred. The report rightly pinpoints defective systems to blame for this sorry state of affairs, but a more honest appraisal quickly exposes a police force, at the time, culturally lagging far behind other forces in its attitude and approach to domestic violence.

Domestic violence and filicide

Some 19 children were killed during the last five years (2008–2012) of the period covered by this study, by fathers who had been responsible on numerous preceding occasions for assault on their partners. One man also allegedly raped his wife, and was due to go on trial when he killed his two children. Often the violence is a recurring feature of the disintegrating relationship. In the 2008–12 cases referred to, the police were called upon at various times in the past to deal with domestic violence incidents. In a number of cases, the police visited, questioned and assessed. The violence was confirmed. But they did not arrest and/or remove.

Assessments can be exceedingly difficult in domestic violence situations, and perpetrators are not always easily removed. If a neighbour reports a domestic violent incident and both perpetrator and victim deny it, who could fault a police officer for not attempting an arrest? If a victim categorically insists that it was a one-off in which she provoked the attack and she definitely does not want the matter pursued, how many officers would go against her wishes? Some officers may be hypersensitive to the possibility of making matters worse. They have formidable supporters in Keeling and van Wormer's (2012) emphatically feminist perspective, the latest of numerous publications exploring the potentially oppressive impact of ill-prepared agency intervention in domestic violence (Allen, 2011; Bui, 2007; Hague, 2000; Stanley *et al.*, 2011).

The assessment of risk

A decade ago, the welfare of children in domestic violence situations would not have been the principal concern of investigative police officers. Today, they are statutorily obliged to consider the impact on children and vulnerable persons. There is abundant research demonstrating that if children witness and hear domestic violence, they are being emotionally and psychologically abused (for example, Jaffe, Hurley et al., 1990; Jaffe, Wolfe et al., 1990; Maker et al., 1998; Rossman, 1998). This was enshrined in legislation, in Section 20 of the Adoption Act, 2002, which amended Section 31 of the Children Act 1989, dealing with the concept of *harm, to include impairment suffered from seeing or hearing the ill-treatment of others*. The research goes further: it demonstrates that *significant harm* is inflicted on very young children who witness their mothers being battered.

The new laws and procedures pertaining to domestic violence are adequate only in so far as practitioners carefully consider these kinds of risk to vulnerable people, particularly young children. There is specific reference to risk assessment in many of the publications already referred to; most are addressed primarily to the police, particularly the Home Office (2009) paper.

The police are nearly always first on the domestic violence scene and see things as they really are: the conflicts, the high tension, the presence of small children; how distressed they are, how they are being exploited. They are now much better trained and equipped for dealing adequately with these situations, thanks to a whole raft of circulars, Acts of Parliament, amendments, new procedures, and not least, additional funding. Individual forces have produced their own frameworks and questionnaires enabling frontline officers to assess the risk of further violence, to both mother and children, and if need be, to intervene quickly and effectively. Yet, as IPCC reports on domestic violence fatalities continuously reveal, there are still far too many occasions when the police response is much less than robust and far below what new procedures and laws demand.

Mental health: another revolution

New legislation, new relationships, new practice and greater specialization

Just as in the field of domestic violence, mental health services too have undergone radical change in practice and culture during the last two decades, culminating in the 2007 Mental Health Act (Department of Health, 1999a, 2001, 2006, 2007; Matthews, 1995). There were numerous aims and objectives, including (i) establishing a *Care Program Approach* (Department of Health, 1990); greater emphasis on social inclusion, human rights, and partnership between health and social care services; (ii) greater service user involvement (Department of Health, 2006); (iii) redefining the relationship between Mental Health Trusts and Local Authority Social Services Departments; and (iv) increasing specialization of mental health teams. Bailey and Liyanage (2012) carried out research in a Mental Health Trust which had gone so far as to create an *Affective Disorder* team and a *Psychosis* team. The 2007 Mental Health Act replaced Approved Social Workers (ASW) with *Approved Mental Health Practitioners*, a title predicated on the assumption that it would be perceived as more specialist than the ASW. Bailey and Liyanage think social workers will regret this change, believing it will diminish the importance of their unique social and family perspective of mental health problems.

A reminder of how it just doesn't work

In studying the case of Raveena in Chapter 6, it seemed the mental health professionals (just like their police officer counterparts in IPCC reports) were not aware of the legislative and organizational changes affecting them, nor of the challenges these brought about. For example, it is hard to envisage how new principles and practice in mental health which were then in force could have tolerated Raveena being assessed by four psychiatrists within nine months and each diagnosing her condition differently.

Even though the more recent policy and legislative changes signal a move towards specialization, the mental health professions as a whole fully support the principles of the *Care Program Approach* initiated by Health and Social Services as far back as 1990 (Department of Health, 1990). This approach has since been reviewed and revised (Department of Health, 1999b, 2008).

Two of the most significant principles of the Care Program Approach are: the provision of a care plan that meets the health and social care needs of the patient; and the appointment of a key worker or care coordinator. In Raveena's case, the inquiry team could find no evidence of a care plan. The 'care-coordinating' was the most heavily criticized aspect of the service, the individual concerned revealing that he or she was unaware of what precisely the role of a care coordinator was, how and why it originated, and of its crucial significance in information gathering and distribution.

Mental health and child protection

As is evident in many mental health cases, Raveena's tragedy was as much about child protection as it was about mental illness. The most important and most widely used government publication advising all professionals about child protection work is *Working Together to Safeguard Children* (DCSF, 2010). It is periodically updated, and is presently being revised once again. It has no less than five full pages on the subject of the children of mentally ill parents. It explores in detail how such illness may adversely impact upon the welfare of the child. It stresses that mental illness does not necessarily preclude good parenting, but it is clear about the obligations on professionals, particularly mental health and child protection workers: 'The consequent likelihood of harm being suffered by a child will range from a minimal effect to a significant one. It is essential to assess the implications of parental ill health for each child in the family' (ibid., p. 266).

Inexplicably, the latest revision of the *Working Together* paper (Department for Education, 2013) has discarded this highly valuable section, which was in Chapter 9: Lessons from Research (DCEF, 2010). This is a serious omission, for both agencies and frontline staff.

Assessment

Assessment is a core concept in family and childcare work and a requirement of the 1989 Children Act. Promoting and safeguarding children's welfare is an objective that can only be achieved on the basis of rigorous assessment of the key aspects of children's lives, their physical, emotional, psychological, social and moral development, and an assessment of the quality of care their parents provide. The Act acknowledges the burdens under which families live, including mental illness, and how these burdens impact adversely on the development of children (Cleaver *et al.*, 1999). Section 10(3) of the Children Act, 2004 stresses that Children's Services 'must have regard to the importance of parents ... in improving the well-being of children'. In the case of a mentally ill parent, proper assessment and support are likely to be more complex, as acknowledged in

The National Framework for Children, Young People and Maternity Services: 'It is important to consider the more specialised forms of support required by families in specific circumstances, such as support for parents with mental health difficulties' (Department of Health, 2000, p. 69, para. 3.4).

Case examples of children killed by discharged parents

Mental health inquiry reports over the decades have often revealed that parents have been discharged from hospital without any assessment of whether or not it would be in the children's interests. The Department of Health (2008) revised its code of practice in relation to the 1983 Mental Health Act, with this in mind. It instructed GPs, psychiatrists, and community mental health professionals to ensure that 'the safety and welfare of dependent children are taken into account when clinicians consider granting leave of absence for parents with a mental disorder' (2008, p. 11).

How more important, then, to consider the welfare of children when mentally ill patients discharge themselves? Unfortunately, far too many cases reveal the absence of this child protection perspective which the code of practice demands, whether the patient is discharged, or discharges him or herself. There are numerous examples in the current restudy. Here are some of them:

- Two-year old Calum was stabbed and strangled by his mother 24 hours after she discharged herself from an Accident and Emergency unit to which she had been taken in a highly distressed state. Her husband had left after the marriage breakdown.
- Ten-year-old Bernard was killed by his father hitting him over the head with a sledgehammer and then setting alight to his house, killing his wife. He had discharged himself on numerous occasions from psychiatric hospital, having suffered depression, delusion and paranoia, coinciding with the marriage breakdown. There was no risk assessment carried out in respect of the child.
- Nine-year-old Lorna was smothered by her mother, who discharged herself from a psychiatric hospital. Both mental health and social services departments were heavily criticized by an official inquiry for ignoring the assessment of risk to the child. Her marriage had just broken up.

- Six-year-old Nahum was burnt alive after his mother set his bed alight. Her arranged marriage had compelled her to move to the UK against her wishes. She was admitted to psychiatric hospital after numerous suicide attempts. A risk assessment in respect of the child had not been carried out.
- Robert, 2, and Daniel, 4 months, were both stabbed repeatedly by a lone single parent mother. The father had left and her mental condition deteriorated rapidly over a two-year period. There is no indication of a risk assessment having been carried out in respect of the children.

Bernard's case is worthy of additional comment, as is the case of Robert, 2, and Daniel, 4 months. Both filicide parents in these cases suffered mental illness coinciding with relationship break-up, and both of them, for very different reasons, had ceased taking their medication weeks and months before the killings. While it is not uncommon for patients generally to stop taking prescribed medicine, it can have fatal consequences for the children of mentally ill patients. A mentally ill parent not taking the prescribed medication has to be assessed as high risk factor, particularly in the case of lone, unsupported parents, male or female. The high risk applies both to the parent and the children he or she is caring for (Ofsted, 2013).

Collective responsibility for safeguarding children

Section 11 of the Children Act 2004 lists the agencies responsible for promoting and safeguarding the welfare of children in whatever context the matter arises: frontline staff in these organizations may encounter parents whose caring capacities are adversely affected due to mental illness. Guidance about their specific duties under Section 11, is contained in Department for Education and Skills (2007).

The new mental health legislation, the accompanying guidelines, the codes of practice, and the departmental policies deriving from them, should, in theory, ensure the safety of children when parents are suffering serious debilitating mental illness (often coinciding with relationship break-up). The culture of change within mental health services is more conducive to recognising the need for swift comprehensive multidisciplinary assessment, particularly the assessment of risk. Should the threshold of risk be judged unacceptably high, there are ample statutory tools that can be invoked to protect both parent and child. The legislative framework is sound; the procedures are robust and comprehensive. Consistently adhering to them is the main challenge.

Childcare and child protection

A feverish outpouring

Few could have anticipated that the 1989 Children Act, the most radical and comprehensive childcare legislative innovation in British history, would also be the precursor of a swath of additional legislation. In that same year the *United Nations Convention on the Rights of the Child*, was published, and ratified by the UK in 1991. A most basic right was protection from abuse. Subsequent legislation included *Children (Leaving Care) Act, 2002*; *Adoption Act, 2002*; *Children Act, 2004* (a direct consequence of the Government's Green Paper, *Every Child Matters*, following the death of Victoria Climbié); the *Children and Adoption Act, 2006*; *The Child Care Act, 2006* (which replaced Part 10A of the Children Act, 1989); the *Safeguarding Vulnerable Groups Act 2006* (following the Bichard inquiry into the circumstances surrounding the murders of Jessica Chapman and Holly Wells (Bichard, 2005)); and the *Borders, Citizenship and Immigration Act, 2009*, which is of increasing importance in safeguarding and promoting the welfare of children of families incarcerated and vetted before entry or expulsion from the UK.

Child sexual abuse led to another strand of legislation: *The Sex Offenders Act, 1997*, aimed chiefly at monitoring offenders, and the *Sexual Offences Act, 2003*, which widened the scope of 'abuse' to include the offences of grooming, abusing positions of trust, intrafamilial abuse and trafficking. It also covers child sexual abuse offences committed by UK citizens while abroad. The *Female Genital Mutilation Act, 2003* sought to protect young women and girls from an abhorrent and dangerous practice within certain minority populations.

A flurry of inquiry reports were also published in this period: on abuse and neglect fatalities (Haringey Safeguarding Children Board, 2010; Harrow, 1999; Laming, 2003); on failures in residential care (Leicestershire County Council, 1993; Social Services Inspectorate Wales (1991); Staffordshire County Council, 1991; Utting, 1991); and on ritual abuse (La Fontaine, 1994).

Among Guidelines issued during this 25-year period, two of the most significant are (i) *Framework for the Assessment of Children in Need and Their Families* (Department of Health, 2000) and the constantly updated *Working Together to Safeguard Children* (Department of Education, 2013). The latter was first published in 1991; and its latest 2013 update replaces the former *Framework* guideline, which had been universally adopted as an effective and systematic means of identifying and assessing children in need.

Common factors in filicide and in child protection social work

In Chapter 2, it was stated that family and childcare workers are familiar with many of the principal features and challenges that predominate in the majority of filicide cases. One common feature that was not mentioned was the prominent role of courts and the use of public and private law. Social services may, for example, be seeking care or supervision orders. Separated, warring parents may be seeking residence orders or contact orders, or prohibited *steps* orders (Section 8 of the *Children Act 1989*). Social workers and/or court welfare officers can be drawn into these private law proceedings. They can be asked to report to the court on matters relating to the welfare of the child (S. 7 and S 37, Children Act 1989). This is particularly likely if the application is being opposed by another parent. Similarly as with public law and child protection proceedings, a social worker compiling a report to help a judge or magistrate in private law applications may have observed aspects of either parent's lives which could be instrumental in the court's decision. For example, severe limitations in caring capacities, a history of violence or specifically, domestic violence, drug or alcohol dependency, mental illness, and not least, a tendency to disregard court decisions of the past. Despite the supremacy of the court, these public and private law proceedings can be a dangerous time, a time of enhanced risk for all concerned, including social workers.

Not so safe

I recall many threats being made in the magistrates courts, and parents who lose their children vowing never to speak to me again. The situation may be even worse in respect of private law applications. District Judge Nicolas Crichton has recently publicized the dangers, even in such a prominent law location as the Principal Registry of the Family Division in central London. He tells of a female judge seriously injured by a family member. He says threats are often shouted at the judges, and books and cups thrown at them. Another circuit judge lamented: 'These are the most volatile sensitive courts in the land ... it's a disaster waiting to happen' (*Daily Telegraph*, 24 December 2012, p. 2).

Case examples of filicide killings around the time of court proceedings

If family court judges and social workers can be the focus of such animosity and threat coming from either or both parents, what if the parents themselves are locked in bitter struggle over which of them the child will reside with, and the nature and extent of contact with the parent they do not reside with? The prospect of jointly losing out to social services and a care order is humiliating enough, but for a parent to lose out to *their former partner* on the matter of caring for their child may be too painful to bear, particular if that partner is in a new relationship.

The case of Sonya earlier in the chapter is one such case. The mother and father were due to appear in court that day to hear a decision on the issue of residence and contact. The father appears not to have been able to face the near certainty of the mother being given care of the child and of his contact being limited. Here are other public and private law examples of parents unable to face the prospect of court decisions which they thought would be made against them.

- The father of Alison, 7, and Oliver, 3, was convinced he was going to lose out in court due to his habitual violence; he was also due to appear in court to hear (almost certainly) that he would lose possession of the family home. He killed the children and himself a few days before.
- The mother of Abraham, 8; Lesley, 8, and Cathleen, 5, failed to turn up to court when decisions were to be made about the children's contact with their father. He was in a new relationship. The

mother had for some time been thwarting contact between him and the children. She killed the three children the next day by multiple stabbing. She attempted but failed to commit suicide.
- The father of Christie, 6, is believed to have smothered him and started a fire only hours after a court ruling which he misinterpreted as meaning he would not be able to have contact with his son. He also believed his wife was in a new relationship.
- The mother of Rose, 5, and David, 11 months, was so terrified at the prospect of care proceedings and losing her children, that she killed them both. She had good reason to know she would lose them, and why: she was a senior manager in Social Service's Children's Services.

There were an additional 17 cases in which 30 children were killed by 7 female and 10 male perpetrators at and around the time of court proceedings.

Acknowledging the depth of loss

Court proceedings that conclude by making permanent decisions about care, contact, residence and parental responsibility are fraught with risk. If parents separate and make opposing applications, courts nearly always award residence to the mother. They are, generally speaking, the principal carers. The 1989 Act also gives prominence to the views and feeling of children themselves. Again, generally speaking, children old enough to express their views and feelings will nearly always choose to remain with the principal carer, their mother. The vast majority of fathers reluctantly accept that and try to get on with their lives. But there is a significant number of fathers who do not accept it and who cannot. Those fathers are likely to have lost numerous other possessions, possibly their home, money, social standing, their job, way of life, routine, their good mental health, their confidence, and not least their authority and control. Court proceedings are like no other challenge they have faced. The law is paramount and will be upheld. Whatever courts decree, a father can only sit and listen. Previously, life may have been intermittently miserable, fractious and even violent, but there was always the opportunity to begin all over again. Court decisions hold out the terrifying prospect of an insufferable permanency, intensifying and perpetuating the hopelessness and helplessness of their predicament. Little wonder a father facing such a prospect may morph into a burning cauldron of hatred and revenge. His only real challenge at this point may be how to conceal his intent.

Contact with fathers

Forty-one children in the current study were killed by their fathers during a contact visit, either formally arranged through the court, or informally arranged by the parents. Despite this, the government's inclination remains set on facilitating contact between children and *both* parents. The *Children and Adoption Act 2006*, for example, made a number of amendments to the *Children Act 1989* to facilitate and promote contact. These amendments introduce the concept of *contact activity directions* and *contact activity conditions*, both of which require the parent seeking contact with children to undertake certain activities conducive to such contact. The activities and conditions may include counselling or guidance classes that help the parent to establish, maintain and improve contact, and understand and accept the challenges and the pitfalls of contact; most important of all (in the context of the domestic violence which precedes so many marital breakdowns) the parent (invariably the father) may have to undergo self-awareness and self-control sessions in which any violent tendencies are exposed, acknowledged and controlled. There is as yet no research indicating that these innovations are being vigorously implemented and the results incorporated within a comprehensive risk assessment. Assessment of the father's current perception of his loss of residence and contact is as important as assessing the significance of previous violent tendencies or convictions.

A final gesture of hatred and contempt

There are at least two cases (though I suspect many more) where the last act of fathers before they killed their children and themselves was hugely symbolic of their feelings for the law and those who uphold it and implement it. In the case of 6-month-old Ewen, his father wrote out a suicide note on the back of the anti-molestation order which his wife had sought only weeks before. In the case of 17-year-old Walter, the father posted to his former home, the copy of an affidavit sworn by his wife when she sought an injunction to keep him out of the home. Around the edges of the affidavit copy, he had scrawled the same kind of abuse and threats which had compelled her to seek the injunction in the first instance.

For such men, childcare law, courts and court proceedings are the ultimate threat. The court's decisions, which are then enshrined in single sheets of paper, each of which constitutes a particular order, may be the last straw, strengthening a conviction long festering: that life is no longer worth living, and somebody must pay the price.

Summary

Three distinct filicide subject areas have emerged from previous chapters: domestic violence, mental illness and child protection. This chapter has focussed on radically new legislation pertinent to all three.

Domestic violence is a pervasive feature of filicide cases. Nearly a million incidents were recorded in the UK in the year 2009–10. While this is a depressingly high figure, of more significance is the response of the police, who prosecuted over 45,000 offenders in the same year. A decade earlier, domestic violence incidents were barely recorded, let alone dealt with. There has been a sea change in public, governmental and police perceptions of domestic violence, coinciding with a raft of new policies, laws, guidelines and funding. Specialist teams, courts and advisors have emerged, and a zero tolerance approach has now been adopted by many police forces. Traditional police attitudes and practices still persist, however, and were exposed as contributory factors in some recent particularly brutal killings of mothers and children by known domestic abuse offenders.

There has been similar radical and structural change in mental health services. As with the police, many frontline mental health staff are unaware of the changes, and how they impact upon their working practices. There are many examples in inquiry reports of the consequences of staff not adhering to the new statutory framework and procedural guidelines which now underpin their service. One of the most significant new challenges for clinical, managerial and administrative mental health workers is in acknowledging and maintaining a child protection perspective when providing services to mentally ill parents, particular single parents of very young children.

There has been a prodigious amount of new childcare legislation since the 1989 Children Act. Childcare law is increasingly invoked in care proceedings initiated by social services, and in disputes about residence and contact. This can be a challenging and dangerous time for all family members. The prospect of a court issuing a child protection or care order, or deciding to grant a residence order to one parent, usually a mother, and restricting contact with the other, may be too much for some parents to bear. It may be the ultimate loss, coming after the break-up of a relationship, the ejection from their home, and a substantial reduction in their status and control. The risks of them then taking some drastic action on or near the day a court is due to decide, will be higher if the court hearing has been preceded by weeks, months or years of bitter wrangling between the parents, or if there has been frequent involvement by social workers unhappy with the care of a child, or when there has been recurring domestic violence, and the issuing of non-molestation and other types of restraining orders. The final decision of a court may leave a parent seething with rage and a desire for revenge or retaliation.

Legislation pertaining to domestic violence, mental health and childcare has improved enormously over the past three decades, and no doubt, countless victims, families, patients and children have benefited. But the law can never be a panacea for all social or marital ills. The implementation of child protection law in particular, in fear- and hate-laden marital disputes, can be a trigger that unleashes powerful destructive forces, culminating in a family cataclysm that mocks all our attempts to safeguard and promote the welfare of children.

9
Jackie's story

Introduction

My research for this study has necessitated the usual trawl through modern data banks and long-forgotten texts in once venerable, now defunct titles. It has also taken me to numerous unlikely places throughout the mainland and beyond; to coroners inquests and Crown Courts and Her Majesty's prisons. I came into contact with many family members and friends during this time, including a woman whose husband had killed their children, and then committed suicide. She had once given a brief anonymous interview to a journalist. I was struck by the degree of similarities in her case and in so many of the cases I had been studying. I asked her if she would be willing to submit to a (much lengthier) questionnaire for my study. She wrote to me saying that she would be 'happy to help in any way possible ... BUT, I do not want my children's pictures or names used, or my surname'. There was no possibility of me doing that, yet during the period which followed, I was preoccupied with discomforting questions. The all-abiding preoccupation for the woman was: could anonymity be maintained? I was reasonably confident it could; I have been writing about and anonymizing actual child abuse and mental health cases for over 30 years. But this was a case which, like every other filicide-suicide case, was so heavily publicized, nationally, in the press, on radio, on television and on the internet. For that reason, I agreed to let her read the chapter before I would submit to a publisher. She didn't ask for that, nor did she seek the right to 'edit' the chapter, she merely wanted to be reassured that anonymity had been maintained. It was not herself she was primarily concerned about; it was her family.

I emailed her a 17-page structured questionnaire, containing 85 questions. The questions were grouped under 10 sections: *Background, Developing problems, Father's relationship with children, Mother's perception of father, Children's perspective of parents in conflict, The killings, Balance of power, Aftermath, The inquest* and *In retrospect*. Many of the questions must have evoked powerful and painful memories, and perhaps much regret. She completed it within about three weeks. The answers were characteristically blunt, honest, incisive and totally without self-pity or sentiment. Some were witty and self-deprecating. Over the following 12 months, we maintained contact. She was remarkably patient and tolerant when I sought clarification and explanation on so many issues her answers raised. The emails we exchanged continuously enhanced my understanding of the person, and of the circumstances and processes by which two people, loving parents, and, at one time deeply in love, can unwittingly and unwillingly choose a course of action that may lead to a catastrophe.

With more licence in altering material facts than usual therefore (in order to protect her anonymity), this is Jackie's story. Her experience, memories, perceptions and opinions have not, however, been altered in any way. Within her tragedy lie lessons for us all.

Origins

Jackie and Martin lived together in the north of England for about eight years before marrying. They had two children during this period, Kevin, aged 7, and Lois, aged 5. They had two more children during marriage, Jonathan, aged 4, and Carina, aged 2.

Jackie recalls a generally happy, privileged childhood and upbringing, unlike Martin, whose family experienced a series of tragedies and ill-health, including the suicide of his sister at the age of 17, an event from which he never fully recovered, nor forgot. Their early education was similar, though Jackie left school at 16 and immediately started work in catering. Martin went on to further education, and completed training in hotel management. It would be a job that would necessitate a good bit of travel and frequent periods away from home, a fact that would have some bearing on their future marital life.

Isolation and dependency

After the birth of their first child, Kevin, Jackie became aware of developing problems in the relationship. Although supported by her own parents who lived nearby, there was a growing sense of isolation and dependency. She was totally dependent on Martin financially, and he exercised maximum control in the running of the home. Yet he wasn't there for much of the time.

Martin's controlling inclinations manifested themselves in a more significant way. Kevin was diagnosed asthmatic, and whereas Jackie was willing to research the subject and be guided by medical opinion, Martin could hardly accept the diagnosis, and was highly sceptical about what advice the doctors were offering. He shared Jackie's intense pride and love of the child, and, when he was there, was the typically hands-on father, immersed in most duties and play. But the differences in perception between him and Jackie about the child's condition and his needs, and about child rearing in general, remained.

The births of the three other children, perfectly healthy, were a joyous and welcome diversion for the couple. But it wasn't long before Jackie was recognizing something else in Martin's behaviour. It seemed to her that even though he doted on the children, he nevertheless seemed to lack empathy with them. He expected too much from them. He could not feel and perceive things as they did. This would sometimes provoke a harsher response than was necessary; not a physical harshness, but an impatience, an irritation, because the kids would not always be conforming to his wishes. Martin's confidence (and stubbornness) about what kids need and how they should be reared seemed to Jackie to be an extension of his confidence and control over all things financial. This rankled with her, accentuating her sense of an imbalance in the relationship.

A break for independence

Jackie returned to work, first part-time, then full-time. Martin didn't like this. Jackie's parents helped out with the child minding. Earning a wage confirmed just how much she had depended upon Martin, and how much she had resented it. Her work was in the catering trade, though unconnected with her husband's job. She was in daily contact with the public. Her circle of friends expanded considerably. She got involved in community work. She also got involved with another man. This was kept secret for a while, but it increasingly convinced Jackie that her marriage was in deep crisis and was not going to last.

She acknowledged to herself that Martin had enough resentment on his plate: he resented her job, her increasing independence, her rising status and integration in the community; her closeness to and her dominant influence over the four children; and all of this steadily weakening his control and influence within the family. He was drinking more on his short periods at home. He and Jackie were conversing less and less. How might he react, she wondered, on hearing that she was having an affair with another man?

The question provoked dread and determination in equal measure; and also, doubt. Jackie was reasonably certain that even if his reaction was verbally explosive, it might not actually be physically aggressive. He had never been violent to her or their children. But she was not at all certain about his emotional and psychological coping mechanisms. She was acutely aware of the shifting balance of power in their relationship, in her favour, and knew that he would instantly perceive this inevitable end of the marriage as a frightening prospect. He had chosen a career and a way of life which, while it provided a comfortable standard of living and status, it offered him neither roots nor structure. His marriage, his children and his family home were in every sense his main roots and structure. When he returned on each of those far-too-rare occasions, it was to his wife and children he was returning, not to the town or mates or to endless shindigs in a local. He had no real roots in this town other than his wife and children. His wife was born and reared in this region; her parents and family lived nearby. His family and roots were at the opposite end of the country.

The children

What about the children? Jackie was determined about that. They would be leaving with her. That's what they would want. That's what they would need. She had reared them virtually single-handedly. And she knew that this would be the greatest threat of all to Martin. She knew that it was primarily the thought of the children that still held some excitement and anticipation for him each time he drove back home (it was certainly not the prospect of returning to an increasingly busier and more independent Jackie). The possibility of losing his kids would be horrendous for him. And the prospect of Jackie leaving for another man, and taking the kids with her, and *his* kids being *looked after* by the person responsible for his world collapsing all round him ... this was just too much to contemplate. Yes, he would erupt. He may disintegrate. But he would fight. He would resist. They would both end up in court. She would in all probability, 'win'. But it would be a mess, a goddamn-awful mess, a protracted and bitter hate-filled, mess, and Martin would most likely be the biggest loser.

Facing only half of the reality

She decided not to tell him about the affair. But, three months before the tragedy, she did tell him that she wanted a divorce. As predicted, he erupted without violence. His tirade contained implicit threats that he would kill himself. She had not anticipated that. But she could sense the avalanche of thoughts and memories that were flooding over him, overwhelming him. If he did not realize it before, he could not escape from it now, the realization that his job, being away for very long periods and being home for only two or three days, had unquestionably contributed to the rot setting in. He must have recalled dozens of fleeting indicators of how the separation between them had begun – maybe it had begun years ago, and how it had accelerated in recent weeks and months. He would have recalled too, their increasing mutual avoidances, their silences, Jackie diverging confidently further and further along a path unfamiliar and threatening to him. Of course, that made him think the unthinkable: there must be another man involved. And however courageous Jackie was in telling him that she wanted a divorce, she could not bring herself to tell him about the affair. She denied any affair. That meant she would have to bear the burden of concealing not just the affair, but her true intent. Repeatedly, she might have to deny it. She was prepared to do so.

He was having none of this divorce business. They would make another go of it. He would give up his lucrative work that took him away for so long. He would get work nearby, less money and status, but greater opportunity to salvage the marriage. He talked and talked in this vein; he talked through her and over her and above her. He exhausted her. But all his efforts were futile. He didn't know the truth. He didn't know her true intent. He had little or no awareness of the parallel forces, the extent of decay in their relationship and the new dawn that his wife desperately aspired to, both hurtling them towards an irreparable separation, both raising infinitely more complex questions, dilemmas and fears in her mind, than in his.

A new start?

He did change job. He still wasn't able to be home every day and night – the nature of his work would not permit that, but it was a heck-of-a-lot better than two or three days a month. In the weeks ahead, he strove to make things better than they had ever been. But he remained preoccupied with the bombshell of his wife asking for a divorce. He felt a sense of 'making up' because of the much greater time he had now with the children. But he also felt that his children were even more wayward and demanding than during those ever-so-briefer periods in the past. He still loved them dearly. Now perhaps, he also loved them desperately.

As for Jackie, Martin instinctively knew her heart was not in this supposedly attempted 'reconciliation'. She made it obvious that she was not going to forgo new friends or the hard-won independence she had gained, nor the status and influence in their local community which she had acquired. On the contrary, his greatly increased presence in the home merely facilitated her deeper immersion in matters outside of the home. Martin himself had *not* changed. He had been wounded, humiliated and angered on hearing from his wife that she wanted a divorce, but it didn't provoke any great self-analysis as to how they had ever got to that point, nor how he might have contributed to it (apart from being away from home so long and his wife being left with four small kids). His attitudes and perceptions did not change, nor did it ever dawn on him that perhaps they might have to change. He thought the challenges his children posed for him were a consequence of the way his wife had reared them. He had little concept of child development.

And there was the basic matter of physical warmth, of sexual relationships; of how they felt merely in each other's presence. Jackie's affair was still very much alive, principally because it had been denied. Among her many burdensome reflections, she often regretted not telling Martin, but she could easily counter that with the realization that its continuance, and all the secrecy and the intrigue necessary for it to continue, somehow made life more bearable; it was a lifeline; it gave her hope. But she knew too, that it was dangerous. Between them, Jackie and Martin were now carrying enough baggage of fear, guilt, deceit and doubt, to guarantee that there would never be sexual fulfilment or satisfaction. There never would be a new start. It was that same baggage that would preclude them from seeking professional help, both of them too independent and too proud to share what they now perceived as their messed-up innermost lives with strangers.

Separation

The strain was too much. Jackie was going to tell Martin about her affair. No matter how he would react, even violently (which she knew was a possibility), telling him might be some kind of relief for her, the beginning of a release. Although he could not possibly perceive it as courageous and honest, she knew it was precisely that, and highly risky. But she was not going to tell him primarily because she suddenly felt the need to be honest and courageous; it was much simpler than that. The strain was just unbearable.

As the words dropped from her mouth and she struggled to look into his eyes, she realized that she was not just telling him about an affair, but also, about a sham. She could tell from the expression on his face that he too was not so much stricken by her affair with another man, of whom he knew nothing, but much more so by the sustained lies and betrayal of the woman, about whom, now, he believed, he knew everything. She had allowed him to delude himself that the marriage might actually be saved, but now she could see him awakening to that delusion, and she could see the hatred in his eyes.

He attacked instantly and viciously, the blows accompanied by the predictable litany of insults and curses. The words seared through her. She was physically and psychologically incapable of defending herself. She wasn't even capable of running away, rushing into the street and yelling for help. She did not know how or when her ordeal would stop. She was terrified, thinking it might never stop. But then she could see that it was over, and he ordered her to 'fuck off'... out of his sight, out of his mind, out of *his* home. She later wrote with self-mocking understatement that Martin had made: 'not an unreasonable request in the circumstances'.

She left the home in the early hours, without her three oldest children. Her youngest, 2-year-old Carina, was not there; she was safely tucked up in bed in the home of Jackie's parents. Carina often stayed with her adoring, indulgent grandparents, particularly at weekends.

Jackie felt bereft and scared. She felt her life was in tatters. She actually thought there was a possibility of losing all four children. If social workers believed half of what she had been called that night, she might indeed lose them.

She was instinctively an organized and competent individual, one who normally prepared well for the vicissitudes of life, for herself and for all her family. She would later dwell on the irony of single-handedly triggering a crisis of this magnitude, yet having made no preparation whatsoever.

The police

The violence had been heard within the neighbourhood. Someone contacted the police. They traced Jackie to another location and interviewed her. She told them everything. They weren't interested in 'affairs', only in the 'when' and the 'how' of the violence. They would interview Martin, and, though they didn't say so at the time, they gave every indication that they would prosecute.

Despite the trauma and the chaos of her mind, the vibes she was getting from the police officers intensified Jackie's predicament. She had been preoccupied by issues such as seeing the children again, divorce proceedings, money, where she was going to live temporarily, and so on, but the police involvement and their obvious intent alarmed her to the extent of near panic. She held herself responsible for what had happened. But what might happen now, she thought, when the police knocked on the door in the middle of the night, and interrogated him and arrested him? He would feel doubly betrayed. She imagined him going berserk with the police officers; maybe striking one of them; then being hauled off and locked up; prosecuted and humiliated, and all because of her, having an affair. How would he cope?

Weird as it felt, Jackie was empathising with Martin. She had turned his world inside out and upside down. He had been violent to her for the first time in his life, but at this moment in time, she wasn't thinking about that; she was thinking about his fragility, and of his implicit threats to kill himself. This led her on to thinking about his sister's suicide at 17. Was suicide a family trait, or was it a probable consequence of all that had happened in the last few hours, to be accelerated in the next 30 minutes by whatever the police might do?

She had made up her mind. She told the police that she did not want them to go after her husband. She did not want them to prosecute him.

It was a decisive stand, the first moment of the night when she felt she was regaining some control, determining events. But she wasn't really. The police made it clear that they were legally obliged to go after Martin. At the very least, they had to interview him.

She asked them not to, and they repeated they must. She begged them, telling them she thought it might tip him over the edge. She got more and more upset, thinking that they weren't taking her seriously, that they had their own legitimate work to do, and would do it regardless of what she thought and felt. She told them about the suicide of his sister, and how he had never really recovered from that. Could they not see the danger? She told them that she had inflicted enough hurt on him for one night; could they not just leave him to recover from that for a while, and see him later?

Are the children safe?

The older officer seemed to have been in this kind of situation many times before: a battered wife begging police not to bother. He probably thought to himself: it never works; they always end up getting called out again. He tried fobbing her off by saying that the final decision on prosecution would be taken by his seniors. Her pleas were so persistent, however, and her anxiety about the mental state of the man who attacked her so genuine, that he eventually told her he would ask his 'boss' not to pursue the case. He and his colleague had not yet visited the home. Jackie was relieved.

But the officer had something else on his mind. If, he asked Jackie, Martin was so 'fragile' and so 'vulnerable' as she made out, and if she seriously thought he might 'top it', what about the three children he was now in charge of? Did she think he might harm them? Did she think they were safe? She assured them that Martin would not 'lay a finger on his children'. The police later reported back to Jackie that their 'boss' had decided not to pursue the domestic violence incident.

The final deed

What happened in the next 48 hours was the subject of the usual protracted forensic investigations and the questioning of dozens of friends, work colleagues, neighbours and professionals. Yet no one knows the full story. What is known for certain is that Martin decided he was going to kill his children … by stabbing them; then he was going to do what many filicide fathers do: set the house on fire and kill himself, with the same knife. This was a 'plan' made in a hurry; in desperation; a messy, risky plan, in which anything might go wrong.

Within the debris of a house almost burnt to the ground, there was evidence that the children had not been killed in their sleep. Their three bodies were discovered in entirely different locations. There were strong indicators that they had been fleeing from their killer, and that the oldest child, Kevin, had succeeded in getting to his bedroom, where he futilely attempted to push his bed against the door. Martin had kicked the panelling of the door right through, an action which must have brought the child's fear, terror and panic to a climax. He was the last to be killed, because Martin then turned the knife on himself, and bled slowly to death as the fire which he had started spread rapidly.

What really *did* happen to the children?

In the weeks and months ahead Jackie would be consumed by 'not knowing' precisely what had happened to the children in the 48 hours before they were killed, and more specifically, how much suffering they had endured before they died. She wondered how many hours it took for her children to realize that she was gone, and how long before the youngest of them, Jonathan, in particular, became anxious as a consequence. Did Martin tell the two older children, Kevin and Lois, why she was gone? Did he attempt to explain it? He would have been hopeless explaining that at the best of times.

Was he able to conceal the fact, that, for him personally, it was the worst of times? Did he frighten them by shouting out angry and fiery judgements of her? Or did he say nothing to them, but rant and rave to himself, which would have been equally frightening to them? In his sense of betrayal and wrath, and in their pining and distress, could he have begun perceiving them not as the children he had always loved, but merely as an extension of the woman he despised?

Last words

Martin sent an email to Jackie before he died. It was full of anger and revenge. He wished her ill. She had destroyed everything precious to them. He hoped she could die painfully and slowly. But as she was alive, he was going to do something that *she* would live to regret for the rest of her life.

Social media comment

If Jackie thought that the tabloid press was grossly insensitive, nothing could have prepared her for the running commentary in social media. Everybody seemed to know her and what she was enduring. Much of the commentary was sincere and sympathetic. Some of it was cruel beyond belief. The would-be philosophers ('we are not in control ... life is unpredictable') and the would-be hell and brimstone moralists ('you reap what you sow ... it's God's will') were particularly oppressive (it would turn her off religion permanently). And there was a bizarre aspect of social media which she found incomprehensible and frightening: complete strangers were erecting internet memorial sites on behalf of her children. This was not merely an intrusion, but a 'virtual' takeover of her life. Later, she would discover that a company was attempting to use the deaths of her children in an internet promotions ad. She could at least challenge the company, which she did, but she could not halt anonymous persons saying whatever they wanted to say on the internet.

Police family liaison officers

The police family liaison officer was well aware of the sense of devastation and helplessness Jackie was experiencing. She was particularly adept at avoiding putting any more pressure on her. She prepared her well for, and to some extent protected her from, additional intrusion and excesses of the press. She was the perfectly unfazed sponge, soaking up all the tears and vitriol which Jackie helplessly, and frequently expressed (sometimes directed at the officer herself). But she could not fulfil Jackie's basic need of knowing precisely what happened and why. She fed her morsels of information about things that did not really matter, but she was as much in the dark as Jackie herself was on how her husband could bring about such a catastrophic end as a consequence of her affair. The officer left the scene at the end of her allocated time. Jackie's description of the impact of that departure was that she *'felt dropped!'*

Recovery

Despite that catastrophic end and all its ramifications, Jackie was not without friends. She had her parents close by, enduring as much suffering as she was, in the loss of their grandchildren in the most violent way. Simon, the man she was having the affair with, was the only one who could comprehend the depth of self-blame she felt, because he felt precisely the same. They needed each other more than ever.

The greatest source of solace and hope for Jackie, however, was Carina, her last remaining child. How did fate decree that Carina slept peacefully in her bed, in the safety of her adoring grandparents, while her siblings were subjected to unthinkable ends? It didn't matter now. Carina, and the joy and love she generated, would be the principal means by which Jackie would recover more quickly than she had ever anticipated.

Inquest

Surviving parents of filicide cases always dread inquests. These usually take place one or two years after the killings. There are often two opposing groups present. One side centres around the family of the surviving parent, and the other side centres around the family of the killer parent.

Jackie was directed to sit near Martin's mother, who had off-loaded much of her condemnatory views and feelings about Jackie to both local and national press. A male stranger sat between them, presumably a court employee ordered to sit there by the coroner. Obviously a precautionary move, but it served only to accentuate the risk of the hearing degenerating into a slanging match. Martin's mother was ordered out of the court because she insisted on questioning witnesses about the 'affair'.

When Jackie was later asked did she agree with the coroner's verdict (unlawful killings and suicide), she replied: 'Didn't make any difference to me – they were still dead.' This answer conveyed something of the detachment she felt on the day, a process that in reality had really nothing to do with her. The fate of her children, which is indelibly imprinted in her mind, was reduced to an autopsy report, presented with the usual cold, clinical detachment. The words 'pain' and 'suffering' were never uttered.

Retrospection

One of the last of the 80+ questions Jackie was asked, was this:

Presumably, you have dwelt long and hard on the question: how could X's killing of your children have been prevented? If that presumption is right, do you have an answer?

To which she replied with characteristic directness and honesty:

Yes, I should never have had an affair and just stuck to my guns about going through with a divorce.

Honest and sincere though this reply was, it does little to enlighten professionals involved in similar tragedies as to how they could respond in a way that actually minimizes the risk of that cataclysmic end. At first sight, the case does indeed seem to be one in which the opportunity for prevention seems non-existent. To prevent a catastrophe, it is helpful to be aware of its origins and of all the processes which are contributing to it. But precious few individuals knew anything of those processes. Martin was totally unaware of them, and Jackie determinedly chose not to share them with anyone other than the man with whom she was having the affair.

Neither predictable nor preventable?

It is now abundantly clear, however, that there *was* one big opportunity to prevent the catastrophe, and that lay in the hands of the police. The whole episode of police involvement was one that perplexed me considerably. Jackie provided additional copious and detailed notes of her recollections to help me understand. Ironically, the more she wrote, the more appreciative she was of the police answering her plea not to pursue Martin. She even went so far as to suggest a reason why:

> Why did they agree? I don't know. Maybe they could see that it was making me very anxious. Maybe the boss had been cheated on himself and thought the guy has been through enough. Don't know.

Knowing about procedures and adhering to procedures

The police response fell drastically short of what was required and what they were procedurally and professionally obliged to do. No matter how passionate and persistent Jackie was in pleading for them not to pursue that investigation, that is precisely what they should have done. Their fobbing her off with a promise to ask their 'boss' not to pursue prosecution was inexplicable. If a senior officer did indeed 'approve' or decide on this response, it was a serious lapse of judgement.

The police failure in respect of the children was much more serious. The training, experience and instincts of the officers led them (and they should be commended for this), to pursue the most important line of inquiry in their investigation, that is, what risk did Martin pose to the children? But that same training, experience and instinct should have instantly told them that the very last person they could depend upon for a rational, professional analysis of risk and for a judgement on whether or not the children were safe, was the frightened, traumatized, guilt-laden, homeless mother of these children, who had just suffered an attack by the very same person the officers were concerned about. It is not the first time professionals were fatally swayed by a wife's reassurances (Saunders, 2004). Of course Jackie knew Martin better than anyone else; and of course she was right: Martin loved his children, and would instinctively have attacked anyone who threatened to harm them ... that's the Martin she knew ... but what she did not know at that precise moment was the metamorphic consequences of events: the Martin she knew no longer existed.

Serious case review

In the serious case review, the police were severely criticized for a failure in not following domestic violence and child protection procedures, and for relying on assurances that the family would ensure that protection (the 'family' actually was a father whose world had just been shattered, rendering him a seething, hate-laden, desolate man capable of exacting a terrible revenge). While the police are not expected to do a quick psychological profile of suspected offenders, the mere sight and sound of Martin (if they had visited, questioned and arrested him) would surely have cast some doubt on his suitability at that particular moment to care for the children.

The review criticizes agencies for not being alert to the need for communication about potential risks in families, particularly in cases in which there is no current involvement by social services children's department. This undoubtedly applies to the police response that night. They should have instantly alerted social services when they learnt about the violent removal and separation of a mother from her three young children. Such action was all the more imperative when the police decided they were going to do nothing themselves.

Highly unusual in serious case reviews, the review panel concluded that if the police had adhered to the force's procedures (for the duration of their investigation and intervention), there might well have been a different outcome.

We will explore some of the lessons to be learnt from Jackie's experiences in Chapter 10.

10
A way forward

Introduction

This chapter considers the implications of the findings for the many different groups of professionals repeatedly referred to in previous chapters. It suggests a way forward in terms of knowledge, awareness, attitude and approach. Given the number and diversity of cases identified and the numerous categories to which they belong, it would be delusional to think one has a solution for ending the carnage of all filicide and familicide killings. The principal objective nevertheless is to formulate a professional and competent attitude and approach which will at least alert and better prepare professionals in cases that have the potential for such killings.

The chapter is going to concentrate on three predominant and related categories among the overall number of cases. In the first category, children are killed by one parent (more likely to be the father) in response to the revelation, announcement or conviction of an affair or new relationship, by the other. The motivation and driving force are predominantly revenge-retaliation, and the killing is premeditated and swiftly executed. In the second related category (more likely the parent is to be a mother), the revelation, announcement or conviction of or about an affair or new relationship triggers off a crisis of such magnitude within the parental partnership, that the offended party has a deteriorating mental health crisis that leads to her killing her child. There may or may not be an element of revenge-retaliation in such killings, but they are less likely to be an instant response to the revelation of third party involvement. In the third much broader category, which may be related to and/or include the other two, the perpetrator experiences a gradual and unmistakeable loss of power and control at the same time as the partner's independence and influence within family and/or community are increasing.

At the end of this final chapter, the knowledge base for frontline practitioners will be considerably extended far beyond essential statistics, and their understanding of the relational and situational dynamics in many filicide cases will be enhanced. These two advances are key to the ultimate objective of ensuring the right *attitude* and *approach*.

Common themes

Jackie's tragedy and the death of her children very much belongs to that category in Table 5.1 (pp. 74–83) of fathers who kill their children and then commit suicide. Although there was some ongoing involvement by specialists in the disability of the older child, there were no childcare workers involved in this case, no history of child abuse or neglect, poverty and deprivation, and no calls for help because a marriage was failing. That might lead one to think that the case has little to offer in terms of learning. But it is actually a highly relevant case, as its most prominent features are identical to those in so many of the other male perpetrator filicide cases included in this study. Those features include: a once stable marriage lasting well over five years; a family well integrated into the local community; good maternal and/or paternal grandparent support; mother more involved and influential in the care of the children; father traditionally exerting excessive control and power in the relationship and in the running of the home; mother steadily acquiring more status and influence within community; the involvement of a third party (disclosure of an affair, or pronouncement of a new relationship); one parent seeking separation and divorce; domestic violence; inadequate police response.

Given this level of similarity, many of the lessons learnt in Jackie's story should be transferable to a substantial number of other cases. Here is one, the main difference being that the perpetrator of the killing was the mother. The information which follows is based upon the overview of the SCR report, inquest proceedings and reported witness statements in both inquest and trial. As with Jackie's case, this one too, is heavily anonymized, and material facts have been altered.

Baby Colin

Alan and Caroline had met in their teens. They were married in their late twenties, and had their first child a few years later. They had a beautiful home, and both had secure well-paid jobs. Their families lived nearby, and were a constant source of support and social life. They were both well integrated in the wider community, and both had leisure interests and pursuits. Baby Colin was planned and much celebrated.

When Colin was three months old, and Caroline still on maternity leave, Alan told her that he had been in a relationship with one of her closest friends, who was six months pregnant with his child. Caroline disintegrated, physically, emotionally and psychologically. She was utterly uncontrollable. She attacked him in as much as her slender body would allow, and he hurt her repeatedly in defending himself. She launched at various items in the home, smashing them. She subjected Alan to a tirade of abuse, and never stopped even when she was gathering her belongings together in a case. She went to Colin's room and took him from the cot. She left the house with suitcase and baby.

It was late at night. Caroline drove anywhere and nowhere. A few hours later, she drove back home, and found the door locked. She had received numerous texts from Alan, saying 'goodbye'. She thought the worst. She went to a neighbour and asked them to help. The police arrived. They forced an entry, and found Alan drunk and a near-overpowering smell of cannabis in the air. Paramedics were called, and Alan quickly recovered. He apologized to everyone. The police and paramedics conferred and agreed that Alan was not a risk to himself. They barely looked at the baby, who was still outside sleeping in the car, with Caroline, and another relative. Caroline disclosed to the police the revelation of her husband's affair which had triggered the incident. No formal assessments were done either in respect of mother, father or child, but a police officer did regard Alan as a 'vulnerable' adult and duly ticked the box on the relevant form. The police and paramedics left.

Some time later, the police Domestic Abuse Unit was contacted with a request to make a risk assessment in respect of mother. The police child abuse investigative unit referred the case by email to the Social Services Children's Dept., but marked the referral: 'For information only'. They provided a detailed account of the incident, concluding there was no further role for the police. The duty manager in social services came to the same conclusion: they had no role to play. The referral was closed. Crucially significant as a subsequent inquiry would reveal, neither police nor social services referred the case to the agency most appropriate to assessing the welfare of a 3-month-old child, the health visiting services.

During the following week, Caroline's distress and unhappiness increased significantly. Her hyper-anxiety led to numerous panic attacks, during one of which, she left Colin alone for a considerable period. She went to her GP in desperation. She had had persistent rows with Alan since the revelation of his affair. She walked out a number of times. During one of the rows, he violently attacked her, leaving bruises on her face and arms and legs. The police were called again, but when they arrived they learnt that she had gone to her mother's home, with the baby. No further action was taken. Caroline's GP referred her to a counsellor.

The police were called out a third time, to the home of Caroline's mother. Alan was there, returning Colin after having been caring for him. A serious row developed. The police found Alan very confrontational. No arrest was made. They reported back to their seniors who decided on no further action. This incident coincided with the imminent birth of the child whom Alan had fathered with Caroline's friend. He attended the birth.

At her first appointment with a therapist, Caroline gave more information about Alan's violence towards her. The therapist told her that this information would have to be referred onto social services. Caroline did not want this to happen, but eventually relented. A social worker made telephone contact with her, and offered advice and a booklet. Caroline told the social worker that she did not want help from social services at this time. The social worker accepted this but warned Caroline that further incidents like those which had occurred could necessitate social services taking action to protect Colin. The referral was then closed.

Friends and relatives reported that Caroline became more anxious and erratic. She was resorting to more and more cannabis use. She was seen curling herself up in the foetal position. She would admit that she no longer could manage Colin. She expressed thoughts about self-harm, talking about the appeal of death.

A few weeks later, Alan discovered Colin dead, and Caroline standing over him, slashing herself with a razor. She had smothered Colin. She was hospitalized, charged with murder, pleaded guilty to infanticide, and was given an indefinite sentence.

The SCR on this tragedy was highly critical of the shortcomings of agency responses (Leicester Safeguarding Children Board, 2012). One of its conclusions was that though Colin's death was not predictable, it was preventable. It pinpoints many key moments when the right attitude and approach might have made that difference. The social services responses in particular, to two separate referrals about a domestic incident and domestic violence in a home in which a 3-month-old child lived, were grievously amiss.

Restoring the status of 'attitude'

In the vast majority of the 128 cases looked at in this text, it is obvious that too many professionals have adopted the wrong attitude and approach. The word 'attitude' has lost much of its original meaning in modern-day usage. Its Latin, French and Spanish heritage linked it very closely to *aptitude*. It basically meant *fitness* and *disposition*. Before saying anything more about the case of baby Colin, it is necessary to very briefly explore this concept further, with the help of a bereaved grandfather from another one of our cases.

Aban, aged 3, and Farrar, aged 2, were asphyxiated by their father, who also killed their mother before hanging himself. The mother had been the subject of intermittent social services involvement since early childhood; she had been in care since the age of 7, due to marital conflict and eventual separation of her own parents. When she gave birth to her own children, she remained a concern. She had three children to two partners. She was subjected to domestic violence in both relationships. On one occasion her head had been smashed against a headboard; on another occasion, petrol had been poured over her and a threat made to set her alight. The police were repeatedly involved, not just because of domestic violence but also because of allegations of criminal activity on the part of both parents. An IPCC report on police responses criticized the officers for not consistently adhering to the force's procedures on domestic violence. The serious case review on this tragedy criticized the social services' failures and incompetence over many years. Once again, the recurring theme was lack of assessment and planning in a family situation that was continually demonstrating a high degree of risk. The attitude and approach of the workers clearly demonstrated that they were unaware of the risks.

Three years after the tragedy, the maternal grandfather gave a lengthy interview on national radio (BBC 4, 2012). He criticized those involved, but he had a more charitable recommendation for the future than perhaps listeners may have anticipated: in order that tragedies like that never occurred again, he said, he wanted a picture of his grandchildren on every social worker's desk. He reckoned that the constant memory of what his grandchildren endured would ensure that workers would have the right attitude and approach to similar cases in the future.

Attitude and approach based on awareness

He may be right, though I suspect that if pressed, this well-intentioned grandfather might concede that photographs of children who were murdered by their parents may not have a lasting effect. But the essence of his message is sound: frontline professionals need something more than experience, knowledge, skills and departmental procedures; they need some kind of trigger that immediately alerts them to the mere possibility that the case or the incident they are exploring has the potential for quickly degenerating into something far worse than the original referral suggests. That will help generate the appropriate attitude and approach.

In the previous chapter, it was seen that police involvement in Jackie's case provided the only opportunity for a different outcome, which might have come about had they (i) arrested and removed the man who seriously assaulted his wife, and (ii) immediately summoned Children's Services through a social services emergency duty team. In the case of baby Colin, numerous opportunities to avoid the eventual outcome were missed; the most important of these were: (i) the mother was not seen when two separate referrals detailing the gravity of the situation were made to social services; (ii) health visiting services, the key agency in the welfare of a 3-month-old baby, were not informed, either initially, or thereafter, about these referrals (the failure to engage health visitors is a common error identified in previous analyses of SCRs) (Ofsted, 2008).

There are two features of both of these cases which figure prominently in filicide killings. One has already been discussed at length: domestic violence. Frontline workers need to know of the high incidence of domestic violence in filicide cases. But the second common feature is in some respects, more significant. When the professionals (and there were a good many in the baby Colin case) learnt that the crisis they were called upon to deal with had been triggered by the revelation of an affair, alarm bells should have been ringing. In this study more children have died, and many of them have suffered shockingly brutal deaths as a direct consequence of one of the following: (i) one parent has told the other that he or she is in a relationship with a third party; (ii) one parent has left the other, revealing that he or she has struck up a new relationship with someone else; (iii) a father has discovered that his partner is having an affair with another; (iv) a mother has discovered that her partner is having an affair with another. Less common but no less explosive in its consequences, (v) a mother has revealed to her husband that she is pregnant with another man's child; (vi) a father has revealed to his wife that another woman is pregnant with his child. The case of Jackie and the case of baby Colin are only two such cases. Although one cannot say (though Jackie will do so) that child A died solely because parent B had an affair, the process and patterning of events are so repetitive and consistent that we must at least acknowledge the potentially dangerous and destructive impact that the revelation of an affair, or of a new relationship, or, even the suspicion of either, can have on *both* parents and children, Here are a number of cases where that potential was realized:

1. James, 11, and David, 3, were strangled by the father who then hanged himself, soon after his former wife announced her new relationship on Facebook.
2. Tansila, 6, was bludgeoned to death and Amina, 5, was strangled, by their mother. She had heard that her estranged husband had returned to their country of origin, to remarry.
3. Aniela, 5, and Kajetan, 1½, were stabbed to death by their father unable to cope with marital breakdown and the discovery of his wife's relationship with another man.

4. Havelock, 3, and Eugenia, 2, were asphyxiated by their mother. She placed their bodies in a hold-all and delivered them to the home of her estranged husband. She had seen intimate emails between him and another woman.

Two cases of special interest in relation to affairs are almost identical. A 'fourth' party became involved in each case.

1. The father of Desmond, 6, and Caroline, 5, was in an extra-marital relationship. The mother found out. She 'retaliated' by starting up a relationship with another man, and letting her husband know. The marriage degenerated into constant rows and mutual recriminations. The mother told a friend in the presence of her husband that her sexual liaison with the fourth party was more pleasurable than with him. That same night he bludgeoned her to death and killed himself and the two children through carbon monoxide poisoning.
2. The father of Harry, 3, and Charles, 1½, had more than one affair. When his wife found out, she 'retaliated' by starting up a relationship with another man. She later told her husband that she was leaving and taking the children with her. He attacked her with a hammer, and after killing her, attacked Harry and Charles. Two other children escaped, though one of them was seriously injured. The marriage had been characterized by extreme violence in which the mother had been attacked many times, even when pregnant.

Possible reasons for workers' reluctance to consider the impact of affairs

Another 38 children in 23 other cases were killed in similar situations. There may well be many more, in which the involvement of a third party and a possible revenge-retaliation motivation has been concealed. Seventeen of the 23 cases were known to more than one agency, including police, Children and Family Court Advisory Service (CAFCASS), mental health services, health visitor, GP, school nursing services, psychotherapy, court welfare and social services. At least 16 of the cases were known to the police because of domestic violence; there were probably more: like clandestine relationships, domestic violence can also be hidden from public view.

Despite the number of killings, and the near identical circumstances relating to the relationship break-up of the parents, professionals still seem largely unaware of the risks. There may be perfectly understandable reasons for that:

- The omission of this subject matter (that is: the heightened risk to children resulting from the impact of affairs on relationships) in filicide literature and in child abuse literature and training.
- Instinctive reluctance. Just like the police in Jackie's case, some professionals may not want to hear about an 'affair' or 'betrayal', or 'treachery' or about any other similar potentially explosive perception of events from the offended party. They may think it's too 'messy', 'awkward', 'embarrassing', but most of all, a very private matter.
- Domestic violence, a common feature in filicide cases, is challenging enough without having to consider the affair which may have provoked it, or the potential killing of children caught up in it. Professionals are often consumed by the crisis of the moment: the passions, the threats, the mutual recriminations, the walkouts, and not least, by the task of ensuring the adult victim is not subjected to another attack.
- Too many other ongoing and long-term challenges. In some cases, couples may be in a permanent semi-crisis state, with issues such as poverty, deprivation, racism, criminal activity, and so on, to contend with. These are the issues which have always, and still do, preoccupy the worker, who may perceive the new crisis of third party involvement as merely an extension of the chaos of the family's life, having little implications for the welfare of the children.
- Professionals themselves may have personal experience of affairs. They may feel exceedingly uncomfortable (and not a little hypocritical) exploring other people's affairs and their impact on relationships. In such circumstances, they may reflect the wider societal unease in dealing with revenge filicide killings triggered by affairs.

Priorities

There may well be more reasons underlying the wrong attitude and approach. This necessitates an honest and rigorous self-exploration.

Professionals can seek out what the reasons are, and, crucially, explore how any such reason may impact adversely upon their work. Their own awkwardness, discomfort, embarrassment, hang-ups or whatever should be discarded or suppressed. The priorities are as always those pertaining to the welfare of the child. On learning that a couple's relationship has erupted in crisis because of the revelation of an affair, a professional from any agency who may become involved in the case should consider the mere possibility that the children's lives are in real danger. The source of that possibility, namely, the injured party, should be seen, interviewed, and assessed. This is a formidable challenge for any worker (including, as we saw in Chapters 8 and 9, police officers). But what is the alternative? To avoid them? To let them stew in their own sense of betrayal, hatred and revenge, while they care for their children? Often there is added urgency to the task of seeing and assessing. In so many cases in this study, and in filicide studies in general, the 'betrayed' parent has reacted to the betrayal by actually threatening to kill, or implying that they might kill, or, saying words to the effect (as Jackie's husband did) that they will do something the other parent will regret for the rest of their lives. These threats, irrespective of whether or not they are genuine, make it imperative to see and to assess. The fact that the overwhelming majority of marital breakdowns triggered by affairs do not end up with a filicide killing, is hardly a good reason for not considering the possibility that such threats may be carried out.

Management replicating frontline staff

Professionals' reticence and awkwardness about affairs, and their failure to see how affairs may heighten risk to some children, are often replicated by management. Many managers are involved in the SCRs which follow. SCRs on children who have been killed by one parent following the revelation of an affair by another, often pay scant regard to such 'scandalous' events. The principal underlying factor in the killing though it may be, an affair is somehow regarded as 'off-limits' in the compilation of many agencies' contribution to the SCR process.

One can understand managerial sensibilities on this matter, just as one can understand the same in their frontline staff. But the same conclusion then has to be drawn about both levels of the organization: this is an institutional failure to link affairs, when professionals find out about them, with increased risk to *the welfare of the child* and a failure to explore this linkage in depth in cases to which it applies. Everyone central to the killing of each of the 50 children in total in the 29 cases referred to earlier knew about the impact of the affair. Many of the perpetrators spelt it out in their suicide notes and recorded messages. For the majority of them, revenge was both the motive and the driving force.

Shifting balance of power, control and influence

The murderous response to the revelation of an affair, which so many of the parents in this study have demonstrated, may not be the whole story. There may well be a wider context in which relationships have already been deteriorating for some time. This brings us to the third clearly identifiable category of filicide killings: those in which a significant shift in the balance of power takes place over a period of time. In these cases, we are likely to see one partner gaining power or control or influence, and the other partner losing it. Or we may see a partner losing it as a consequence of external factors having nothing to do with the relationship. But what is this power, control and influence?

- Power, control and influence over one's partner. This is so predominantly a male feature in the beginning of relationships in filicide and familicide cases. It may take a long time for the woman to acquire the confidence, status, financial independence, and so on, to challenge it. She may not actually challenge it directly, but, over time, achieve a slow, gradual and subtle loosening of the bonds, well advanced and irrevocable by the time a male partner realizes it.
- Power, control and influence in relation to the children. Once the dominant partner, a father may not only see, but also hear and feel his influence over his children rapidly dissipating in the throes of marital breakdown, losing custody, being granted limited access, and worst of all, his children rapidly developing intellectually, socially and emotionally, and having the confidence to tell him that they prefer to stay with their mother.
- Power, control and influence dependent upon material wealth and social status. Unemployment, bankruptcy, overburdening

debts, repossession of homes, and so on, can have a devastating effect in reducing one's ability to control events and influence family members. Fathers are more likely to experience this kind of loss, and to be more adversely affected by it.
- Power, control and influence dependent upon good physical and mental health. Debilitating illnesses, mental and physical, can reduce a parent's power, control and influence in many aspects of marital and family life. The onset of mental illness in particular can have a devastating effect on whatever influence that parent has been exerting, in running the home, rearing the children, and maintaining the family's status within the community.
- Returning to the first and second category of cases already discussed, the power, control and influence instantly lost in the revelation that one's partner is having an affair, or about to leave and start up a partnership with someone else. This may be perceived and felt as the ultimate loss of power and control.

Case examples of filicide perpetrators losing power, control and influence

The loss of power, control and influence is the predominant feature in the following examples.

1. The parents of Elisa, 3, and Eleanor, 14 months, separated after months of fierce rows, threats and domestic incidents requiring police visits. The mother took the initiative in getting the father to leave. He stayed in a caravan in a field close to his work. He became increasingly isolated and estranged. He made threats to kill himself. He dreaded the prospect of mother getting custody. His performance at work suffered. He walked out of his job. His contacts with others became more fraught. His wife allowed him to have the children one weekend, thinking it might help him. He smothered them and hung himself.
2. The mother of Nicola, 4, a child mildly disabled, drowned her in a bath. She perceived the child's mild disability as a major handicap, a perception that was not shared by her husband, nor family members, nor by professionals who offered good support services. Long before the killing, the relationship between the parents was deteriorating. The mother was still subject to mental health crises

which she had first experienced as a teenager. Hospitalizations seriously jeopardized her well-paid job. She began drinking heavily, and became alcohol-dependent. The state of the marriage worsened. The father eventually ordered her out of the marital home.
3. The father of Angela, 12, and Stan, 5, stabbed them, their mother and their uncle over 300 times. The mother was in employment. He was not. She was well supported by her family who lived locally. He was not. She was totally integrated into the community, well known and liked among parents at the children's schools and her work colleagues. He was not. She told him the relationship was finished, numerous times. He didn't and couldn't accept that. He suspected she was having an affair with his best friend, and planned to kill him. His mental health was deteriorating. His use of cannabis was increasing. The judge acknowledged his depression during his trial, but agreed with a psychiatrist who testified that he was in control of his actions during the killings. He was sentenced to a minimum of 35 years.
4. The mother of Ewen, 6-months-old, had a history of drug and alcohol abuse, mental illness, a victim of domestic violence, committing serious crime, and self-harming. She had three children from previous relationships removed by social services, because of neglect. But, now, prospects looked a bit better. She had met a man older than herself. He had been previously married. He seemed more mature, more experienced, and he was not on drugs. The perception of some of the professionals who had worked with the mother was that he may be a positive and controlling influence on her. He turned out to be excessively controlling. In baby care, running the home, and in managing the finances, his controlling tendencies were becoming oppressive. She had initially accepted them, but then resented and began to resist them. That would sometimes provoke an attack. There were many domestic violence incidents, even during the pregnancy. They continued after Ewen was born. The police were often called. She eventually told her partner to leave. He threatened suicide if he had to leave. He once simulated the act of hanging himself as if to drive home the point. She finally got him removed and obtained a Non-molestation Order against him. On the first occasion he had access, he drowned Ewen in his bath, laid him out on the bed surrounded by flowers and toys, and then hanged himself.

A metaphor denoting the shifting balance of power, control and influence

At least another 23 cases in which 35 children were killed, reveal similar imbalances of power. One of those cases was that of 5-year-old Gillian, which was the first case to be examined in detail in Chapter 1. I now want to look in more detail at the very last case in this final chapter, that of Ewen, aged 6 months.

Ewen's mother's earlier life was, predominantly, one of abuse and self-destruction, misery and brutality. Her experience therefore, of another failed, physically and psychologically abusive relationship preceding the murder of her baby must have seemed as though the whole pattern of her earlier life was being re-enacted. Yet somehow, she was emboldened not just to resist what had become a stifling, controlling influence, but to enlist the authority's help in getting rid of it. Such resistance contributed to a growing crisis for her partner, a crisis that would drive him to an action more destructive than anything she had ever witnessed or experienced in her own miserable life.

The case raises crucial questions about agency involvement, to which I will return, but at this point I merely want to emphasize that it is a case which classically represents the dramatic change of fortune which may befall a filicide perpetrator, drastically altering the balance of power in a relationship, and dwindling to zero the level of power, or control, or influence they once exerted. It is hugely ironical that in looking at this case from the outset, there seems already to be a massive imbalance of power. The upbringing and misfortune of the mother are such that one can easily see her initially agreeing to her new partner assuming maximum control. This imbalance of power, however, will not only shift, but will be turned on its head, as the mother herself informed me in a most unexpected but convincing way. During one of three separate meetings which I had with her, in the company of her solicitor, I asked her a series of questions revolving around this balance of power theme. She thought carefully about these questions, and at one point, stretched over, asking could she borrow a pen and some paper. I saw her drawing what appeared to be two ladders, upright and parallel. Then she said, pointing to the sketch throughout her reply:

> All that stuff changed. The only way I can describe it is that when we met, it was like he was at the top of the ladder and I was at

the bottom. As we got going, and we understood more about each other, I realized that he was coming down the ladder, and I was going up. His position was getting worse; mine was getting better. He was doing more gambling too. At the end of the day I have to say that I was in the stronger position. And I had the baby.

It was a rather impressive metaphor from an unlikely source, and it gave some insight (with no small amount of empathy) into the mind of her partner.

Agency involvement

The SCR of the death of Ewen tells us nothing about this dynamic between the parents, simply because its authors and those who contributed to it knew nothing about it (Lancashire Safeguarding Children's Board, 2012). This is not being unkind to the authors; they actually allude to this omission numerous times:

> This case indicated a pattern whereby assessment of parental relationships is inadequate.
>
> (p. 21)

It asks the authority rather pointedly:

> Is the LSCB [Local Safeguarding Children Board] aware of the degree to which professionals are prepared for understanding the nature of the relationships of parents they are working with ...?
>
> (p. 22)

Incredulity in the guise of a conundrum

As one would expect, given the history of this case, many professionals were involved, over 30 according to the SCR. They included social workers, family support workers, health visitors, drug and alcohol addiction workers, psychiatrists, a specialist drug addiction midwife, the GP, the police and probation officers. This formidable array of professionals is referred to as the Case Group. The review avoids criticism of the professionals and their practice and decision-making by the rather unusual method of presenting various 'conundrums'. But these 'conundrums' are in effect, if not in intent, the expression of incredulity. For example, the first conundrum asks how was it considered possible that Ewen's parents would, in the light of the mother's background in particular, be able to meet the needs of a new baby? She had a lifelong addiction problem, and a heroin addiction four months into the pregnancy; she had serious mental health problems, a history of self-harm and convictions for criminal activity, and she'd lost three children to social services through neglect. The review panel could not understand that, given those kinds of antecedents, there was no multi-agency pre-birth meeting to assess the risks, nor a Section 47 child protection inquiry.

Who's scrutinizing the potential killer?

So, what was the Case Group, the 30-plus different professionals involved in the case, doing? The review repeatedly refers to their 'unfounded optimism' as the incidents of real concern mounted during and after the pregnancy. Such optimism, it declares, made child-focused decision-making unlikely.

Where precisely, or on whom, was the focus of this massive professional effort? The review makes it abundantly clear that it wasn't on the man who was about to kill Ewen. It is highly critical of how this man escaped the child protective radar of umpteen agencies and professionals, and was 'barely included within the focus of the core assessment undertaken before the birth' (p. 20). This was despite the fact that one or two individual workers, to their credit, had misgivings about his 'bossiness' and his controlling tendencies, which they thought might eventually trigger off a reaction in the mother. Such intuition and insight were not sufficiently asserted, and were swallowed up in the cascade of optimism enveloping the 'core assessment' process. Indeed, testing out the workers' intuitive instincts was judged by some managers to risk 'destabilising mother's recovery' (p. 20).

The review declares that no assessment of any kind took place, on how the couple related, or on how, collectively, they would care for the baby. Whereas the mother was being seen virtually on a daily basis, neither father, nor the couple together, were seen other than fleetingly, and never seen for the purpose of in-depth assessment. This is all the more incredulous when one considers that the father was making formal and informal complaints about the mother's child-caring, and was, according to the mother, subjecting her to violent attacks which she initially reported, and was threatening to kill both her and himself should they part. On the matter of domestic violence, the review asserts:

> There was never an assessment or analysis of the dynamics of the domestic abuse, who was a perpetrator, who was being consistently harmed and what power and control dynamic was being played out. This meant that no one understood what was happening, and therefore what would help to make it stop. Without this understanding, the reassurances from parents were meaningless.
> (p. 28)

The Case Group, to its credit, admits that: 'although they were aware of the importance of domestic abuse, they did not always feel confident to assess it or address it effectively' (p. 28). In an era of nearly one million incidents of domestic violence each year, and a decade-long crusade at every level of local and national government to combat it, their admission is alarming.

The perennial challenge of engaging men

The review spends more critical time on one particular issue than on any other: the failure of the professionals to engage the man central to the case: the father. It highlights 'the danger of incorporating only a one-dimensional interpretation of the role of the father' (p. 21). It acknowledges how difficult it is for many workers to engage men, and says they should have the maximum support from their agencies in dealing with fathers, 'particularly those who are known to have been violent, or appear frightening' (p. 21).

This endemic tendency to avoid men is repeatedly exposed in all the child abuse inquiries preceding serious case reviews, particularly in the Tyra Henry, Kimberley Carlile and Jasmine Beckford Reports (London Borough of Lambeth, 1987; London Borough of Greenwich, 1987; London Borough of Brent, 1985); also, in child abuse literature (Farmer and Owen, 1995; Haskett,*et al.*, 1996; Hegarty, 1994; Milner, 1993; O'Hagan, 1997, 1993; O'Hagan and Dillenburger, 1995), and in serious case reviews.

In Ofsted's (2008) report on 50 SCRs, it highlights the lack of assessment of fathers generally, and gives examples of where 'there is no contribution to the SCR by the child's father ...' and where there was 'a failure to report the involvement of mental health services with father' (p. 15). Brandon *et al.*'s (2009) biennial analysis of SCRs commented: 'Information about men was very often missing' (p. 1) In a more recent analysis of 147 SCRs which took place 2009–10, Ofsted (2010) concluded: 'Many of the SCRs commented on the lack of attention to the role of fathers and what was known about them' (p. 20).

The knowledge base

Whatever the shortcomings of professionals in known filicide cases, it should always be acknowledged and stressed that they have no responsibility whatsoever for either the perpetrator's motivation or the killing. But they and their managers and trainers do have overriding ethical, statutory and professional obligations nonetheless. The first of these is an adequate knowledge base giving them a half-decent chance to respond more effectively than has been demonstrated throughout this chapter. For all professionals working in one of the many agencies designated under S. 11 of the Children Act 2004 with the task of *safeguarding and promoting the welfare of children*, there are five basic pillars of knowledge and understanding about filicide killings emanating from this and previous chapters. Each of them necessitates a good deal of study. We shall conclude the chapter by providing a synopsis of each.

1. Knowledge about filicide killings in the context of marital, separation and divorce proceedings. This includes relevant statistics (numbers of children killed, ages, methods of killings, and so on) and predominant features (disintegrating relationships, domestic violence, and disputes about custody and access). A thorough knowledge is required of two or three specific cases of filicide provided in recent SCRs (for example, Leicester Safeguarding Children Board, 2012; Warwickshire Safeguarding Children Board, 2012).
2. Within that very broad category of filicide, professionals need to know of a prominent sub-category of cases in which third party involvement has come to light. The evidence from this study suggests that the risk to children may be significantly heightened when their parents' marriage or partnership erupts in crisis largely because of a clandestine third party involvement.

3. Awareness of the reasons why the revelation about an affair can trigger a process in which a failing relationship degenerates to a level of hatred, revenge and murderous intent. Whether man or woman, this revelation may be perceived as an attack upon the emotional and psychological self, upon every conceivable aspect of one's identity, one's pride and confidence, sexuality and parenthood, one's social status. It may render some parents utterly devastated, humiliated, and exceedingly dangerous.
4. Many cases of filicide reveal a dramatic shift in the balance of power, control and influence between parents. There are often numerous manifestations of this development, both visible and audible. If it is generating strife within the relationship, and rendering the 'losing' parent increasingly helpless and unhappy, the question as to how it is impacting upon the children's welfare and safety should arise. If in the wider context of family life in general, it is coinciding with known features of pre-filicide killings, such as bitter rows, repetitive domestic violence or deteriorating mental health, then the risk to the children may be increased well beyond the threshold necessitating statutory protective action.
5. The avoidance of men is endemic in childcare and child protection work. The knowledge base that can make a difference to this appalling situation begins not with managers or trainers or organizations. It can only begin with rigorous self-exploration by workers. They are more likely than anyone else to know the reasons why they personally avoid or marginalize men in their daily work. Is it the culture of their agency, an ingrained attitude and approach that have never seriously contemplated the role men might play in the lives and welfare of children? Is it fear, an anticipation of loud, foul-mouthed, threatening, aggressive behaviour from men known to behave precisely like that? Is it a conviction that men who treat women abominably don't actually deserve to be involved? Is it because men themselves are seldom about, and the professional doesn't think it's their job to track them down, and encourage them to participate? It is up to professionals themselves to identify the problem. Only then can they and their supervisors, trainers and managers, collectively, attempt to do something about it. Historically, avoiding men has proved to be counter-productive in child protection work generally. In many cases of filicide, it has proved disastrous.

Summary

When a parental relationship erupts in crisis because of an affair, the risk of children being harmed may increase. But many child protection workers may not be aware of that. The danger of such situations has never been a focus of interest in child protection literature and training. Even filicide literature and research has not yet considered this prominent category of killings.

There may be additional reasons for professionals not feeling comfortable and confident about involvement when parental relationships erupt because of an affair. They may regard it as too messy, awkward and embarrassing, far too intimate and private a matter for outsiders to be inquiring about. If the family is one in which agencies have been involved for a long time because of repetitive crises, professionals may see the affair and the passions it has unleashed as little more than an extension of the chaos which is a prominent feature of that family's life.

A shifting balance of power, control and influence between parents is another feature of many of the filicide cases in this study. Losing control and influence over one's partner, or one's children, or the running of the home, can prove intolerable for many. If this coincides with sudden unemployment or bankruptcy, it may heighten risk to the children. If it coincides with or is a direct consequence of a deteriorating or recurring mental illness, that may heighten the risk to children even more.

In one of the sample cases in which this shift in the balance of power occurred preceding the murder of a 6-month-old baby, the professional response verged on the incredulous. Over 30 professionals concentrated their efforts on the mother. The father, who committed the murder, was largely ignored. The avoidance or marginalization of men has been an endemic problem in child protection, exposed repeatedly in child abuse inquiry reports, SCRs and childcare and child protection literature. The 'practice' may be culturally embedded, habitual and instinctive. Any solution can only be based on professionals themselves rigorously self-exploring and identifying the reasons why, for them personally, it is so challenging to routinely engage men effectively. Reversing the practice will have a dramatic effect on the quality of assessment, and in determining the degree of risk to which children are exposed.

Postscript

I was glad to see the end of 2012. I would no longer be adding to the files of 128 filicide killings already accumulated. There would be no more additional inquests and trials to attend. I did actually attend an inquest in Spring, 2013, and I'm due to attend another. But these obligations stem from filicide killings which occurred in 2011 and 2012. The point I'm making is that in December, 2012, the end of this project was in sight. There were many times during the previous two years when I thought it would have to end prematurely. Whatever lessons there are in the contents of this book, there is another overriding personal lesson for me: how this project impacted upon me emotionally and psychologically. In 40 years of writing books and articles on child abuse and child protection, there has never been anything like that impact. Let me assure the reader at the outset, however, that this postscript is about the book's contents, and not about me!

But the killings continue:

2013

- *January*: a mother is charged with murdering her 2-year-old.
- *March*: a mother throws herself and her 3-year-old in front of a train.
- *April* (in one week): (1) a mother kills her three children and throws herself from a tower block; (2) a father kills his partner and 6-year-old son; and (3) a mother apparently poisons herself and her two children.

- *May*: (1) a mother disappears after the body of her 2-year-old son is found; police open a murder inquiry; and (2) in France, a British father, having his first access with his children, kills them by slitting their throats.
- *June*: a father is charged with the murder of his partner and baby son.
- *July*: (1) a father is charged with the sudden murder of his 11-year-old daughter, he apparently then made a suicide attempt; (2) a mother is seen throwing herself and her 5-year-old child from a cliff to their deaths below. Police discover her 2-year-old dead son in the home.

These tragedies occurred within a period of six months. It is a killing rate that should alarm us. By the time this book is published, it is highly likely that a good many more children and their parents will have been killed in the remainder of 2013. There were six such cases in the whole of 2012. In the first two years covered by this study, 1994–95, there were 11 filicide and familicide cases combined; in the last two years of the study, 2011–12, there were 19.

The majority, if not all of these ten 2013 cases, in which 15 children and two mothers were killed, and three mothers committed suicide, are very much in the context of marital difficulties, or separation or custody and access disputes; and mental illness appears to have played a part in some of them. One cannot help wondering how many of these types of killings would it take to cause a public outcry? Or, how many more might provoke a government response?

What is it about filicide killings that provokes a litany of platitudes about family tragedy coupled with a near-paralysis on what to do about them? The contrast with the response to a single child murdered by someone outside the family could not be starker. In the recent case of April Jones, abducted and murdered by Mark Bridger, the police were overwhelmed by volunteers descending from every part of the UK onto a little Welsh village, willing to undergo any privation in the dark days of October, in order to find the child.

In contrast, people want to bury their heads, or block their ears, or run away, when they hear of a brutal filicide killing. Even if I'd given actual names, few members of the public would have recognized a single one of the 224 child victims mentioned in this text. The authorities contribute to this amnesia. There is little said until a post-mortem is carried out; then a great big block of silence, which can be up to two years long, until an inquest or a trial is held. The redacted, anonymized serious case review is published, by which time, few outside of the family can remember the case.

Anyone willing to step into the breach of silence is made welcome by the various media outlets. Plenty do so. A public traumatized and baffled by the brutality of many filicide killings willingly digest in private whatever 'expert' explanation is put in front of them. I've given up counting the number of articles in newspapers entitled: 'Why do fathers kill their children …?' 'Expert' commentators who are always consulted when these incidents occur do not deny that mothers kill their children, but they invariably perceive such a phenomenon in terms of its 'rarity' and believe that its origins lie exclusively within the realms of a depressive illness, particularly postnatal depression. They may also stress that mothers are not likely to kill children so brutally.

The most cursory glance at the tables in Chapter 5 suggest otherwise. Killings by mothers are neither rare (41 per cent of filicide total) nor without excessive violence (16 children died of multiple stab wounds; two children were burnt to death). Nor are they incapable of killing their children for revenge or retaliation (13 such cases). Had this study included cases beyond the confines of marital break-up, separation, custody and access disputes, and included cases in which once perfectly healthy mothers suffer catastrophic breakdowns (postnatal depression or puerperal psychosis), and who then kill their children (usually new-borns and infants), there probably would have been more female filicides than male.

But this is a pointless debate. As Chapter 4 clearly showed, research findings on the gender of filicide perpetrators is inconsistent at best, more often contradictory. Select the target group and you will produce the findings that so many, perhaps for their own particular ideological and personal reasons, instinctively apply to the population as a whole. There are far more important questions about filicide killings and about how society and its agencies respond to them.

In the Acknowledgements, due thanks was given to coroners. Their contribution, through discussion, correspondence and facilitating my presence at a particularly harrowing inquest over which one of them presided, was invaluable. In Chapter 9, I tried to convey just how great a challenge it is for bereaved parents and family members to attend an inquest on their murdered children. The seemingly interminable details about the injuries and the testimony of pathologists and forensic etymologists often provoke a pain and anguish that are too much even for strangers to bear. But something even more challenging may follow: hours upon hours of testimony from family and friends and working colleagues, about the context and processes preceding the killings: who said or did what, when and where? This may be excruciating for the surviving parent, but it may also be helpful in understanding why a loving father or mother has killed.

Before an inquest, the public may know nothing other than the reported views of neighbours and friends, all recalling memories of a gentle, kind, 'loving', dedicated, hard-working parent; a successful parent, employed, happily married, well integrated within the community. The only explanation, therefore, is that the parent 'snapped'.

Two such cases come to mind (there are literally, dozens more). In the first case, a mother, an academic, killed her two children, aged 6 and 1. The community and her working colleagues were stunned. No one was aware of any serious problem in her marriage. There were no health problems, physical or mental; no money problems. She was popular and highly respected in her work. The family was wholly integrated within the local community. A devastated, yet perceptive neighbour lamented that: 'I suppose people will say now that it was postnatal depression ...'

Many might have thought so, but the coroner said no such thing. During the inquest, it was revealed that all was not well in the relationship. Two days before the killings, just before the couple sat down for their evening meal, the mother casually told her husband the latest piece of gossip circulating at her place of work: a colleague's husband was leaving her. She could hardly have anticipated her own husband's response: he said he was leaving too, just like that! Less than 48 hours later, the children were asphyxiated and the mother hung herself. She left a chilling suicide note reeking of revenge and cruel irony.

In the second case, a father, similarly described as 'loving', 'kind', and 'gentle', lured his children, aged 12, 8 and 7, to a stunning beauty spot, killed them by slitting their throats as well as inflicting multiple stab wounds, and then threw himself off a cliff. Within the next few days, a truly inspirational act of charity and forgiveness was made, not by the mother of the children, but by her father. He, the grandfather to the three children, wrote an extraordinary open letter to the public: here are some quotes from it:

> Perhaps some of you feel anger toward him. You know him only as the man who did this ... I know him as the man who fell in love with my daughter. I know him as the man who worked tirelessly to support the family he worshipped. I know him as the man who, with my daughter, raised my beautiful grandchildren in an environment of love and joy and laughter ... Perhaps we will never understand the torment in XXX's mind that drove him to such an act, but I know this was not an act of malice or spite.

This reaffirmation of the goodness of the perpetrator, coming from his *father-in-law* only days after the murders, made a powerful impact. Who could doubt now that this was nothing other than a human tragedy of monumental proportions, in which a fundamentally decent loving father had 'snapped'?

If the coroner who presided over the inquest, had confined his efforts to the basic coroner's goals of establishing *who died,* and *how, when* and *where,* we would be none the wiser. But he didn't. First, he took the trouble to visit the location and spend some time there. In his summing up, he referred to it as 'a scene of unimaginable horror ... the sort of things nightmares are made of'. Second, he also explored the life histories, personalities, and the social, emotional and psychological lives of the parents. I don't think this was the aim, but it was the consequence of questioning key witnesses: the children's maternal grandparents and aunt and uncle, all living close by and very much involved, and the father's many working colleagues. These witnesses in themselves quickly conveyed the impression that the public's perception of this tragedy, forged in the father-in-law's open letter, was merely an illusion.

And there was another 'witness' who did more: the mother of the murdered children. She wasn't at the inquest, having been under the care of psychiatric services since the killings nine months before. But she presented her testimony in the form of a substantial letter, which the coroner chose to read out in its entirety.

Even in the very early stages of the parents' relationship, which was during the father's student years, there were rows, serious domestic violence, drug use, walkouts, mental illness, suicidal attempts, and separations. This was not exactly the 'environment of love and joy and laughter' that the father-in-law had written about. The parents nevertheless survived all that, but it does suggest a fragility in the structure and dynamic of the relationship, which the mother herself confirmed in a blog six years before her children were killed: 'For the longest time my relationship with XXXX was very fragile and sometimes I still find it hard to have faith in our strength as a couple.' That fragility would again surface in the year preceding the killings, when the relationship was facing an infinitely greater challenge: a potential third party involvement.

This was a case with identical features and patterns as those discernible in so many cases in this study. The father may well have been a loving and dedicated one, but he was also over-possessive and controlling. The mother, less educated and less qualified than he, devoted much of her energies and time to the children. She had a history of intermittent mental health crises stretching back to her teens. She had attempted suicide on a number of occasions.

She sought an outlet from what she regarded as the oppressiveness of her existence. She had artistic potential and aspirations. She began attending Open University classes. She sensed liberation and confidence increasing. 'I was changing and getting happier', she wrote, and acknowledged that 'it was difficult for XXXX to see me becoming more intelligent, happier, and interacting with other people because he was so possessive.'

She was also developing some kind of relationship with her tutor. 'Flirty' texts were exchanged. They were texting each other on the day of the killings. Her husband saw the earlier texts. His wife's newfound confidence and independence were challenging enough for him, but the revelation of what he perceived as a developing intimacy between her and her tutor provoked a massive crisis for both of them.

On the evening before the killings, they discussed matters over dinner. The mother said she was leaving. The father cried and pointedly held his wedding ring, asking her should he take it with him. She was in her words, 'pushing him away' because, she 'couldn't stand his closeness'.

She was also entering a psychotic phase. During the morning of the next day, her husband, at her prompting, had taken the children 'for a drive' (she said in her letter that she wanted to 'keep my distance from my kids' and wouldn't talk to them, in case 'anything I said would cause them harm'). She went to her parents' home for help. She was rambling and incoherent, identifying the cat as one of her children. She attempted to take an overdose. Her father prevented it. She attempted to kill herself with a knife. Again her father saved her. She was admitted to hospital. By that time her children were probably already dead.

This deeply moving and honest testimony ends with a judgement on her husband's actions. Unlike her own father's public letter of charity and tolerance, asserting that the actions were without 'malice' and 'spite', his wife interpreted the killings as 'hateful, cruel and horrible'. If the motive was revenge-retaliation, as was implied in her judgement, it could not have been more wholly accomplished: she was at the time of the inquest, still under psychiatric care. The indescribable suffering the killings have inflicted upon her will ensure a lifetime of vulnerability and profound grief.

The coroner's final comment was that in his opinion, the father was of 'sound mind' when he killed his children and himself.

These types of inquests I believe, though harrowing, make a substantial contribution to filicide study, and therein, have the potential for enhancing the training and preparation of relevant professionals. But they are not typical of all inquests. There are enormous variations in how coroners perceive what is in the public interest, and, in deference to the pain and suffering of relatives, how much information should be released. The coroner in Jackie's case (Chapter 9) ordered a witness out of the court for daring to mention the word 'affair' to another witness. In contrast, the coroner in the case of a father and his four children chose not only to reveal an affair, but also, the recorded revenge-laden telephone call he made to their mother in the process of killing them, and his dying wish that she would bear a grudge against the child in her womb (another man's child), for the rest of her life. Perhaps that much detail was not necessary.

What of the future, then? Filicide and familicide killings are on the increase. The underlying processes and trends fuelling that increase, some of which were discussed in Chapters 2 and 10, are, to a large extent, uncontrollable and unstoppable: they are (1) separation and/or divorce of married or unmarried parents; (2) increasingly bitter and unresolved custody and access disputes; (3) clandestine third party involvement; and (4) use of and dependency on social media. On this last point, texting and the discovery of texts have been a potent factor in many of the cases. Some day, a professor and his or her team will research the impact of social media on parental relationships which have broken down. One cannot help anticipating that they will learn the impact is considerable.

Even governments are helpless in stemming this tide, and the present coalition government has no inclination to resist. In the recent debate on same sex marriages, for example, the Equalities Minister in the House of Lords, Baroness Stowell, said: 'Marriage does not require the fidelity of couples. It is open to each couple to decide for themselves on the importance of fidelity in their own relationship' (Bingham, 2013).

At which point, we might lose sight of the victims, past, present and future, whom I have tried to place at the centre of every chapter in this book. It is both bizarre and discomforting to be able to predict that within the next 12 months, in the UK, children who are at this moment playing happily in supposedly happy homes, or sitting among their peers in classrooms, will be asphyxiated, burnt alive, shot dead, drowned, poisoned, bludgeoned or stabbed to death. Such incidents may occur within 200 miles of where I live, or maybe 50 miles, or 10, or perhaps, in the same neighbourhood.

Let's consider for a moment what has been done for other potential victims. Due credit must be given to this and previous governments for their efforts in terms of new legislation and expenditure in ensuring that professionals are much better equipped and prepared for the victims of child sexual abuse and domestic violence, crimes which will, just as assuredly, occur in abundance within the next 12 months. Those victims are recognized, their suffering anticipated, and the new laws that will rescue and protect many of them have already been implemented.

Due credit also to the police and the Crown Prosecution Services for their relentless pursuit of sexual abuse offenders of decades ago, in the interests of the victims who felt justice would never come.

Now let's return to the filicide and familicide victims of tomorrow. Do the authorities still believe that absolutely nothing can be done about *them*? I do not believe that.

Politicians are unlikely to share the prediction about filicide killings which I have just made. But that is hardly a reason why frontline professionals who are trying to protect children should not be thinking of that possibility. Part of the foundation for the necessary change of attitude and approach to this carnage is to talk about filicide, think about filicide, anticipate it, and prepare for it. Every serious case review on a filicide case, and every inquiry report reveals that that is precisely what professionals never did.

It is mystifying to me that so many authors of serious case reviews still cannot see the irony of 'learning lessons' (the *raison d'être* of serious case reviews), by discovering major shortcomings, like ignoring procedures, not carrying out risk assessments, being eternally over-optimistic without being vigilant, botching official records ... and so on, but then concluding that the filicide outcome was neither predictable nor preventable! Thankfully, since beginning this book, I have discovered two SCRs, mentioned in Chapters 9 and 10, in which the authors actually said the opposite!

It is mystifying that judges and lawyers and social workers are still repeatedly supporting unsupervised contact between particular fathers and their children, when everyone knows, including the professionals themselves, that the father is a seething cauldron of hatred and bitterness because he lost out on the custody battle, and his wife has successfully settled in a new relationship. Are they aware of how many children have died in similar circumstances? Are they aware of the methods of death?

It is mystifying that mental health professionals, such as psychiatrists and social workers and GPs, do not see the dangers of young mothers, enduring bouts of severe depression following the break-up of marriage, yet caring alone and unsupported for their one, two or three very young children. Are they aware of how many children have died in similar circumstances?

How many more children need to die?

I did cast doubt in Chapter 10 on the charitable advice of a bereaved grandfather who wanted a photograph of his two murdered grandchildren placed on the desk of every social worker. I wonder if the three tables in Chapter 5 providing the details of 224 murdered children would have any greater impact.

There is a ghastly symmetry in the two statements:

Filicide killings are neither predicable nor preventable.
(therefore)
There is absolutely nothing that can be done about them.

Agencies and their frontline staff are more than capable of ensuring that this doom-laden complacency of convenience is not a contributory factor in the deaths of another 224 children.

References

Abrams, F. (2005) 'The family no one could save', the *Guardian*, 7 June.
Addley, E. (2004) 'Men who kill', the *Guardian*, 6 April.
Alder, C. and Polk, K. (2001) *Child Homicide in Australia*, Cambridge: Cambridge University Press,
Al-Khalili, J., Perry, P., Baggini, J., Moyes, J. and Wybourne, C. (2012) 'Five theories on the greatest emotion of all', the *Guardian*, 13 September.
Allen, M. (2011) *Narrative Therapy for Women Experiencing Domestic Violence*, London: Jessica Kingsley.
Association of Chief Police Officers (2009) *Tackling Perpetrators of Violence against Women and Girls*, London: ACPO.
Bailey, D. and Liyanage, L. (2012) 'The role of the mental health social worker: political pawns in the reconfiguration of adult health and social care', *British Journal of Social Work*, 42(6): 1113–31.
Bakan, D. (1971) *Slaughter of the Innocents*, San Francisco: Jossey-Bass.
Baldwin, A. L., Cole, R. E., and Baldwin, C. T. (1982) 'Parent pathology, family interaction, the competence of the child in school', *Monographs of the Society for Research in Child Development*, Serial No. 197.
BBC News Online (2001) 'What drives a father to kill his children?', 30 August.
BBC News Online (2007) 'Bridge leap mother freed by court', 14 February.
BBC News Online (2008) 'Failures allowed mother to kill', 17 January.
BBC News Online (2011) 'Divorce: senior family law judge on warring parents', 11 February.
BBC4 (2012) File on 4: *Family Annihilation*, 6 March.
Belsky, J., and Vondra, J. (1989) 'Lessons from child abuse: the determinants of parenting', in D. Cicchetti and V. Carlson (eds) *Child Maltreatment: Theory and Research on the Causes and Consequences of Child Abuse and Neglect*, New York: Cambridge University Press, pp. 153–202.
Bennewith, O., Hawton, K., Simkin, S., Sutton, L., Kapur, N., Turnbull, P. and Gunnell, D. (2005) 'The usefulness of coroners' data on suicides for providing information relevant to prevention', *Suicide Life Threat Behaviour*, 35(6): 607–14.
Benson, P. (2009) *Married and Unmarried Family Breakdown: Key Statistics Explained*. Bristol: Bristol Community Family Trust.
Bhugra, D., Baldwin, D. S., Desai, M. and Jacob, K. S. (1999) 'Attempted suicide in West London: II. Intergroup comparisons', *Psychological Medicine*, 29: 1131–9.
Bichard, M. (2005) *The Bichard Inquiry: Final Report*. London: Cabinet Office. Available at: http://www.bichardinquiry.org.uk/10663/report.pdf.
Bingham, J. (2013) 'Being faithful isn't always important', *Daily Telegraph*, 21 June.

Birmingham Safeguarding Children Board (2012) *Serious Case Review Case Reference BSCB/2009-10/2*, Birmingham: BSCB.
Blom-Cooper, L. (1985) *A Child in Trust: The Report of the Panel of Inquiry into the Circumstances Surrounding the Death of Jasmine Beckford*, London: London Borough of Brent.
Bourget, D. and Gagne, P. (2002) 'Maternal filicide in Quebec', *Journal of the American Academy and the Law*, 30: 345–51.
Bourget, D. and Gagne, P. (2005) 'Paternal filicide in Quebec', *Journal of the American Academy and the Law*, 33: 354–60.
Bourget, D., Grace, J. and Whitehurst, L. (2007) 'A review of maternal and paternal filicide', *Journal of American Academy of Psychiatry and Law*, 35: 74–92.
Boyd, D. (2008) *Report of the Independent Inquiry Panel to the Western and Eastern Health and Social Services Board, May 2007: Madeline and Lauren O'Neill*, Belfast and Londonderry: WHSSB and EHSSB.
Brandon, M., Bailey, S., Belderson, P., Gardner, R., Sidebotham, P., Dodsworth, J., Warren. C. and Black, J. (2009) *Understanding Serious Case Reviews and Their Impact: A Biennial Analysis of Serious Case Reviews 2005–07*, London: Department for Children, Schools and Families.
Brandon, M., Sidebotham, P., Bailey, S., Belderson, P. (2011) *A Study of Recommendations Arising from Serious Case Reviews, 2009-2010*, London: Department of Education.
Bui, H. (2007) 'The limitations of current approaches to domestic violence', in R. Muraskin (ed.) *It's a Crime: Women and Justice*, 4th edn, Upper Saddle River, NJ: Prentice Hall, pp. 261–76.
Channel 4 (2003) *Cutting Edge: Behind Closed Doors*, 29 July.
Chesler, P. (1972) *Women and Madness*, New York: Doubleday.
Cheung, P. T. K. (1986) 'Maternal filicide in Hong Kong', *Medicine, Science and Law*, 26: 185–92.
Chew-Graham, C., Bashir, C., Chantler, K., Burman, E., and Batsleer, J. (2002) 'South Asian women, psychological distress and self-harm: lessons for primary care trusts', *Health and Social Care in the Community*, 10: 339–47.
Chinese Academy of Social Sciences (2010) Quoted in 'The worldwide war on baby girls', *The Economist*, 6 March.
Christiansen, S., Rollmann, D., Mygind Leth, P. and Thomsen, J. L. (2007) 'Drab på børn' [Children as victims of homicide, 1972–2005], *Ugeskrift for Læger*, 169(47): 4070–4.
Cleaver, H., Unell, I. and Aldgate, J (1999) *Children's Needs: Parenting Capacity: The Impact of Parental Mental Illness, Problem Alcohol and Drug Abuse, and Domestic Violence on Children's Development*, London: The Stationery Office.
Cook, D., Burton, M., Robinson, A. and Vallely, C. (2004) *Evaluation of Specialist Domestic Violence Courts: Fast Track Systems*. Available at: http://www.cps.gov.uk/publications/docs/specialistdvcourts.pdf.
Cooper, J., Husain, N., Webb, R., Waheed, W., Kapur, N., Guthrie, E. and Appleby, L. (2006) 'Self-harm in the UK: differences between South Asians and Whites in rates, characteristics, provision of service and repetition', *Social Psychiatry and Psychiatric Epidemiology*, 41(10): 782–8.

Corby, B. (2000) *Child Abuse: Towards a Knowledge Base*, Buckingham: Open University Press.

Cox, J. L., Holden, J. M. and Sagovsky, K. (1987) 'Detection of postnatal depression: development of the 10-item Edinburgh Postnatal Depression Scale', *British Journal of Psychiatry*, 150: 782–6.

Crittenden, P. and Craig, S. (1990) 'Development trends in the nature of child homicide', *Journal of Interpersonal Violence*, 5: 202–16.

Daily Telegraph (2012) 'Family court judges call for greater protection', 24 December.

Daly, M. and Wilson. M. (1988) *Homicide*. New York: Aldine de Gruyter.

Davies, N. (1973) *The Aztecs*, Houndsmills: Macmillan.

Davies, N. (1995) *The Incas*, Boulder, CO: The University of Colorado Press.

Department for Children, Schools and Families (2010) *Working Together under the Children's Act: A Guide to Inter-agency Working to Safeguard and Promote the Welfare of Children*, London: DCSF.

Department for Education (2008a) *Analysing Childhood Deaths and Serious Injury Through Abuse and Neglect: What Can We Learn? A Biennial Analysis of Serious Case Reviews, 2003–05*, London: Department of Education.

Department for Education (2008b) *Improving Safeguarding Practice: Study of Serious Case Reviews, 2001–03*, London: Department of Education.

Department for Education (2009) *Understanding Serious Case Reviews and Their Impact: A Biennial Analysis of Serious Case Reviews, 2005–07*, London: Department of Education.

Department for Education, (2013) *Working Together under the Children's Act: A Guide to Inter-agency Working to Safeguard and Promote the Welfare of Children*. Available at: www.education.gov.uk/aboutdfe/statutory.

Department for Education and Skills (DfES) (2003) *Every Child Matters*. Cm. Paper 5860. London: HMSO.

Department for Education and Skills (2007) *Statutory Guidance on Making Arrangements to Safeguard and Promote the Welfare of Children Under Section 11 of the Children Act 2004*, London: HMSO.

Department of Health (1990) *The Care Programme Approach for People with a Mental Illness Referred to the Specialist Psychiatric Services*, Joint Health/Social Services Circular HC (90) 23/LASS (90) 11. London: Department of Health.

Department of Health (1991a) *The Care of Children: Principles and Practice in Guidance and Legislation*, London: HMSO.

Department of Health (1991b) *Working Together under the Children's Act; A Guide to Arrangements for Inter-agency Cooperation for the Protection of Children from Abuse*, London: HMSO.

Department of Health (1999a) *The National Service Framework for Mental Health: Modern Standards and Service Models*, London: HMSO.

Department of Health (1999b) *Effective Care Coordination in Mental Health Services: Modernising the Care Programme Approach*, London: HMSO.

Department of Health (2000) *Framework for the Assessment of Children in Need and Their Families*, London: The Stationery Office. Available at: http://www.dh.gov.uk/assetRoot/04/01/44/30/04014430.pdf.

Department of Health (2001) *The Mental Health Policy Implementation Guide*, London: HMSO.
Department of Health (2004) *The National Framework for Children, Young People and Maternity Services*, London: Department of Health.
Department of Health (2006) *Our Health, Our Care, Our Say: A New Direction for Community Services*, London: HMSO.
Department of Health (2007) *New Ways of Working for Everyone: A Best Practice Implementation Guide*, London: National Institute for Mental Health in England.
Department of Health (2008a) *Code of Practice: Mental Health Act 1983*, London: The Stationery Office.
Department of Health (2008b) *Refocusing the Care Program Approach: Policy and Positive Practice Guidance*, London: HMSO.
Department of Health and Social Security (1974) *Report of the Committee of Inquiry into the Care and Supervision Provided in Relation to Maria Colwell*, London: HMSO.
Derbyshire Safeguarding Children Board (2008) *Report to Derbyshire Safeguarding Children Board Concerning Child K*, Derby: Derbyshire SCB.
d'Orbán, P.T. (1979) 'Women who kill their children', *British Journal of Psychiatry*, 134: 560–71.
Drever, J. (1953) *A Dictionary of Psychology*, Harmondsworth: Penguin.
Duffy, C. (2003) 'Two year sentence for role in abduction of child', *Irish Times*, 27 February.
Eberstadt, N. (2010) Quoted in 'The worldwide war on baby girls', *The Economist*, 6 March.
Emery, J. L. (1985) 'Infanticide, filicide and cot death', *Archives of Disease in Childhood*, 60: 505–7.
Ewing, C. (1997) *Fatal Families: The Dynamics of Intrafamilial Homicide*, Thousand Oaks, CA: Sage.
Falcov, A. (1996) *Study of Working Together, Part 8: Reports: Fatal Child Abuse and Parental Psychiatric Disorder: An Analysis of 100 Area Child Protection Committee Case Reviews under the Children Act 1989*, London: Department of Health.
Farmer, E. and Owen, M. (1995) *Child Protection Practice: Private Risks and Public Remedies: A Study of Decision-making, Intervention and Outcomes in Child Protection Work*, London: HMSO.
Flynn, S., Shaw, J. J. and Abel, K. M. (2013) 'Filicide: mental illness in those who kill their children', *PLoS ONE*, 8(4): e58981. doi: 10. 1371/journal.pone.0058981.
Flynn, S., Windfuhr, K. and Shaw, J. (2009) *Filicide: A Literature Review*, Manchester, University of Manchester Press.
Friedman, S. H., Holden, C., Hrouda, D. R. and Resnick, P. J. (2008) 'Maternal filicide and its interaction with suicide', *Brief Treatment and Crisis Intervention*, 8: 283–91.
Friedman, S. H., Hrouda, D. R., Holden, C., Noffsinger, S. G. and Resnick, P.J. (2005) 'Filicide-suicide: common factors in parents who kill their children

and themselves', *Journal of the American Academy of Psychiatry Law*, 33(4): 496–504.

Friedman, S. H., McCue-Horowitz, S. M., and Resnick, P. J. (2005) 'Child murder by mothers: a critical analysis of the current state of knowledge and a research agenda', *American Journal of Psychiatry*, 162: 1578–87.

Friedman, S. H. and Resnick, P. J. (2007) 'Child murder by mothers: patterns and prevention', *World Psychiatry*, 6(3): 137–41.

Geen, G. G. (2001) *Human Aggression*, 2nd edn, Buckingham: Open University Press.

Gilbert, C. (2008) *Safeguarding Children: The Third Joint Chief Inspectors' Report on Arrangements to Safeguard Children*, London: Ofsted.

Grave, R. (1955) *The Greek Myths*, Harmondsworth: Penguin.

Hackney Safeguarding Children Board (2008) Internal review on the deaths of Antoine Ogunkoya, and Keniece Ogunkoya, reported in the *Guardian*, 17 July.

Hague, G. (2000) 'The voices and views of women experiencing domestic violence', *Criminal Justice Matters*, 42(1): 18–19.

Hamilton, R. P. (2006) 'Love as a contested concept', *Journal for the Theory of Social Behaviour*, 36(3): 239–54.

Hammond, N. (1982) *Ancient Maya Civilization*, New Brunswick, NJ: Rutgers University Press.

Hampshire Safeguarding Children Board (2009) *Executive Summary of Serious Case Review in Respect of Child H & Child G*, Hampshire: Hampshire SCB.

Hannah, S. (2008) *The Point of Rescue*, London: Hodder.

Harder, T. (1967) 'The psychopathology of infanticide', *Acta Psychiatrica Scandinavica*, 43: 196–245.

Haringey Safeguarding Children Board (2010) *Serious Case Review, Child A, November, 2008*, Haringey: Department of Education.

Harrow Area Child Protection Committee (1999) *Part 8 Summary Report*, Harrow: Harrow Area Child Protection Committee.

Haskett, M., Marziano, B. and Dover, E. (1996) 'Absence of males in maltreatment research: a survey of recent literature', *Child Abuse & Neglect*, 20: 1175–82.

Health Service Executive (2011) *Responding to Murder Suicide and Suicide Clusters*, Dublin: Health Service Executive.

Hegarty, M. (1994) 'Women deserve more', *Irish Social Worker*, 11(4): 8–9.

Hetherington, R., Baistow, K., Katz, I. Mesie, J. and Trowell, J. (2002) *The Welfare of Children with Mentally Ill Parents: Learning from Inter-Country Comparisons*, Chichester: John Wiley & Sons, Ltd.

Hogan, D. (2001) 'Father who killed his daughter acted out of love', *Irish Times*, 5 September.

Home Office (2003) *Safety and Justice: The Government's Proposals on Domestic Violence*, Cm. 5847, London: Home Office.

Home Office (2008) *Saving Lives, Reducing Harm, Protecting the Public: An Action Plan for Tackling Violence, 2008–11*, London: Home Office.

Home Office (2009) *Together We Can End Violence against Women and Girls*, London: Home Office.

Home Office (2010) 'Call to end violence against women and girls'. Available at: http://www.homeoffice.gov.uk/publications/crime/call-end-violence-women-girls/vawg-paper?view=Binary.
Home Office (2011) *Call to End Violence to Women and Girls: An Action Plan*, London: Home Office.
Honigsbaum, M. and Barton, L. (2005) 'A short walk to tragedy', the *Guardian*, 8 September.
Houghton, R. (1970) *Love*, Harmondsworth: Penguin.
Independent Police Complaints Commission (2012) *Christine and Shania Chambers Deceased: Independent Investigation: Summary Report*, London: IPCC.
Jaffe, P. G., Hurley, D. J. and Wolfe, D. (1990) 'Children's observations of violence: I. Critical issues in child development and intervention planning', *Canadian Journal of Psychiatry*, 35: 466–70.
Jaffe, P. G., Wolfe, D. A. and Wilson, S. K. (1990) *Children of Battered Women*, Thousand Oaks, CA: Sage.
Johnson, C. H. (2005) *Come with Daddy: Child Murder-Suicide After Family Breakdown*, Crawley, Western Australia: University of Western Australia Press.
Kaplun, D. and Reich, R. (1976) 'The murdered child and his killers', *American Journal of Psychiatry*, 133: 809–13.
Karakus, M., Ince, H., Ince1, N., Arican, N. and Sozen, S. (2003) 'Filicide cases in Turkey', *Croatian Medical Journal*, 44(5): 592–5.
Kauppi, A., Kumpulainen, K., Karkola, K., Vanamo, T., and Merikanto, J. (2010) 'Maternal and paternal filicides: a retrospective review of filicides in Finland', *Journal of American Academy of Psychiatry Law*, 38: 229–38.
Kauppi, A., Kumpulainen, K., Vanamo, T., Merikanto, J. and Karkola, K. (2008) 'Maternal depression and filicide: cases of ten mothers', *Archives of Women's Mental Health*, 11(3): 201–6.
Keeling, J. and van Wormer, K. (2012) 'Social worker interventions in situations of domestic violence: what we can learn from survivors' personal narratives?' *British Journal of Social Work*, 42(7): 1354–70.
Kirkwood, D. (2012) *'Just Say Goodbye': Parents Who Kill Their Children in the Context of Separation*, Victoria, Australia: Domestic Violence Resource Centre Victoria (DVRCV).
Korbin, J. E. (1989) 'Fatal maltreatment by mothers: a proposed framework', *Child Abuse and Neglect*, 13: 481–9.
Kunz, J. and Bahr, S. (1996) 'A profile of parental homicide against children', *Journal of Family Violence*, 11: 347–62.
Kuono, A. and Johnson, C. F. (1995) 'Child abuse and neglect in Japan: coin-operated-locker babies', *Child Abuse and Neglect*, 19: 25–31.
La Fontaine (1994) *The Extent and Nature of Organised and Ritual Abuse: Research Findings*, London: HMSO.
Laming, H. (2003) *The Victoria Climbié Inquiry*, Cm 5730, London: Department of Health and the Home Office.
Lancashire Safeguarding Children's Board (2012) *Serious Case Review, Baby J*. Lancashire: Lancashire Safeguarding Children's Board.

Leicester Safeguarding Children Board (2011) *Serious Case Review in Respect of Children Known as Child 1 and Child 2*, Leicester: Leicester LSCB.

Leicester Safeguarding Children Board (2012) *Serious Case Review Relating to Baby L*, Leicester: Leicester LSCB.

Leicestershire County Council (1980) *Carly Taylor: Report of an Independent Inquiry*, Leicester: Leicestershire County Council and Leicestershire Area Health Authority.

Leicestershire County Council (1993) *The Leicestershire Inquiry*, Leicester: Leicestershire County Council.

Leslie, S. (1932) *Plato's Symposium or Supper*, London: Fortune Press.

Léveillée, S., Marleau, J. D. and Dubé, M. (2007) 'Filicide: a comparison by sex and presence or absence of self-destructive behaviour', *Journal of Family Violence*, 22: 287–95.

Lewis, C. F., Baronoski, M. V., Buchanon, J. A. and Benedek, E. P. (1998) 'Factors associated with weapon use in maternal filicide', *Journal of Forensic Science*, 43(3): 613–18.

Lewis, C. F. and Bunce, S. C. (2003) 'Filicidal mothers and the impact of psychosis on maternal filicide', *Journal of American Academy of Psychiatry and Law*, 31: 459–70.

Liem, M. and Koenraadt, F. (2008) 'Filicide: a comparative study of maternal verses paternal child homicide', *Criminal Behaviour and Mental Health*; 18: 166–76.

Liem, M., Postulart, M. and Nieuwbeerta, P. (2009) 'Homicide-suicide in the Netherlands: an epidemiology', *Homicide Studies*, 13(2): 99–123.

London Borough of Brent (1985) *A Child in Trust: The Report of the Panel of Inquiry into the Circumstances Surrounding the Death of Jasmine Beckford*. London: London Borough of Brent.

London Borough of Greenwich (1987) *A Child in Mind: Protection of Children in a Responsible Society: The Report of the Commission of Inquiry into the Circumstances Surrounding the Death of Kimberley Carlile*, London: London Borough of Greenwich.

London Borough of Lambeth (1987) *Whose Child? The Report of the Public Inquiry into the Death of Tyra Henry*, London: London Borough of Lambeth.

Loughton, T. (2010a) *Child Protection: Back to the Front Line*, Conservative Party Policy,. Available at: http://www.timloughton.com/pdf/CONSERVATIVE%20 PAPER%20Back%20to%20the%20Frontline.pdf.

Loughton, T. (2010b) *A Letter to DCSs and LSCBs: Publication of Serious Case Review Overview Reports and Munro Review of Child Protection*. Available at: http://media.education.gov.uk/assets/files/pdf/t/tim%20loughton%20 letter%20to%20dcss%20and%20lscb%20chairs.pdf.

Lucas, D. R., Wezner, K. C., Milner, J. S., McCanne, T. R., Harris, I. N., Monroe-Posey, C. and Nelson, J. P. (2002) 'Victim, perpetrator, family, and incident characteristics of infant and child homicide in the United States Air Force', *Child Abuse and Neglect*, 26: 167–86.

MacLaughlin, C. (2000) Extracts from suicide note read out at inquest in Galway, 15 June.

Maker, A. H., Kemmelmeier M. and Peterson, C. (1998) 'Long-term psychological consequences in women of witnessing parental physical conflict and experiencing abuse in childhood', *Journal of Interpersonal Violence*, 13: 574–89.
Manchester Safeguarding Children's Board (2013) *Serious Case Review in Respect of Child U*, Manchester: Manchester SCB.
Marks, M. N. and Kumar, R. (1993) 'Infanticide in England and Wales', *Medical Science Law*, 33: 329–39.
Marleua, J. D., Poulin, B., Webanck, T., Roy, R. and Laporte, L. (1999) 'Paternal filicide: a study of 10 men', *Canadian Journal of Psychiatry*, 44: 57–63.
Marzuk, P. M., Tardiff, K. and Hirsch, C. S. (1992) 'The epidemiology of murder-suicide', *Journal of the American Medical Association*, 267: 3179–83.
Matthews, B. (1995) 'Introducing the care programme approach to a multidisciplinary team: the impact on clinical practice', *Psychiatric Bulletin*, 19: 143–5.
Mauriac, F. (1959) *Thérèse*, Harmondsworth: Penguin.
McGrath, P. (1992) 'Maternal filicide in Broadmoor Hospital', *Journal of Forensic Psychiatry*, 3: 271–97.
McGuire, K., Pastore, A. and Flanagan T. (eds) (1993) *Sourcebook of Criminal Justice Statistics 1992*, Washington, DC: U.S. Department of Justice.
McKee, G. R., and Shea, S. J. (1998) 'Maternal filicide: a cross-national comparison', *Journal of Clinical Psychology*, 54: 679–87.
Meadows, N. (2012) Testimony during inquest into the deaths of two children, Manchester Crown Court (Coroner's Office), 2 May.
Mendlowicz, M., Jean-Louis, G., Gekker, M., and Rapaport, M. (1999) 'Neonaticide in the city of Rio de Janeiro: forensic and psychological perspectives', *Journal of Forensic Sciences*, 44: 741–5.
Merril, J. and Owens, J. (1986) 'Ethnic differences in self-poisoning: a comparison of Asian and white groups', *British Journal of Psychiatry*, 148: 708–12.
Milner, J. (1993) 'A disappearing act: the differing career paths of fathers and mothers in child protection investigations', *Critical Social Policy*, 38: 48–63.
Montaldo, C. (2010) *The Dear John Letter Sent by Tom Findlay to Susan Smith*. Available at: http://crime.about.com/od/murder/a/susan_smith_4.htm.
Mouzos, J. and Rushford, C. (2003) *Family Homicide in Australia*, Canberra: Australian Institute of Criminology.
Munro, E. (2011) *The Munro Review of Child Protection: Final Report: A Child-Centred System*, Norwich: The Stationery Office (TSO). Available at: http://www.education.gov.uk/munroreview/downloads/8875_DfE_Munro_Report_TAGGED.pdf.
Myers, S. A.(1970) 'Maternal filicide', *American Journal of Diseases in Childhood*, 120: 534–36.
Navqi, S. (2013) 'A serious case for review', *Professional Social Work*, March, 14–15.
Neu, J. (2002) *A Tear Is an Intellectual Thing*, Oxford: Oxford University Press.
Neustatter, A. (2001) 'What drives a father to kill his entire family?' the *Guardian*, 2 May.

NHS London Strategic Health Authority (2010) *Independent Investigation into the Care and Treatment Provided to Mrs S by the West London Mental Health Trust and Ealing Primary Care Trust*, London: NHSLSHA.

North East London Strategic Health Authority (2002) *Report of an Independent Inquiry into the Care and Treatment of Daksha Emson M.B.B.S., MRCPsych., MSc. and Her Daughter Freya*, London: NELSHA.

Office of National Statistics (2011) *Information Paper: Summary Quality Report for Divorces in England and* Wales, Newport: Office of National Statistics.

Office of National Statistics (2013) *Release: Birth Summary Tables, England and Wales, 2012*, Newport: Office of National Statistics.

Ofsted (2008) *Learning Lessons, Taking Action: Ofsted's Evaluations of Serious Case Reviews, 1 April 2007 to 31 March*, 2008, London: Ofsted.

Ofsted (2010) *Learning Lessons from Serious Case Reviews, 2009–2010*. Available at: http://www.ofsted.gov.uk/resources/learning-lessons-serious-case-reviews-2009-2010.

Ofsted (2013) *What About the Children? Joint Working Between Adult and Children's Services When Parents or Carers Have Mental Ill Health and/or Drug and Alcohol Problems*, London: Ofsted.

O'Hagan, K. P. (1993) *Emotional and Psychological Abuse of Children*, Buckingham: Open University Press.

O'Hagan, K. P. (1997) 'The problem of engaging men in child protection work', *British Journal of Social Work*, 27(1): 25–42.

O'Hagan, K. P. (2006) *Identifying Emotional and Psychological Abuse*, Maidenhead: Open University Press.

O'Hagan, K. P. and Dillenburger, K. (1995) *The Abuse of Women in Childcare Work*, Buckingham: Open University Press.

Oliver, J. (1985) 'Successive generations of child maltreatment', *British Journal of Psychiatry*, 147: 484–90.

O'Malley, S. (2005) *Are You There Alone?: The Unspeakable Crime of Andrea Yates*, New York: Pocket Star Books.

Orr, D. (2002) 'The confused role of the modern father', *Independent*, 16 July.

Orraschel, H., Weissman, M. M., and Kidd, K. K. (1980) 'Children and depression: the children of depressed parents: the childhood of depressed patients; depression in children', *Journal of Affective Disorders*, 2(1): 1–16.

Parker, A. (2011) '3 children drowned by mother are buried', *New York Times*, 26 April.

Paulozzi, L. and Sells, M. (2002) 'Variation in homicide risk during infancy in the United States, 1989–1998.' *MMWR Weekly*, 51: 187–9.

Pilgrim, D. and Rogers, A. (1993) *A Sociology of Mental Health and Illness*, Buckingham: Open University Press.

Pollitt, J. (1965) *Depression and its Treatment*, London: Heinemann.

Porter, T. and Gavin, H. (2010) 'Infanticide and neonaticide: a review of 40 years of research literature on incidence and causes', *Trauma, Violence & Abuse*, 11(3): 99–112.

Pritchard, C. (2004) *The Child Abusers: Research and Controversy*, Maidenhead: Open University Press.

Putkonen, H., Amon, S., Eronen, M., Klier, C., Almiron, M. P., Cederwall, J. Y. and Weizmann-Henelius, G. (2011) 'Gender differences in filicide offence characteristics: a comprehensive register-based study of child murder in the European countries', *Child Abuse and Neglect*, 35(5): 319–28.

Putkonen, H., Weizmann-Henelius, G., Lindburgh, N., Eronen, M. and Häkkänen, H. (2009) 'Differences between homicide and filicide offenders: results of a nationwide register-based case-control study', *BMC Psychiatry*, 9(7). Available at: http://www.biomedcentral.com/1471-244X/9/27.

Radbill, S. X. (1974) 'A history of child abuse and infanticide', in R. Helfer and C. H. Kempe (eds) *The Battered Child*, 2nd edn, Chicago: University of Chicago Press.

Radford, J. and Russell, D. E. H. (eds) (1992) *Femicide: The Politics of Woman Killing*, Buckinghamshire: Open University Press.

Reder, P., Duncan, S. and Gray, M. (1993) *Beyond Blame: Child Abuse Tragedies Revisited*, London: Routledge.

Rekers, G. (1998) *Susan Smith, Victim or Murderer?* Glenbridge: Glenbridge Publishers Limited.

Resnick P. J. (1969) 'Child murder by parents: a psychiatric review of filicide', *American Journal of Psychiatry*, 126: 73–82.

Resnick P. J. (1970) 'Murder of the newborn: a psychiatric review of neonaticide', *American Journal of Psychiatry*, 126: 1414–20.

Rodenburg, M. (1971) 'Child murder by depressed parents', *Canadian Psychiatric Association Journal*, 16: 41–8.

Rogers, L. (2013) 'I will do everything to protect our baby from evil', *Sunday Times Magazine*, 13 January.

Rossman B. B. (1998) 'Descartes' error and posttraumatic stress disorder: cognition and emotion in children who are exposed to parental violence', in G. W. Holden, R. A. Geffner and E. N. Jouriles (eds) *Children Exposed to Marital Violence*, Washington, DC: American Psychological Association.

Saunders, H. (2004) *Twenty-Nine Child Homicides: Lessons Still to Be Learnt on Domestic Violence and Child Protection*, Bristol: Women's Aid.

Schaap, C. and Korsgaard, H. (2008) *Den sidste gave: tragedien i Odense [The last gift: tragedy in Odense]*, Copenhagen: Lindhardt and Ringhof.

Scott, P.D (1973a) 'Parents who kill their children', *Medicine, Science and the Law*, 13: 120–6.

Scott, P. D. (1973b) 'Fatal battered baby cases', *Medicine, Science and the Law*, 13: 196–206.

Shaw, R. (1992) *Drowning: A Search for Answers*. Available at: http://www.lib.niu.edu/1992/ip920721.html.

Showalter, E. (1987) *The Female Malady* London: Virago.

Sidebotham, P. (2012) 'What do serious case reviews achieve?' *Archives of Diseases in Childhood*, 97(3): 189–92.

Smith, K., Osborne, S., Lau, I. and Britton, A. (2012) *Homicides, Firearm Offences and Intimate Violence 2010/11: Supplementary Volume 2 to Crime in England and Wales 2010/11*, London: Home Office. Available at:

http://www.homeoffice.gov.uk/publications/science-research-statistics/research-statistics/crime-research/hosb0212/hosb0212?view=Binary.

Social Services Inspectorate, Wales (1991) *Accommodating Children: A Review of Children's Homes in Wales*, Cardiff: Welsh Office.

Somander, L. K. and Rammer, L. M (1991) 'Intra and extra-familial child homicide in Sweden 1971–1980', *Child Abuse and Neglect*, 15: 45–55.

Spinelli, M. G. (2001) 'A systematic investigation of 16 cases of neonaticide', *The American Journal of Psychiatry*, 158 (5): 811–13.

Staffordshire County Council (1991) *The Pindown Experience and the Protection of Children: The Report of the Staffordshire Child Care Inquiry 1990*, Stafford: Staffordshire County Council.

Stanley, N., Miller, P., Richardson-Foster, H. and Thompson, G. (2011) 'A stop-start response: social services interventions with children and families notified following domestic violence incidents', *British Journal of Social Work*, 41(2): 296–313.

Stanton, J. and Simpson, A. (2002) 'Filicide: a review', *International Journal of Law and Psychiatry*, 25: 1–14.

Starmer, K. (2011) 'Domestic violence: the facts, the issues, the future', speech by the Director of Public Prosecutions, Keir Starmer QC. Available at: http://www.cps.gov.uk/news/articles/domestic_violence_-_the_facts_the_issues_the_future/, 12 April.

Stern, E. S. (1948) 'The Medea complex: the mother's homicidal wishes to her child', *British Journal of Psychiatry*, 94: 321–31.

Stokes, P. (2006) 'Mother who jumped from bridge with baby is jailed for 18 months', *Daily Telegraph*, 24 November.

Tallant, N. (2011) *Flesh and Blood: Familicides and Murder-Suicides that Haunt Ireland*, Dublin: Hachette Books Ireland.

Thomson, J. and Ross, G. (2011) *Beyond All Evil*, London: Harper Element.

Toner, H. (2008) *Independent Review Report of Agency Involvement with Mr Arthur McElhill, Ms Lorraine McGovern and Their Children*, Belfast: Department of Health, Social Services and Public Policy.

U.S. Dept of Justice (2011) *Homicide Trends in the United States, 1980–2008*, Washington, DC: Bureau of Justice. Available at: http://www.bjs.gov/content/pub/ascii/htus8008.txt.

Utting, W. (1991) *Children in the Public Care: A Review of Residential Child Care*, London: HMSO.

Walby, S. and Allen, J. (2004) *Domestic Violence, Sexual Assault and Stalking: Findings from the British Crime Survey*, Home Office Research Study 276, London: Home Office Research, Development and Statistics Directorate.

Walker, M., McGlade, M. and Gamble, J (2008) *A Domestic Homicide Review into the Deaths of Julia and William Pemberton*, West Berkshire Safer Communities Partnership. Available at: http://www.thamesvalley.police.uk/pemberton-review.pdf.

Warwickshire Safeguarding Children Board (2012) *Serious Case Review in Respect of the Death of a Child*, Warwickshire: Warwickshire SCB.

Warren, J. I. and Kovnick, J. (1999) 'Women who kill', in V. B. van Hasselt and M. Hersen (eds) *Handbook of Psychological Approaches with Violent Offenders: Contemporary Strategies and Issues*, New York: Plenum Press, pp. 189–204.

Warren, M. A. (1985) *Gendercide: The Implications of Sex Selection*, New York: Rowman & Allanfield Publishers.

Watkins, B. (2011) 'LaShanda Armstrong: mother drives her kids in the Hudson River'. Available at: http://thyblackman.com/2011/04/14/dr-boyce-watkins-lashanda-armstrong-mother-drives-her-kids-into-the-hudson-river/.

Werner, O. H. (1917) *The Unmarried Mother in German Literature*, New York: Columbia University Press.

West, D. J. (1965) *Murder Followed by Suicide*, London: Heinemann.

West, S. G., Friedman, S. H. and Resnick, P. J. (2009) 'Fathers who kill their children: an analysis of the literature', *Journal of Forensic Science*, 54(2): 463–8.

Williams, S. (2013) 'Our children were murdered by our husbands', *You*, 28 April.

Wilson, M., Daly, M. and Daniele, A. (1995) 'Familicide: the killing of spouse and children', *Aggressive Behavior*, 21: 275–91.

Women's Aid (2000) *Child Protection and Woman Protection: Links and Schisms*. Available at: http://www.womensaid.org.uk/domestic-violence-articles.asp?section=00010001002200020001&itemid=1198.

Wu, Z., Viisainen, K. and Hemminki, E. (2006) 'Determinants of high sex ratio among newborns: a cohort study from rural Anhui province, China', *Reproductive Health Matters*, 14: 172–80.

Wybourne, C. (2012) 'Love is free yet binds us', the *Guardian*, 13 December.

Yardley, E. (2013) 'Why ever more fathers are killing their own children', *Daily Mail*, 22 May.

Zhu, W.X., Lu, L. and Hesketh, T. (2009) 'China's excess males: sex selection, abortion and one child policy: analysis of data from 2005 national inter-census survey', *British Medical Journal*, 338b: 1211.

Zigler, E. and Hall, N. W. (1989) 'Physical child abuse in America: past, present and future', in D. Cicchetti and V. Carlson (eds) *Child Maltreatment: Theory and Research on the Causes and Consequences of Child Abuse and Neglect*, Cambridge: Cambridge University Press.

Index

abandonment, 34, 56
abusive relationships, 65–72
accident and emergency centres, 22
Adoption Act, 2002, 157, 162
adversarial court cases, 23
affective disorder team, 158
aggression, 69, 72, 139, 142, 144, 149, 153
alcohol-dependent, 117, 196
altruistic filicide, 63, 135, 139
ancient Greece, 39, 45, 137
  Greek myth, 37
anniversaries, 105
anti-depressants, 7, 124, 143
approved social workers, 158
approved mental health practitioners, 158
Aristotle and Plato, 37
  Plato's *Symposium*, 137
Assyria, 38
avoidance of men, 199–203

baby P., 6. 27–8
Balls, Ed., 27
Beckford, Jasmine, 6, 24, 25, 37

cannabis, 108, 116, 142, 186, 187, 196
care coordinator, 158–9
care planning, 128, 129
care program approach, 129, 158
Carthaginians, 38
case management reports, 97
child abuse, 6, 18, 22, 24, 25, 27, 37, 53, 67, 125, 200
  and neglect, 59, 106
  fatalities, 36, 37, 67, 162
  literature and research, 53
child protection, 20, 22, 26, 31, 115, 123, 125, 126, 128–9

agencies, 17, 22, 36, 128
  and mental health, 159–62
  failings of, 27
  legislative context of, 162–7
  literature and research, 53
  court proceedings for, 163, 164–5
  strategies for, 22
child sacrifice, 37–8
child sexual abuse, 162
children
  age of, 59, 60, 107–9
  as filicide victims, 74–96
  concealing identity of, 73
  escaping/surviving attempted filicide, 102–4
  exploitation of, 6–14, 23
  gender of, 60
  of parents suffering mental illness, 129, 159, 161
  perceptions of, 73
  relationship with perpetrator, 61
  used as pawns, 6, 22, 144
  used as weapons, 23
  watching siblings die, 102
Children Act, 2004, 159, 161
Children Act, 1989, 157, 162, 163
Children and Adoption Act, 2006, 166
Children and Families Team, 123
Climbié, Victoria, 6, 24, 25, 26, 37
coalition, 28
cognitive distortions, 145
Colwell, Maria, 6, 24
community mental health team (CMHT), 122, 124
confidentiality and data protection, 26
coroner, 45, 57, 98–9, 102, 111, 114, 146, 119

225

coroner's inquests, 47, 97, 180–1, 206–10
coroner's reports, 97, 119, 120
Court of Appeal, 14
Crichton, Nicolas, District Judge, 164
crisis intervention teams, 22
Crown Prosecution Service, 152
cultural diversity, 125–6
custody and access disputes, 5, 6, 20, 33, 61, 73

Denmark
  filicide and familicide killings in, 97–8
divorce, 23, 33, 61, 69, 173–4, 181, 185, 201, 210
divorce rates, 19–21
Domestic Abuse Stalking and Harrassment Model, 153
domestic homicide reviews, 153, 155
domestic violence
  as child abuse, 127–8
  police response to, *see* police
  prevalence of, 21, 152
  preceding filicide, 5, 13, 21–2, 65, 97, 122, 156–7, 175–6, 187–8
  legislative context of, 153–6
domestic violence courts, 154
Domestic Violence, Crime and Victim's Act 2004, 153
Domestic Violence Risk Indicator Model, 153

Edinburgh Postnatal Depression Scale, 122
emergency services, 10, 99, 189
emotional and psychological abuse, 9, 13–14, 22–3, 69, 127–8, 147, 157
emotional and psychological development, 108
emotional interactions, 139, 141, 149
ethical dilemma, 73
Euripides, 39
Exodus, book of, 37

extra-marital affairs, 5, 143, 172–6
  professionals' response to, 191–4

Facebook, 13, 14, 16 190
familicide, 30, 34, 58, 92–7
  definition of, 35–6
femicide, 30, 34
feminist-sociological perspective, 65–8
feticide, 34
filicide
  antecedents of, 34, 37
  attempted filicides, 64
  classifications and definitions of, 34–6
  cultural and historical perspective of, 30, 33, 37–8
  days on which it occurs, 104–5
  inexplicability of, 33, 36
  predictability and prevention of, 17, 29, 65, 69, 131, 146
  prevalence of, 56
  processes leading to, 46
  suddenness of, 33, 36
filicide research
  basic data in, 51, 53, 56–68
  criticism of, 70, 118–19
  different strands of, 52–68
  focus on female perpetrators, 30, 51, 52–5
  reviews of, 51, 52, 55–6
filicide-suicide, 62–3, 109
final solution, 21
Findley, Tom, 42–3
Finland, 56
food treats before killing, 101
forensic entymologists, 207
foster and adoptive parents, 61
Framework for the Assessment of Children, 163, 53

gendercide, 34
guardian ad litems, 20
Guardian, The, 137

Haringey, 27, 28, 162
Health Service Executive, 35

health visiting services, 187, 189
helpless neighbours, 45
Home Office, 57–8, 152, 154
homicide, 34, 57, 116, 117, 136
　Australia's Homicide Monitoring Program, 62
　differentiating from filicide, 57
Humber Bridge 13

ideological perspectives, 72
imbalance of power, 41, 69, 138, 194, 197
Independent Domestic Violence Advisers, 154, 156
Independent Police Complaints Commission (IPCC), 155–7, 188
infanticide, 34, 35, 38, 54, 57–9, 188
inquiry reports
　on child abuse, 24, 25, 61, 97, 125, 162
　on mental illness and filicide, 31, 55, 61, 114, 125, 128–9, 130, 160, 167, 203
Ireland
　filicide and familicide killings in, 98
Izzat, 125

Jeremiah, Book of, 37
Johnson, Carolyn, 66–7, 148
Joshua, Book of, 37
judges, 6, 7, 11, 12, 15, 22, 101, 102, 212

Kings (II) Book of, 37
Kirkwood, Debbie, 67–8
knowledge base, 201–2

La Llorana, 39
legal system and family courts, 66
Lord Chief Justice, 16
Loughton, Tim, 28, 29
love, 31
　absence of, 37
　antithesis of, 141
　as delusion, 139–40
　as motivator in filicide, 135–6, 141, 144
　attempts to understand and define, 137
　combined with fear, 140
　filicide killings attributed to, 140–1, 143–4, 147
　misguided, 140
　mutual bonds of, 40
　pathological, 145
　professions of, 33, 36, 68, 143
　Socrates' view on, 131
　synonymous with altruism, 63, 136

Mauriac, François
　Thérèse Desqueyroux, 39, 44
Mayas, Incas and Aztecs, 38
Medea, 39–47
　doubts of, 44–5
　guilt of 45
　resolve and cunning of, 43–4
　revenge motivation of, 39, 40–2
　synopsis of play, 39–40
Medea complex, 39
media interest, 5, 27, 121, 179
mental health, 3, 13, 17, 22, 53, 61, 69, 124–5, 130, 140
　legislative context of, 157–61
Mental Health Act, 1983, 160
Mental Health Act, 2007, 157–8
mental illness, 5, 22, 30, 31, 33, 36, 64, 68
　affective disorders, 116
　bipolar disorder, 111
　delusions, 3, 14–17, 62, 131, 139, 141, 143, 149
　depression, 14, 22, 68, 80, 100, 116, 120–9 145, 160; severe, 126, 129, 131, 141
　dissociative hallucinations, 116
　narcissistic personality disorders, 117
　paranoid schizophrenia, 116
　perinatal depression, 129
　postnatal depression, 35, 122, 206, 207

mental illness – *continued*
  postpartum psychosis, 35
  prevalence of, 151–2
  puerperal psychosis, 206
  schizophrenia, 136, 141
  schizoid-affective type, 136
mercy killing, 64, 138, 142
metamorphosis, 14
method of killing, 62, 74–96,
    109–11
  asphyxiation, 62, 101, 141
  battering, 25, 60, 64, 117, 143
  carbon monoxide poisoning, 101,
    103, 109, 191
  carried/thrown over bridge/
    balcony/cliff, 4, 5, 13, 54, 103,
    104, 205
  detonating a bomb, 69
  drowning, 3–5, 11, 101, 103, 111,
    141
  electrocution, 62
  fire and/or smoke inhalation,
    38, 62, 98–9, 109, 111, 206,
    211
  gassed, 62
  neglect and abandonment, 62
  poisoned, 111, 140, 141
  scalded, 62
  shot, 62, 103, 111
  stabbing, 62, 100, 101, 103, 104,
    111, 141
  stabbing and battered, 103, 111
  strangulation, 62, 102, 111, 143,
    160, 190
  throats slit, 103, 104, 111
Mochrie, Robert, 144
motivation for killing, 63
  altruistic, 63, 64
  gender differences in, 67–8
  psychotic episode, 63
  rage and jealously, 68
  revenge, 12, 14, 16, 19, 22, 39, 44,
    47, 63–4, 65, 67, 110–11, 131,
    144, 194, 210
  unwanted child, 63
Multi Agency Public Protection
  Arrangements (MAPPA), 154

Multi Agency Risk Assessment
  Conference (MARAC), 154, 156
multiple killings, 62
murder trials, 97

negative emotions, 68, 139, 143
neonaticide, 35, 37, 47, 54, 56, 58,
    62, 63, 119
  definition of, 34
non-biological parents, 61
Non-molestation Order, 152, 196

Office of National Statistics, 19, 57
O'Neill, Madeleine, 128

paedophile, 99
Parliament, 28
pathologists, 102, 146, 207
patients discharging themselves,
    160–1
Pemberton, Alan, 154–5
personal testimonies, 51, 52, 68–70
perpetrators
  age of, 59, 106
  gender of, 58, 106
  maternal, 4, 30, 59, 60, 62, 68,
    84–91, 100, 117, 140–1
  paternal, 30, 56, 58, 63, 65–70,
    74–83, 100, 116, 118, 143–4
  relationship with spouse/partner,
    61
  relationship with victims, 61
police, 8, 10, 13, 102, 151–7, 182–3,
    191, 192–3, 196, 205, 211
  police domestic violence unit,
    122, 152, 186
  response to domestic violence,
    22, 66, 123, 147, 176–9, 182–3,
    186–8
police family liaison officers, 179–80
Police Protection Order, 153
post-mortem examination, 99
possession and control, 69, 209
power and control, 183, 195–8
premeditation, 7, 68, 99–102
prisons, 70, 115, 169
probation officers, 20, 198

Prohibited Steps Orders, 163
Protection from Harassment Act 1997, 153
psychiatry, 54
psychiatrists, 54, 111, 115, 116, 121–3, 138, 139, 149, 159
psychiatric construct, 138
psychiatric evaluation, 116
psychiatric institutions, 116
psychoanalysis, 55
psychoanalytical interpretation, 55, 136
psychological and psychiatric perspective, 67
psychologists, 111, 139, 144, 149
public and private law, 20, 163, 164

refuge centres, 22
Relate, 123
relationship breakdown, 17, 19–21, 30, 67, 113
residence and contact disputes, 151, 168
Residence and Contact Orders, 163, 164, 165, 166
Resnick, Phillip 34, 54–5, 63–4, 115, 119, 129, 136, 138
Restraining Orders, 153–4
retaliation, 14, 16, 17, 105, 168
retaliatory killing, 61, 64
retaliatory mothers, 60
revenge
  category of, 64
  in Medea, 39–46
revenge-retaliation, 67, 72, 110–12, 138, 184, 191, 210
revenge notes, 68, 100, 101
risk assessment, 30, 66, 124, 126, 129, 139, 156–7, 161, 186, 212
risk indicators, 128
Roman Law Patria Potestas, 38
Royal College of Psychiatrists, 129

safe haven laws in USA, 56
safeguarding children boards, 6, 29, 129

Sartre, Jean-Paul
  No Exit, 38
Saunders, Hilary, 65
sentencing, 97, 102
separation, 5, 6, 11, 20, 21, 36, 61, 66, 67, 68, 118, 127, 173–5, 183, 210
  of unmarried couples, 20
  impact on children, 20, 178–9
  different meanings of, 36
serial lying, 101
Serious and Organised Crime and Police Act, 153
serious case reviews, 18, 23–30, 129, 183
  anonymised and redacted, 28, 72, 206
  confidentiality and data protection of, 26
  criticism of, 28, 29
  executive summary of, 18, 25, 28
  language of, 24, 46
  learning the lessons of, 28
  number of, 26
  on baby P., 27–8
  origins of, 24
  publication of, 28–30
  raison d'être of, 24–5, 29
  recommendations in, 29
  secrecy of, 25–6
sexual abuse, 162, 211
significant harm, 65
Smith, Susan, 42–3
social deprivation, 18, 147
social services, 123, 127, 130, 141, 163–4, 168, 183, 187–9, 191, 196, 199
social workers, 20–2, 27, 53, 126–7, 141, 158, 163, 164, 168, 176, 198, 212
statistics
  limitations of, 3, 5, 12, 17, 72
  use of, 14, 46, 119, 185, 201
suicidal tendencies, 144
suicidal thoughts, 124, 126
suicide, 4, 12, 13, 34, 35, 42, 52, 57, 60, 73, 80, 97, 109–10, 118–20, 165

suicide – *continued*
  of male perpetrators, 47, 54, 55, 58, 62, 104, 155, 169, 185
  of female perpetrators, 31, 55, 62, 68, 109, 113, 114, 121–30, 140
suicide attempts, 7–11, 13–14, 54, 73, 97, 109, 110, 113, 129, 141, 205, 209
suicide internet sites, 148
suicide notes, 10, 13, 14, 42, 63, 68, 111, 141, 142, 143, 166, 194, 207
survivors, 14, 66, 69, 73, 99

tabloid press, 26, 179
trainers, 101, 201

unborn, 33, 106, 107, 108, 109, 113
United Nations Convention on Rights of the Child, 162
university of Manchester centre for suicide prevention, 55

US government, 56
uxoricide 34

Violence Restraining Orders, 66
Violent Offender Orders, 154
von Goethe, Johann Wolfgang
  Faust, 38

Wall, Sir Nicholas, 22
White Paper, Safety and Justice, 152, 154
women incarcerated in institutions, 54
Women's Aid, 24
women's refuges, 152
Working Together to Safeguard Children, 65, 159, 163
Working Together under the Children Act, 24, 32

Yates, Andrea, 4

Printed and bound by CPI Group (UK) Ltd, Croydon, CR0 4YY